Where Does Mind End?

A RADICAL HISTORY OF CONSCIOUSNESS AND THE AWAKENED SELF

MARC J. SEIFER, Ph.D.

FOREWORD BY URI GELLER

D1294538

Park Street Press
One Park Street
Rochester, Vermont 05767
www.ParkStPress.com

Text stock is SFI certified

Park Street Press is a division of Inner Traditions International

Library of Congress Cataloging-in-Publication Data
Seifer, Marc J.
  Where does mind end? : a radical history of consciousness and the awakened self / Marc J. Seifer.
      p. cm.
  Rev. ed. of: Inward journey. 2003.
  Includes bibliographical references and index.
  ISBN 978-1-59477-430-0 (pbk.) — ISBN 978-1-59477-804-9 (e-book)
  1. Thought and thinking—History. 2. Consciousness—History. I. Seifer, Marc J. Inward journey. II. Title.
  BF441.S447 2011
  150—dc23

                                                          2011036015

Printed and bound in the United States by Lake Book Manufacturing
The text stock is SFI certified. The Sustainable Forestry Initiative® program promotes sustainable forest management.

10   9   8   7   6   5   4   3   2   1

Text design and layout by Virginia Scott Bowman
This book was typeset in Garamond Premier Pro and Gill Sans with Caslon, Grajon, and Gill Sans used as display typefaces

To send correspondence to the author of this book, mail a first-class letter to the author c/o Inner Traditions • Bear & Company, One Park Street, Rochester, VT 05767, and we will forward the communication, or contact the author directly at **www.MarcSeifer.com**.

To Bentley Davis Seifer

1998–2011

A youngster of Great Spirit

Contents

Foreword

Uri Geller

The English poet John Donne wrote, "No man is an island." We all exist in relationship to each other, and we all live and work and play within an extraordinarily complex network of human relationships. In chapter 26 of *Where Does Mind End?* Marc Seifer quotes Lev Vygotsky, the Russian psychologist who covers this same territory, but from a neurological point of view, namely that as the mind and brain of the child grows and learns, it must, by necessity, interact with the minds and brains of his or her parents, siblings, and friends. We are all open systems, and so, by necessity, the individual mind cannot end where the brain ends.

Even when the person dies, as stated in the Jewish tradition, the person lives on in his or her deeds and in the memories of loved ones. Some aspect of who we are remains.

When Marc asked me to write the foreword to *Where Does Mind End?* he stated that one of the reasons was because I was a relative of Sigmund Freud, who plays a central role in this work. My mother's maiden name was Freud. Born in Berlin, her grandfather, Solomon Freud, was Sigmund's nephew. She told me of this relationship when I was about six years old. Marc wanted to know if my knowledge of this connection played any role in my interest in psychic development, and I told him, I didn't think so.

But as I look through *Where Does Mind End?* I realize that if consciously my connection to Freud has meant little, unconsciously it may be a different story. I am interested in the unconscious, not in the way Freud generally meant, that is, as a repository for childhood conflicts and repressions, but rather as a source or gateway to higher human development.

In my own case, I have a distinct memory of being struck in the forehead by a ray of light when I was about four years old, and since that time I have displayed strange abilities. For instance, my soupspoon bent when I was eating, the hands of the watch my father had given me also bent, and I began to connect with my mother in telepathic ways. As I grew older and had my abilities tested at laboratories around the world, I began to realize that what was more important than my own abilities was the need to help others enhance their mind power in the arena of positive thinking and inspiration.

Take nature as an example. Why do you think a queen bee is special? Is it heredity? No, all the larvae produced in a hive are the same. The young pupae that develop into queen bees are different because they are fed a diet of royal jelly in special cells, and were it not for this, they would be the same as any of the other worker bees. Now, obviously, we can't all be born princes or princesses, but we can develop special qualities just like the bees if we are trained properly and fed the right information in order to develop our dormant talents and skills. And as Marc points out in this book, beyond the bees, we humans have an extra dimension. We can learn about the true source of our mind power. We can influence our destiny. We have the choice to be special.

Where Does Mind End? starts with the teachings of such sages as Zoroaster and Aristotle and then takes the reader to modern times and the works of Sigmund Freud and Carl Jung. What Marc has done here is resurrect the true majesty of the Freudian paradigm and link it to Jung's great work on the spiritual dimension of the collective unconscious and on Gurdjieff's teachings regarding will, psychology, and self-evolution. Unlike the worker bees, all of us humans have the ability to taste the royal jelly. No one really knows where the mind ends, but we all know where it begins, and that is with the self. So find a comfortable chair, turn the page, and take the journey within.

Uri Geller first came onto the world scene in the early 1970s. He has been tested successfully at numerous scientific laboratories for his abilities, such as bending keys and spoons psychokinetically. He has conferred with many of the greatest minds of our age, including Salvador Dali, Golda Meir, Deepak Chopra, Henry Kissinger, Roselyn Carter (wife of former president Jimmy Carter), former vice president Al Gore, Senator Claiborne Pell, Elvis Presley, Mohammad Ali, Michael Jackson, Dr. Andrija Puharich, astronaut and moon walker Edgar Mitchell, quantum physicist David Bohm, author Arthur Koestler, Clint Eastwood, and John Lennon. His TV show *Phenomena* plays in over a dozen countries.

Introduction

The White Rabbit put on his spectacles. "Where shall I begin, please your Majesty?"

"Begin at the beginning," the King said very gravely, "and go on till you come to the end; then stop."

LEWIS CARROLL,

ALICE'S ADVENTURES IN WONDERLAND, 1870

What is consciousness? How does one go about finding an answer? These are two questions that have been the focus of my research and teachings for over forty years. My first foray into the field began in college with a course I took on abnormal psychology, which included Freud's discussion of the defense mechanisms. Everything clicked; it all made sense to me, particularly the idea that the unconscious could influence supposed conscious decisions.

When I went to graduate school, I chose my schools based on one criterion: whether or not they taught courses on dreams. This led me to the University of Chicago, where I was able to study with several world leaders in the field of consciousness research, most notably Daniel G. Freedman, an ethologist who was studying one-day-old babies to uncover the biological underpinnings of behavior; Herbert Meltzer, M.D., who had expertise in the study of schizophrenia; and Bruno Bettelheim, the world's leading psychoanalyst at the time.

My dorm was located outside the campus. Thus I had a good walk to get to class, which took me by a number of secondhand bookstores. An early key purchase was a compact thousand-page compendium, which was a collected works of Sigmund Freud, who had been Bettelheim's teacher. What better way would there be to learn Bettelheim's course than to study the master himself? To my surprise, I found that of all of Freud's works, *Wit and Its Relation to the Unconscious* was the most beneficial in terms of explaining precisely how the mind really worked. Freud's most important contribution was his realization that the unconscious has its own separate consciousness. In other words, the unconscious *thinks,* and through this complex subliminal process, the conscious is influenced. The profundity of this realization never ceases to amaze me. Like it or not, we are of two minds, one of which we hardly know.

For another class on ego psychology, I studied David Rapaport's little-known weighty essay "Activity and Passivity of the Ego with Regards to Reality" and also the works of Anna Freud and Heinz Hartmann on the dynamics of mind and the problems of adaptation. Where Rapaport led me to a Freudian model to explain the link between neurosis, creative expression, and longevity, Anna Freud further explained the defense mechanisms and Hartmann introduced me to the concept of the automatism, which included symbolic behavior and the preconscious habit. Hartmann explained that people can perform the most complex behaviors, including even driving a car, and not be "conscious." Hartmann also came up with the idea of the "conflict-free ego sphere," a part of the psyche that was simply curious, not born from the endless battle between the conscience of the superego and the animal id.

For my master's thesis, I decided to explore theories of the unconscious beyond Freud, many of which were in Ellenberger's book on this topic, and also the works of Carl Jung on the collective psyche and J. B. Rhine's studies in parapsychology, including telepathy. This paper, which ran about a hundred pages, was written under the direction of my mentor, Daniel G. Freedman, who gave me the freedom to explore essentially whatever I wanted as long as I cited my sources.

At about this same time, I discovered the writings by and about Gurdjieff, a Russian mystic who had traveled to such places as Egypt, Mongolia, and the Himalayas to piece together a comprehensive theory on the highest states of consciousness. Where Freud and his followers took the journeyman into complexities of one's childhood and the depths of the unconscious, Gurdjieff was more pragmatic. Higher states are equated with self-observation, the idea of continual self-improvement or self-evolution, and acts of one's own willpower. Where one theoretician took me way inside, such as into the world of dreams, defense mechanisms, and neurotic complexes, the other forced me outside. Intentional doing, in Gurdjieff's scheme, is the real key to the higher states. Thus, it seems, a truly comprehensive model of mind must take both views into account, and that is what this book attempts to achieve.

In the year 2000, I began teaching at Roger Williams University, and shortly thereafter I was asked to teach a core course in human behavior. There was no textbook, and I struggled to find one. The focuses of the course, aside from human behavior, were such themes as human aggression, the different ways the two sexes think, and the idea of identity and one's coming role in society. What will these students do with their lives, and how will they contribute to society once they graduate?

These were the concepts that the course covered, and so it occurred to me that the best way I could help prepare these students for the so-called "real world" would be to equip them with knowledge about the higher states of consciousness. I wanted to structure a course in psychology that truly helped students not only with the complex issue of self-understanding but also with the practical reality associated with learning how to best choreograph their future. Society programs us in many ways that we remain unaware of, and so I wanted to cover topics that would help these students see how we are indeed programmed and see how we can combat this pressure by learning to be truly self-reliant. These are some of the core issues and key goals that I cover inside this book.

The structure of the course brought up the issue of the individual in relation to society and the concept of psychohistory, which was the subject of my doctoral dissertation undertaken at Saybrook Institute with Stanley Krippner. One of the things that such psychohistorians as Adorno and Marcuse did was to combine Marxist theory with that of psychoanalysis; in other words, they explored how social and economic or exterior forces structure our consciousness as compared to psychoanalytic or interior imperatives.

In order to gain a handle on exactly what human consciousness is, what forces shape it, what the unconscious is, and what the higher states are, I decided to start at the beginning. This brought me to the question: When did the so-called cradle of civilization actually begin? Although biologically modern man may have been around for hundreds of thousands of years, the general consensus is that what we would call modern society began about ten thousand years ago in Mesopotamia in the Fertile Crescent—now part of Iraq—around the Tigris and Euphrates rivers. Why there? Because the climate allowed one to grow crops, and because the rivers themselves, by their nature, promoted commerce. But how would one keep inventory? Buying and selling products would help

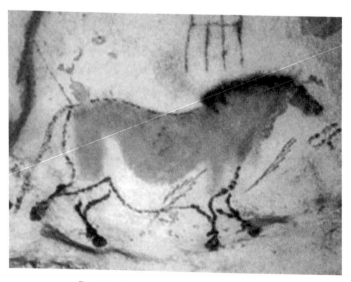

Fig. I.1. The cave drawings of Lascaux

promote not only social interaction and language but also the need to create goods to trade with and the idea of counting. This would evolve into the ability to write down how many of each item one had and how, in written form, to differentiate one object from another. Here is where written language began.

But what about those cave drawings in France, which go back thirty-five thousand years, and the question of why Cro-Magnon man survived and Neanderthal died out? As I understand it, where Neanderthal man may have had a larger brain in relation to body size, Cro-Magnon man had a more highly developed larynx or voice box. Thus, Cro-Magnon man had more developed language skills, and this led to greater cerebral complexity, which would enable him to better plan and coordinate troop movements and so on. Odds are, although there may have been some interbreeding, Cro-Magnon man probably wiped out Neanderthal man, who stayed more primitive because his language skills were no match. So when did civilization really begin? Was it a half million years ago, when man emerged from Africa; thirty-five thousand years ago with the cave drawings in France; or ten thousand years ago in Mesopotamia? One way or another, on the time scale of life on Earth, which goes back hundreds of millions of years, man as a civilized being is a recent development. Like it or not, we are the new kids on the block.

1

The Philosophers

Now this connection or adaptation of all created things to each and of each to all means that each simple substance [monad] has relations which express all the others, and, consequently, that it is a perpetual living mirror of the universe.

GOTTFRIED WILHELM LEIBNIZ

When I began my research to find the earliest writings on the topic of consciousness, I came upon Zoroaster (628–551 BCE), who lived about six hundred years before the birth of Christ and about a thousand years after the birth of the first great monotheist, Moses. Probably influenced by the idea of the Ten Commandments, Zoroaster's thinking was so powerful that he founded a new philosophy, Zoroastrianism, which became the dominant religion of the Persian Empire for hundreds of years before and during the time of Christ: a religion that still exists today. The word *Zoroaster* according to Wikipedia is a combination of two words, *zoro* or zero and *aster* or stars. Zoroaster can be seen not only as the first star but also, as implied, the first to come up with the amazing concept of zero. A circle, when seen in this light, can represent both nothing (zero) and everything (circle), all of which reflect the numinous contradictory nature of God himself. Kabbalistically, this can be set up as the numerical equation 0 = 1, which, of course, is impossible, and yet it represents the essence of the mystery of our existence. Note how this concept is revealed in the Book of Genesis:

In the beginning God created the heaven and the earth. . . . And the earth was without form, and void; and darkness was upon the face of the deep. And the Spirit of God moved upon the face of the waters.

Zarathustra, Zoroaster was a Persian prophet, teacher of Pythagoras, and spiritual guide to Cyrus the Great (589–529 BCE). Zoroaster, who saw a benevolent God, taught the ancient wisdom that "only those who develop conscience can be sons of Mithra." Cyrus is credited as the father of human rights. A Persian king, Cyrus the Great entered Babylon with a peaceful agenda, which included the freeing of slaves. Tolerant of all ethnic peoples, he enabled the Jews to resurrect their civilization in Jerusalem, and thus he is mentioned in the Old Testament, which establishes that at least that section of the Bible had to have been written after 600 BCE. Zoroaster's philosophy has been explained in an ancient cuneiform cylinder found in 1879 that resides in the British Museum.

Unlike the prevailing view of the divine right of kings (e.g., the pharaohs), Zoroaster, a Sufi, taught that each man could find his own salvation because "the possibility of liberation was inherent in every human soul." Zoroaster, much like Moses, proclaimed through revelation that every soul was "sacred,"[1] a direct link to the creator. His esoteric worldview saw Mithra as the light of wisdom and the world as torn apart because of an "eternal struggle between good and evil." Through ethical living a person could achieve God's graces and immortality. This view, espoused by Jesus and much later by Gurdjieff, developed in a sense into a form of esoteric Christianity, highly simplified down to the credo "If you are good, you get to go to heaven." Zoroaster preached that "real men are those who create their own reality,"[2] and in doing so, they aid Mithra in his task. Here, in such simplified form, is the essence of the key to the very highest states of consciousness, what people from the East call "dharma," or right living, and what Gurdjieff espouses in his

Fig.1.1. The solar system

will psychology. In this scheme, humans are in partnership with God, where godliness and the good are closely linked.

One of Zoroaster's students was Pythagoras of Samos (582–500 BCE), the founder of modern science. Having studied with the atheist Anaximander as well as the mystic Pherekydes, Pythagoras came to believe that "at its deepest level, reality is mathematical in nature."[3] Traveling through Greece, the area around the Fertile Crescent, and Egypt, Pythagoras settled in Italy near Naples to set up his mystic order. According to Arthur Koestler, "by Aristotle's time, Pythagoras had achieved a semi-divine status,"[4] a philosopher who created a bridge between science and religion.

Pythagoras split the study of the world into three branches, the "trivium," which was the threefold field of the humanities: grammar, rhetoric, and logic; the "quadrivium," or fourfold fields of the sciences: arithmetic, geometry, astronomy, and music; and "esotericism," which lay at the basis of the gnostic tradition, neoplatonic thought, and the Kabbalah.[5] Where the first two areas are still the mainstay of modern education, esoteric teaching has stayed on the periphery, even though these mystical views have influenced such fields as psychology, cosmology, and quantum physics.

Astronomy for Pythagoras revealed "the order of the heavens and the harmonies of the celestial spheres,"[6] because the great thinker was linked to a mystical understanding of music. Beginning with his realization that the "pitch of a note was dependent upon the length of its string," Pythagoras began to see the relationship between music, numbers, and the construction of the heavens.[7] This correspondence, which lies at the basis of modern recordings, whereby books, music, and films are stored as digital codes, was extended to man himself, portrayed in such vivid form by Leonardo da Vinci in his Vitruvian man, where da Vinci theorized that the construction of the human body mirrored the construction of the universe. Having studied the stars, Pythagoras claimed that he could hear the very movement of the planets across the night sky. This became known as the "music of the spheres." The world was set up in a harmonic fashion, and numbers held the sacred key.

Just as crystals form "pure number shapes . . . reality could [also] be reduced to number-series and number-ratios."[8] This idea that reality could be reduced to numbers had an enormous impact on the Greeks and thus on Western culture. In particular, fully two thousand years later, it influenced both Johannes Kepler and Isaac Newton who found,

Fig. I.2. Vitruvian man, by Leonardo da Vinci

respectively, the laws of planetary motion and gravitational attraction.

Astronomer, mathematics teacher, and court astrologer Johannes Kepler (1571–1630) was convinced, because of Pythagoras, that the motion of the planets around the Sun had to be as perfect circles. As Arthur Koestler explains in his great book *The Sleepwalkers,* one of Kepler's bitter rivals was Galileo who, to Kepler's dismay, had the only telescope in town. Wanting to borrow it but unable to approach his nemesis, Kepler had a nobleman request the use of the scope, and then Kepler clandestinely used it.

After studying the movement of the planets, Kepler eventually discovered that Pythagoras's view of the planets as moving in perfect circles was in error; their orbits were instead perfect ellipses. This led Kepler to discover his *harmonic law of planetary motion,* $p^2/d^3 = K$, whereby p = period, the time it takes a planet to circle the Sun, squared, divided by d, the distance from the planet to the Sun, cubed, was the same for all the planets, K = constant. For instance, this constant ratio, K, for Earth would be one year, or 365 days, squared divided by 93 million miles cubed. This in turn led Newton (1642–1727) to his *law of gravitational attraction:* m_1m_2/d^2, where m_1 = the mass of one planet, m_2, the mass of a second planet, and d = the distance between the planets squared. Kepler's harmonic law also helped Newton and Leibniz discover or invent calculus. God was, indeed, a mathematician. The only planet this did not work for was Mercury. This anomaly was overlooked for centuries until Albert Einstein came along and stated that Mercury's great speed had to be taken into account, and this was linked to his theory of relativity. The point here is that in essence Pythagoras was right. There was an underlying harmony to the universe, and with that knowledge its great secrets could be revealed.

If there is indeed structure, harmony, and mathematical precision to the physical world, was this not evidence of a design maker? Can there be laws to the universe without a lawmaker? The trend during this time was to ascribe to our origins a supernatural explanation. Where ancient Greek and Roman mythology was polytheistic, both Moses and

Zoroaster suggest one creator, and thus one set of laws for one universe. And yet the debate still rages.

In 1859 Charles Darwin (1809–1882) published *The Origin of the Species,* a comprehensive theory of evolution, which was revolutionary for a number of reasons. Not only did Darwin suggest that humans evolved from apelike primates, Darwin also suggested that the key mechanism behind evolution was a combination of random mutation, natural selection, and survival of the fittest. This theory was in counterpoint to Jean-Baptiste Lamarck's (1744–1829) theory of use and disuse. According to Lamarck's theory, giraffes got long necks and cheetahs became faster because they used those parts of their bodies. In the same sense, the human appendix is disappearing because it is not being used. Where Lamarck has the animal participating through its actions in its own evolution, Darwin's theory is simpler. The giraffes with the longer necks and the cheetahs that run faster survived; the others died out.

It is not commonly realized, but Darwin did not oppose Lamarck's use and disuse theory. He devoted a chapter to the idea in his book. For instance, Darwin points out that domestic ducks have weaker bone structure than wild ducks because wild ducks fly south in the winter, (i.e., use and disuse). But Darwin instead was saying that the *dominant* force behind evolution was the simple idea that animals constantly changed, and the ones that were better able to adapt to the environment tended to live, and the other animals died out. A good example of this is finding squirrels instead of porcupines or cougars in urban environments. Over time, because squirrels are better adapted to such enclaves, they tend to live, and other animals not as well suited to such environments die out.

The problem with Darwin's theory is that he bases life purely on a chance process. There is no God directing the evolution. It is all chance; ergo, there really is no reason for life and also no reason for religion. This prevailing paradigm, which has dominated the scientific view since the late 1800s, is opposed by the religious view, which elevates humans to a higher plane and places God back as the creator. Is Darwin right and the religious view wrong, or vice versa? Or is there some compromise in between? Certainly Darwin's theory explains much of how animals evolve. Clearly those that can adapt to the environment live, and those that don't die out. However, it does beg a key question, and that is the driving force inherent in the animal that makes it want to live in the first place, what Henri Bergson called the *élan vital*. From this vantage point, even if life is, to a great extent, a chance process, there is still an underlying force that started it all, which still lies inside of life, which propels animals to try to survive: known theologically as First Cause.

This dialectical view as to the cause of the cosmos and impetus to evolution, chance versus directionality, brings us to our next mind explorer, Socrates (469–399 BCE), the great ancient Greek philosopher. Born approximately forty years after the death of Pythagoras, Socrates stated, "The unexamined life is not worth living." Thriving on paradox and contradiction, a theory that truth was related to some type of compromise between opposites, Socrates said, "No one is wiser than you."

Socrates calls for his students to be self-reliant, to seek truth above all else. Thus, the student must, by necessity, question the prevailing worldview, including the authority. And yet Socrates also advocated the need to show unwavering allegiance to the state. When students would come to him for answers, Socrates would avoid giving any. He wanted people to make up their own minds. These ideas would lie at the basis of René Descartes' need to doubt even the existence of God, in humanistic psychology, which strives in nondirective therapy for people in analysis to come to their own realizations and decisions, and in Gurdjieff's requirement that to be in a high state of consciousness means to be master of one's own ship. Because Socrates was such a thorn in the side, questioning people in power and yet by design never being able to suggest a better alternative, he was tried at age seventy by the state and given a sentence of either exile or silence. Because he refused to honor either restriction, instead of exile he was sentenced to death. Although he could have fled, he accepted the sentence. Consoled by his friends in his last hours, he "drank the hemlock poison."[9]

The concepts of the importance of innate ideas and of recognizing individual differences are attributed to Socrates' student, Plato (427–347 BCE). Some people had artistic ability, others musical talent, mathematical propensity, and so on. Further, Plato believed that "the world of ideas is just as real as the world of objects, and it is through ideas that man attains consciousness of the absolute."[10]

Founding a school that would last nine hundred years, Plato said that "only those who knew geometry" could enter his academy.[11] God, for Plato, was a mathematician: God "geometrizes." This sacred ability became the physical forms that Aristotle identified as the essence of things that determines their destiny. Fish were destined to swim; birds were destined to fly. Secrets to one's nature and to the ultimate structure of mind could also be understood in the pure forms, which could be represented in mathematical terms. Experiences and innate ideas were stored in the soul, which, for Plato, consisted of "reason and appetite," translated two thousand years later into what Freud called the ego and the id.

Obviously neither Aristotle nor Plato knew about DNA. Nevertheless, if DNA were broken down into its atomic constituents, on one level the genetic code could certainly be understood from a mathematical/geometric arrangement of electrons orbiting protons and neutrons coding for the essential nature of living things. When viewed from the molecular level, at its core biological life can indeed be seen as mathematical in structure.

Plato's student Aristotle (384–322 BCE) is often credited as the first major psychologist because of his attempts to create a systematic study of the mind. A seeker of knowledge, Aristotle equated the ability of the soul or psyche to incorporate novel data with the property of intelligence. Man was the only being that had this capability to acquire new information, deliberate about it, and explain things.

Aristotle attributed a purpose, and thus a *teleological* principle, to the universe and its parts. The purpose or final cause of each of its constituents was defined by its essential nature or essence, which was determined by its form, which we have seen from Pythagoras is geometrical in structure. Everything in the universe had a potentiality and an actuality. The acorn is not coaxed into becoming an oak tree. It is predetermined by its essence, a dynamic life-giving principle, and its form to grow into that culmination. Obviously an acorn will not grow into an apple or pine tree and certainly not a squirrel. Its final cause is built into its essence.

If we extrapolate to man, his final cause is predetermined by the form of his soul. Aristotle would say that the ultimate aim for man is the understanding of his being. Endowed with a mind, the ability to think was based upon the capacity for creating images and making associations between them. As a precursor to many theories that followed, Aristotle stated that humans were motivated to seek pleasure and avoid pain. Since man could reason, he was also motivated by benefits based upon future considerations. These ideas would be morphed by Freud into the pleasure principle and the reality principle.

The idea of the "tabula rasa" is also attributed to Aristotle. As a counterhypothesis to Plato's theory of innate ideas, Aristotle theorized that the mind was born a blank slate. Experiences would be impressed upon this tablet, and this would form the basis and contents of the mind. All ideas were the result of experience. In a simplistic sense, this idea was compatible with behaviorism, which throughout most of the twentieth century sought to eliminate the invisible mind from the study of psychology and only deal with behavior, what happens after birth, motivations molded through stimulus and response, rewards, and punishment.

Aristotle placed the "seat of thought" in the heart, not the brain. This was an idea with ancient roots comparable to the "Ba spirit" of the Egyptians, who stated that "Ba" lay in the chest and bowels, not in the head. This view has been misunderstood by most modern psychologists, as the seat of thought seems obviously to be in the brain. But let us reconsider.

"On the subject of the heart," Islamic scholar Henry Corbin writes, "in . . . Sufism in general, the heart is the organ which produces true knowledge, comprehensive intuition, the gnosis of God and the divine mysteries, in short, the organ of everything connoted by the term *esoteric science*. It is the organ of a perception."[12]

This idea is further developed by Hadrad Abd al-Qadir al-Jilani, a Sufi mystic and saint of Islam who lived in the twelfth century:

> Some of the properties of this darkness are arrogance, pride, envy, miserliness, vengeance, lying, gossiping, backbiting, and so many other hateful traits. . . . To rid one of these evils one has to cleanse and shine the mirror of the heart. This cleansing is done by acquiring knowledge, by acting upon this knowledge, by effort and valour, fighting against one's ego within and without oneself, by ridding oneself of one's multiplicity of being, by achieving unity. This struggle will continue until the heart becomes alive with the light of unity—and with that light of unity, the eye of the clean heart will see the reality of Allah's attributes around and in it.

Aristotle understood that the entire being of the person, his or her essence/form, was the whole body, not just the brain. Heart transplants notwithstanding, it *is* possible to think with the heart. This is simply another way of saying that a person is in touch with his or her feelings and thinks with emotion. It is a more primal form of thought and more visceral. There is a consciousness to the heart. Sit for a moment and think and feel with your heart. The higher states of consciousness are directly linked to this organ as the centerpiece for the entire human organism, for here one is in touch with not only one's emotions, but also with compassion, empathy, and conscience. Anatomically, it is well known that there is a major feedback circuit between the heart and the brain via the medulla, so it can also be argued that there is a cerebral counterpart to heart activities. True knowing involves sensing with the entire being as a gestalt, the Ba spirit of the Egyptians, that gut feeling that truly is not located in the head. As the Sufis tell us, and as Aristotle has intimated, we must learn to "polish our heart."

2
The Industrial Revolution

That which creates but is not created is God.

JOHN THE SCOT ERIGENA

There are a number of key figures worthy of note from the next fifteen hundred years, such as Plotinus (ca. 200 CE), St. Augustine (ca. 400 CE), John the Scot Erigena (ca. 800 CE), Roger Bacon, and Thomas Aquinas (both ca. 1200 CE). Except for Bacon, much of their work expounded on the theories of the ancient Greeks cited in the chapter 1 or on the discussion of church doctrine. Whereas Plotinus, St. Augustine, and Thomas Aquinas all believed in an everlasting soul and its potential ascension to heaven, Augustine and Aquinas emphasized the importance of introspection and the realization of a free will that can choose to do good or evil.

ROGER BACON

Roger Bacon (1214–1294) is in a separate category because he revived interest in a Pythagorean view of the cosmos and an approach to science based on the empirical method of observation and experimentation. Having studied mathematics, geometry, astronomy, and music at the University of Oxford, Bacon worked with mirrors and lenses to create the precursors to what became eyeglasses, the microscope, and the telescope. As an academician, he sought to coordinate scholars with the help of the church to create an encyclopedia of science. This request was misunderstood by Pope Clement IV, who thought that the encyclopedia had already been written. With little choice, Bacon rapidly put together *Opus Maius* (The Great Work) and two other books, which he sent to Rome. Like Augustine, Bacon hoped to fashion a science that would evolve in concert with religious doctrine, but this, of course, was opposed by factions of the clergy, particularly after Pope Clement IV passed away. Bacon thought that the earth was round and that it could be circumnavigated. He also calculated that the stars were about 130 million miles away.[1] Like Galileo, who was to follow, Bacon was arrested for his beliefs by the following pontiff, Pope Nicholas IV. Imprisoned for ten years, he nevertheless survived to write *A Compendium of the Study of Theology* and died two years later in 1294 at the age of eighty.

This period has been called the Dark Ages for the simple reason that the church, as it gained power, also began to severely restrict the flow of information. Following in the tradition set up by Pope Nicholas IV, three hundred years later Pope Paul IV published his *Index Librobrum Prohibitorum,* or list of banned books. During this period there were numerous inquisitions, and various prominent scientists such as Copernicus, Descartes, Kepler, and most tragically Galileo suffered. I've never fully understood why a heliocentric view of the cosmos was such a threat to religion, but that was the case, and so the fact that the sun and not the earth was the center of our universe was banned. Interestingly, the *Index* continued all the way up to the present era, when it was finally dismissed by Pope Paul VI in 1966. Our discussion will continue with Hobbes, Descartes, Locke, and Spinoza: all thinkers who made this illustrious *Index*.

During the time of the great explorers, such as Magellan and Christopher Columbus, the view of the world was changing. Many of the great thinkers of the past such as Pythagoras, Ptolemy, and Copernicus knew that the Sun was the center of the solar system, but church doctrine, which was anthropomorphic, opposed this finding.

God created the heavens and the earth for man, and thus, the earth was the center of the universe.

As late as the 1600s, the church continued to doggedly hold to this primitive view. Johannes Kepler (1571–1630) was in difficult straits. Even though he was the court astrologer to Holy Roman Emperor Rudolf II, king of Hungary and Bohemia, his mother was being accused of witchcraft. In those days, the accused were given little choice: renounce witchcraft or get tortured or burned at the stake. During this period, tens of thousands of people were killed this way. With this kind of pressure on Kepler and his mother, he still maintained that the Sun was the center of our planetary solar system.

Like Kepler, Galileo (1564–1642) also subscribed to the heliocentric view. He had discovered this in a roundabout way. By improving on previous designs, Galileo had constructed the first modern telescope, and with it he was able to see the rings of Saturn and the moons of Jupiter. If Jupiter had moons, then Earth could not be the center of the heavens. The church was so powerful at that time that scientists were simply unable to publicize their findings.

To scientists, it was obvious that the church was not infallible, but no scientist of repute could espouse this view. The proof, of course, was that the greatest scientist of the day, Galileo, was arrested and sent to prison for the last ten years of his life. This act created a schism between the church view and scientific view on the nature of reality. At the same time, humans had created great ships that could traverse oceans and machines that could produce goods. To the scientific minded, humans had become smarter than God. This situation would impact greatly the philosophers of the day, who would now do their best to shape a worldview that would even explain consciousness as an act having nothing to do with a mythological creator. Thus an atheistic bent edged its way into the scientific mainstream. The upside was the development of the scientific method and corresponding advances in biology, physics, and medicine. The downside was that the idea of a sentient basis for the development of the cosmos would never again be placed at the heart of any science. Natural law had nothing to do with higher intelligence. Life evolved as a chance process. There was no ultimate design maker.

THOMAS HOBBES

A secretary of the highly regarded philosopher and barrister Sir Francis Bacon, Thomas Hobbes (1588–1679) was a contemporary of Kepler and Newton and an acquaintance of Descartes and Galileo. An empiricist, Hobbes set a materialistic agenda because he believed that all knowledge was derived from the senses and experience. The one internal component Hobbes adhered to was that humans, by nature, were aggressive. As predators, humans not only killed animals, they killed each other. Thus societies were formed not so much for the social imperative but as a way to protect the self and the clan from other aggressive clans. But Hobbes also believed in the intrinsic equality of men, the necessity of a civil society and social contracts so as to avoid wars, and the need for "legitimate political power to be based on the consent of the people."[2] Paradoxically, Hobbes was also a proponent of the idea of the divine right of kings, not because he believed in God (he had his doubts), but because he theorized that humans needed strong leaders, otherwise chaos would ensue. A modern example of this can be seen in Iraq. Once Saddam Hussein was ousted, starting in 2003, warring factions of Shiites, Sunnis, Kurds, and the terrorist group al-Qaeda tore the country apart. Even if Hobbes tended to remove God from his theories, Hobbes was still an avid churchgoer. It was for that reason that he supported King Charles I in a civil war against Oliver Cromwell. When Charles was executed in 1649, Hobbes fled to France and stayed there for the next decade until the monarchy in England was reestablished.

Hobbes, as a materialist, wrote in his main treatise *The Leviathan,* "all knowledge is derived through sensation." Moreover, he went on to profoundly suggest that "nothing exists, internal or external to us, except *matter and motion,*" [emphasis added] thus grouping psychology firmly with materialism and also setting the stage for the physicists to construct their explanation for birth of the universe in a way that completely removed the mystical element. Sensations, then, are "reduced to motion in the form of change."[3] These form "the rules of mechanical association to derive ideas and memory," which, in turn, explains how "the mind acquires knowledge. . . . For Hobbes, the contiguity in time or place of events provided the association of sensations to form the idea unit, which is then stored in the mind as memory."[4] Humans were motivated by the desire to seek pleasure and avoid pain, and it was this process that had been labeled wrongly by other philosophers as free will. Hobbes discounted the concept of innate ideas and set up essentially an atheistic paradigm, which provided the scientific basis for the various theories of the modern psychologists who followed, like Stumpf, Wundt, and Fechner in the late 1800s, and behaviorists like Pavlov, Watson, and Skinner in the 1900s. According to this view, all human action was extrinsically motivated. Nothing came from within. Ideas stem from sensations and associations, which come from the environment. Dreams, which heretofore were most often seen as having a divine origin, became, for Hobbes, the random action of thought sequences.

RENÉ DESCARTES

The Frenchman René Descartes (1596–1650), a contemporary of Hobbes, was a transitionary philosopher influenced by both the atheistic trend and the supposition that there was indeed a sentient creator. Blessed with a stipend to cover his expenses throughout his life, Descartes was schooled by the Jesuits and then followed in his father's footsteps and obtained a law degree. Descartes was also interested in geometry, theology, and cosmology. At the age of twenty-two he moved to Holland, and it was there that he came up with his most famous creation, the Cartesian coordinates. Descartes got the idea of the graph with its x, y, and z axes by sitting in an empty room and contemplating how to locate a fly that was buzzing about.

Shortly thereafter, Descartes had a dream on the nature of reality that changed his life. Devoting himself to finding "truth" and to discovering the ultimate nature of things, he started with the premise of doubting everything, including the existence of the Almighty. After a time, he realized that there was one thing that he *was* certain of, and thus was born his famous credo, "I think, therefore I am."

Ironically, this great insight, which became for him the first principle of a new philosophy of the mind, also served unwittingly to separate man and God from the universe. The world, which he accepted as having been created by God, operated like a great machine, and it was something physical. This was different from the human mind and soul, which, like God, were free and lacking in substance. However, this mental realm does indeed control the body, and it was Descartes' theory that the transducer for this action was located in the center of the brain in the pineal gland.

Descartes identified six primary passions: wonder, desire, love, hate, joy, and sadness. All other feelings were derived from combinations of these six. He separated ideas into two classes, those that came from experiences (Aristotle) and those that were innate (Plato). The sense of self, God, time, space, motion, and geometry were all innate ideas. Animals, according to his theory, did not have a soul because they lacked the human qualities of language and self-awareness.[5]

Descartes lived at a pivotal time in modern human history because part of the great mystery of our existence—the movements of the stars and planets—was being explained by astronomers. The earth was no longer the center of the universe, and further, the laws of how the planets orbited the Sun and how they were attracted to each other were being formulated by scientists like Kepler and Newton. Even though, like Descartes, most of these great thinkers accepted the premise of divine creation, once it was surmised that the world operated like a great clock, a duality emerged: God and his creation. If the planets were simply traversing the heavens in a prescribed, orderly fashion, then the universe would have no more purpose than a machine.

Descartes would expand this idea to suggest that animals, like machines, were no more than self-propelled automata. God and man could give purpose to their existence, but the human soul, like God, was separate from the machine-like/animal-like aspects of existence.

This, as Arthur Koestler noted, became the "ghost in the machine."

Descartes argued persuasively that the mental domain, the world of ideas and imagination, was distinct from the physical world. In the realm of inner space, mental objects could have properties unrelated to properties of physical objects. The subjective world now was a separate realm from the objective world.

T. H. Leahey points out that this new scientific view "began to alienate human beings from the universe,"[6] and so the world, instead of being permeated with a living dynamic God, now became a separate "cold impersonal universe."[7] Before Descartes, Leahey suggests, there had been a tacit assumption that God and the universe were one, and man thereby would be part of this totality. Now, in the early 1600s, with the advent of Descartes' mind/body dualism, just as God became separated out from his mechanically run cosmos, man, too, became separate. At the same time, the church was losing its prestige because of its inability to recognize the obvious truth to the findings of such men as Copernicus, Galileo, Kepler, and Newton. And so a new mechanistic paradigm began to emerge: one where scientists like Heisenberg and Einstein, three hundred years later, could discuss and even include the role of the observer in their schemas, but not the *consciousness* of the observer as a force in and of itself. The mind was separate, and therefore not part of the physical world, and thus not subject to the laws of physics. Further, if one tried to reintegrate the mind into the structure of the cosmos, that thinker was branded as unscientific and a mystic.

Descartes' dualistic paradigm is appealing but also problematic. According to this theory, only humans have a soul and thus only humans have a vehicle to take them to the next world after death. But what about our pets? Surely, if I have a soul, then Geno, our amazing little Maltese who ruled the house and broke up fights for fourteen years; Lady M, a miniature German Shepherd who once saved me from a pack of angry dogs; Fluffer P. Nutter, our quiet, gentle cat who greeted all the children on the block and who entered my dreams on a regular basis, and Tiger Lilly, who scolded me once when I didn't help her down from a tree during the Superbowl, have souls too. So here is the problem: Where does one draw the line? If our pets have souls, what about that pesky crow that shoos all the other birds away, or the fisher cat or coyote who makes meals of our precious pets, or that big ugly spider who was too fast to capture and disappeared under the furniture? Wouldn't they have souls too? And if so, heaven suddenly becomes a vastly more complicated place.

JOHN LOCKE

For Locke, as for Descartes, the paradigm of genuine knowledge is mathematics.

NICHOLAS JOLLY, 1984

John Locke (1632–1704), like so many other great theoreticians who struggled with the problem of consciousness, made major contributions to the body of knowledge in other fields as well. A Puritan from Oxford University, Locke became the scholar to the king at the age of fifteen and later a member of the Royal Society of London. Although close to the monarchy, Locke preferred the idea of representation of elected officials by popular consent. Seeing government as a contract between the leaders and the people, Locke believed that if the leaders violated the trust of their office, the people had the right to overthrow such a government. His *Two Treatises on Government* also described the idea of three branches—executive, legislative, and judicial—with a system of checks and balances. All of these ideas became the cornerstone of the American Constitution.

Expanding on the work of Hobbes, Locke, as the ultimate empiricist, was heavily influenced by Isaac Newton's clockwork model for the construction of the cosmos. Completely ignoring the more mysterious aspects of the invisible mind, Locke's idea was to "find a similar set of rules" as Newton had, but apply it to the study of consciousness. His goal was to "refract" the mind into its "basic elements, just as Newton had refracted light." Consciousness, for Locke, was, like Newton's paradigm, "atomistic and reductionistic."[8] All of this put Locke squarely in the tabula rasa school: *Nihil est in intellectu nisi quod prius ferit in sensu* ["There is nothing in the mind that was not first in the senses"]. There was no innate sense of the Divine and no theological basis for the soul. Everything happened after birth. This philosophy became the basis for the rise of behaviorism two hundred years later. However, where the behaviorists attempted to strip the human of a cogitating mind, Locke stated that thought did occur and that it proceeded through a process of associations and reflections, which were derived from impressions received from the senses. Complex thoughts are derived from simple ones.

Fig. 2.1. Moses on Mount Zion. Drawing by Lynn Sevigny.

BARUCH SPINOZA

Baruch Spinoza (1632–1677) grew up in Amsterdam, the son of a Jewish merchant who made his living polishing lenses for eyeglasses and microscopes. Spinoza came from a long line of "crypto-Jews," those who were forced to convert to Christianity during the Spanish Inquisition but who practiced their religion in secret. By the time Baruch was born, the veil had been lifted, and he was raised as a traditional Jew.

Influenced by the other philosophers of his day, like Locke and Hobbes, Spinoza wrote extensively about God, but underneath it all he stripped God of his miraculous cloth. Although Christ, for Spinoza, was God's spokesman for both Christian and Jew, in Spinoza's opinion Christ would reveal a God that followed natural law. Every effect had to have a cause. This idea would later surface in psychoanalysis under the term "the Freudian slip." Even odd or irrational behaviors, when understood, had to have a root cause. God himself could not disobey natural law. In fact, God was one with Mother Nature. "Thus, Spinoza sought to reconcile the conflict between science and religion by redefining the deity in terms of the universe"[9] as revealed by the scientists and astronomers.

Whereas the universe essentially followed its mechanical laws, the mind was in a different category, therefore it could overcome bodily emotions through reason and adherence to an ethical standard. But when the brain died, so did the mind. However, while alive, the mind did indeed have transcendent properties. Spinoza's nonbelief in an afterlife greatly influenced modern Jewish thinking, as opposed to the Catholic view, which seemed to construct a religion based on the promise of an afterlife. Where Catholics generally believe in a heaven, Jews emphasize the idea that people live on in their deeds and in the memories of those still living.

GOTTFRIED WILHELM LEIBNIZ

Certainly one of the most important philosophers of this period was Gottfried Wilhelm Leibniz (1646–1716). A lawyer by profession and factotum to princes, Leibniz stands out as a kingpin because of his monad theory. Along with Newton, Leibniz is the cofounder of the mathematical discipline calculus. Coming from a brilliant and original thinker, Leibniz's ideas would turn out to have profound implications for modern man, for his monad theory not only foresaw, in some derivative way, such advances as cloning, whereby a single cell contains a map for the entire organism, but also in the still-developing field of holography, three-dimensional photography, whereby even a small part of a hologram carries information about the whole.

Descartes had laid down the gauntlet. From his perspective, the mind and the body were two separate things. The Aristotelian concept of the tabula rasa embraced by Hobbes and Locke became another benchmark. And a third belief, which was essentially atheistic, set forth by Spinoza tied God to the mechanical action of nature. A new scientific outlook was emerging, which disavowed the idea of a sentient substrate for the construction of the universe and thus was a disavowal of church doctrine as well.

One could start with Copernicus and then Galileo, who both had to subvert their heliocentric view to the will of a church that obtusely demanded, against all evidence, that the earth remain the center of the universe. Kepler, like many great scientists, was indeed ruled by the premise that the universe had divine organization. However, once he uncovered the law of planetary motion, which explained very well the mechanical action of the solar system, Kepler unwittingly helped support a tendency away from a God-based universe because this law supported the contention that the universe worked in blind fashion.

Leibniz was troubled by the atheistic trend, because he respected such thinkers as Hobbes, Locke, and Spinoza but disagreed with them. His answer to Locke's famous quote was the addendum: *Nihil est in intellectu quod non fuerit in sensu, nisi ipse intellectua* ["Nothing is in the intellect that has not been in the senses, *except the intellect itself*"].[10] Leibniz had identified the crux of the issue. Perhaps Hobbes can explain, to a great extent, *how* we think, but he cannot explain *why* we think. Leibniz believed in the concept of innate ideas because he assumed there was a sentient God who created the world, and from this entity came the infinite monads: our minds.

A modern analog to Leibniz's concept can be seen in the home computer. The parents proudly purchase a new computer for their child who is about to go off to college. Much like Aristotle's tabula rasa, this virgin machine is, indeed, a blank slate. But is it really? The hard drive may be blank, but the machine is filled with software, for without the software, the fancy device would be useless. In the same sense, Leibniz is telling us that infants, much like computers, are born with a ton of preprogramming. These are our instincts, called by Plato, innate ideas. So, the question remains, where does the inherent intelligence stem from?

Leibniz stated outright, in his treatise *The Monadology,* that just as a "preform" precedes a seed, humans are born with a soul, which preceded the body at birth and persists with the dissolution of the body after death. Leibniz was concerned with the new atheistic trend of the philosophers. An early culprit was Machiavelli, who condoned the use of evil if the ends were justified. But the work of such think-ers as Hobbes and Spinoza was more subversive, because the removal of God from a model of the mind became less obvious. Hobbes had written about God "giving grace to his disciples," but he also questioned whether or not "the kingdom of God [would ever] come."[11] Leibniz too, was concerned about the potential arrival of the Messiah. With total faith in the majesty of existence, he believed that God had created the best of all possible worlds. Leibniz envisioned a benevolent God, one accessible to all individuals, because each person/monad reflected the divine overarching monad. We are all in a fellowship with God, and each monad strives to understand his or her divine connection.

Leibniz's theories have wide-ranging implications for such emerg-ing fields as holography, and holographic paradigms of the universe and biophysics, whereby large monads, like animals, are made from smaller monads, cells. We know from cloning that just as Leibniz propounded, each part, in this case each cell, does indeed code for the whole. Leibniz's monad theory whereby the microcosm reflects the macrocosm greatly influenced both the religious outlook and the scientific view. Leibniz's monad theory was also linked to the metaphysical credo "As above, so below," and the biblical saying "We are made in God's image." From the scientific standpoint, if each part of the universe reflected the source, this implied some inner connection between all things. This theory would permeate such far-ranging realms as Kabbalism, Buddhism, Sufism, and mainstream science.

Coupled with Newton's law of gravitational attraction, Ernst Mach in the late 1800s could come up with Mach's Principle, which stated that all bodies (stars) act on each other; every part of the universe is connected to every other part. So Leibniz's monad theory can be expanded to view the world to be holographic in construction. An example of this would be to take the Hubble telescope and place it anywhere in the universe. At each point in space a map of the entire universe is present. No matter where one goes, the intersecting light from every star is there (or potentially there). Would not this moving telescope have, at any point in space, information about the whole? Now, with the advent of holography, or 3-D photography, whereby a part of a hologram does indeed code for the whole, cosmologists can step beyond simple philosophizing because they now have a *physical mechanism* that proves the theoretical axiom. In other words, if one says that each part of the universe codes for the whole, we now see an actual invention—holography—which supports the theory.

> One is led to a new notion of unbroken wholeness which denies the classical idea of analyzability of the world into separately and existing parts. . . . We have reversed the usual classical notion that the independent "elementary parts" of the world are the fundamental reality, and that the various systems are merely particular contingent forms and arrangements of these parts. Rather, we say that inseparable quantum interconnectedness of the whole universe is the fundamental reality, and that relatively independent behaving parts are merely particular and contingent forms within this whole.[12]

Leibniz also had an original view of evil. Since God was benevolent, how could one then explain evil? According to Leibniz's view, one must have faith that what looks like evil in the short run will be beneficent in the long run.[13] An interesting example of this would be the AIDS virus. Casualties from this late twentieth-century disease include both the innocent and the reckless. In the short run (say, in a time span of twenty-five to forty years), the disease has caused and will cause horrific hardship and death. However, in the long run, with greater understanding of how the virus cripples the immune system (e.g., attacks the T-cells), new medicines and technologies will emerge, which will help man treat other powerful diseases such as cancer, and we will also learn more about how the immune system works.

Having an infinite number of worlds to choose from, God chose the best one. Every monad has input, and a change in any one monad will affect the whole. Conversely, as the universe changes, the monads change along with it, and also each monad will reflect, in some way, every other monad. Leibniz's great philosophy starts with the premise that life develops out of some unifying and intelligent life force. So, in some way, his theories also serve to resurrect the authority of the church. Nevertheless, his microcosm/macrocosm monad theory remained simply too powerful an idea to be ignored by emerging scientific paradigms. We conclude this section with Leibniz quoting Hippocrates, *sumpoia panta*, "Everything breathes together."[14]

3

The Laws of History

HEISENBERG AND BOHR

In September of 1941, during World War II, the German physicist, Nobel Prize winner, and discoverer of the uncertainty principle, Werner Heisenberg, forty years old, in the prime of his manhood, took a trip to occupied Denmark to meet with Niels Bohr, his mentor, sixteen years his senior and close associate of Albert Einstein. The Nazis had already taken most of Europe. Having successfully invaded Poland, Holland, Belgium, and northern France by the spring of 1940, and in a debilitating bombing campaign on London, by this time Germany also controlled Austria, Czechoslovakia, Hungary, Denmark, and Norway, most of Yugoslavia, Romania, and Greece, and also a good part of northern Africa. Now Hitler could launch his next move, Operation Barbarossa, which was the invasion of Russia begun in June of 1941. By September, the time of the Heisenberg/Bohr meeting, Germany was, by far, the dominant force in Europe. The Germans had taken over the Ukraine by decimating the Red Army in the Battle of Kiev, and they were on their way to Leningrad in the north. However, with England still viable, the Third Reich was involved in a two-front war, and so they had the ghost of World War I to contend with, as that was the key reason for their demise. Nevertheless, in September, Nazi Germany was at its height. It would be three months until the attack on Pearl Harbor, so at this very moment, the United States was yet to enter the fray.

Influenced by the yin-yang insignia, Niels Bohr, also a Nobel Prize winner, solved one of the key problems in physics, namely that sometimes an elementary particle could operate as a wave and sometimes it could operate as a particle. Bohr agreed simply that this was so, and further, that these two attributes were complementary to each other. Thus he formulated a holistic principle that accepted the dual nature of the elementary particle as its fundamental property. Years earlier, working under Ernest Rutherford, Bohr helped describe the first workable model for the structure of the atom with electrons circling the nucleus in specified orbits. This mini solar system–like model was derived from nineteenth-century speculations reported by inventor Nikola Tesla in speeches in the 1890s studied by Rutherford.

Another problem at that time was the inability to measure both the speed and position of an electron simultaneously. That is where Heisenberg came in. He noted that the very act of trying to measure one of these variables influenced the other because one needed light particles to observe electrons. However, once photons were used, the electron's position or speed would be altered. At this fundamental level, there was no way to detach the observer from what was being observed. This became the uncertainty principle, and a key basis for quantum mechanics.

This theory suggested that the observer could not be separated from the universe as Descartes had speculated, because the very attempt to observe the elementary particles influenced them. Together, Heisenberg's uncertainty principle and Bohr's principle of complementarity were combined to create the Copenhagen interpretation of quantum theory. Heisenberg tells us that this interpretation is based on the paradox that the scientist needs the instruments of classical physics to describe the fundamental structure of matter, but the scientist is also aware that these instruments can never fully reveal what is really going on. At its most basic level, nature is contradictory: it has dual properties and fuzzy edges.[1]

Although Einstein disagreed with the premise that the ultimate substructure of the universe had an uncertain base, "God does not play dice" was Einstein's famous quote, Heisenberg's position became the prevailing view. For psychologists studying the nature of consciousness, Heisenberg's principle also provided a basis for allowing the mind of the observed to be intrinsically related to the structure of matter, because ultimately one could not separate the observer from what was being observed.

From a theoretical point of view, the principle of uncertainty was a radical departure from the Newtonian worldview whereby the universe operated much like a clock, with extreme precision and predictability. This new model allowed for ambiguity and thus, in some derivative sense, more free will. The ramifications of this simple theory were staggering, because it implied that the Great Designer had an arbitrary aspect.

During World War II, it was Heisenberg himself who was in charge of the Nazi plan to construct a nuclear bomb. Bohr, a Dane and half-Jewish, trapped in his homeland, was, like all other Jews there, forced to wear a yellow star on his sleeve. And like many, he was hoping and waiting for the war to end, or to find a means of escape.

At this specific moment, that is, 1940–43, with the Third Reich at its pinnacle, Hitler had placed Denmark in a separate category. Unlike Poland, Hungary, or Romania, where Hitler was expeditiously rounding up Jews, shooting them outright, or shipping them off to extermination camps, the Jews in Denmark, for this period, were relatively free. Since Hitler had not invaded Denmark but rather had taken it over in a peaceful fashion, part of the deal with the king of Denmark was to limit interference with interior politics. Further, Hitler needed a symbol to show the outside world how humane he was, and for one reason or another, he chose Denmark to be that symbol.

So why does Heisenberg visit Bohr in September of 1941?

In Michael Frayn's play *Copenhagen*, the playwright tries to answer this question in the way of *Roshamon,* that is, by telling the story from a number of points of view, some of which may be contradictory.

Heisenberg visits Bohr to tell him that at this moment in history, the scientists still control the potential power of this awful weapon. If both sides, that is, all scientists, agree *not* to build a bomb, it cannot be built.

Heisenberg visits Bohr to hint that he should leave Denmark as soon as possible because the hiatus cannot last. Or he comes to tell him, without telling him, that he is in control of the Nazi plan to build the bomb, and he has no plans to build it. In his autobiography, Heisenberg suggests that he was essentially stalling the Nazis, because he knew that eventually Hitler would be defeated, in part because Germany was fighting a two-front war, now that they had attacked Russia. Heisenberg says later that he stayed in Germany because it was important for some sane people to remain there, so that order could be restored after Hitler was defeated.

But maybe he visits Bohr because the building of a nuclear weapon involves uncharted territory in mathematical theory, and Heisenberg is seeking how to solve remaining dilemmas. He doesn't know how to do it without Bohr.

Or is Heisenberg there to try and find out how far along the Allies are in their quest? Or perhaps it is simply to show off to his teacher his new fancy uniform, to assure him that he, Heisenberg, could have the power to save Bohr's life, should the need arise.

What is the real reason? Is it any one of these reasons, some of which are contradictory, or is it perhaps some combination? Frayn as playwright suggests all of these scenarios, in separate gripping scenes. But no one really knows, and maybe Heisenberg, in September of 1941, was not totally certain himself of the reason.

The play suggests that at that moment, the fate of the world hinged on the minds of two men. If Heisenberg could solve the conundrum by wrestling a needed clue from Bohr, either through what Bohr would say or what he would not say, Hitler could have gotten the bomb, and then what? As it turned out, Bohr did not reveal what he knew to Heisenberg, and there is clear evidence that Heisenberg was, indeed, actively trying to build a nuclear weapon. For instance, Heisenberg had obtained heavy water from Norway, which was needed for the device. Where Heisenberg erred was in his premise. Heisenberg thought that a nuclear weapon would have to be huge, at least the size of a large room, whereas Bohr knew that a nuclear bomb could be built on a much smaller scale. It would seem likely that, one way or another, Bohr not only kept this information from Heisenberg but that he also, most likely subtly, encouraged Heisenberg to continue along the lines he was going, that is, to think on a large scale.

Heisenberg describes the meeting as a respite, where Bohr read poetry and Heisenberg played Mozart on the piano. A third scientist privy to the meeting, Carl von Weizsäcker, said that he and Heisenberg were definitely interested in finding out if a chain reaction were possible with nuclear power and Bohr was quite adept at deflecting this kind of discussion.

As the war progressed, policies changed. In 1943, Hitler broke yet another treaty and decided to round up the Jews of Denmark. Fortunately, however, nearly all escaped, with fellow Danes providing small boats to take those fleeing to Sweden. From there, Bohr went to England, and then he made his way to the United States and Los Alamos, where he would actively participate in the Manhattan Project.

There are many ironies to this story. By the time the United States finally dropped the bomb on Japan, Heisenberg was incarcerated. He was both shocked and appalled that such a horrible instrument was used. The world would never be the same. What did occur and what may have occurred fell into the exciting field of psychohistory, the place where psychological theories are applied to the historical process. The brilliance of Michael Frayn's play remains imbedded in Heisenberg's gift to science, the principle of uncertainty, which, in this instance, not only applied to the understanding of atomic structure but also to human inclinations.

MACHIAVELLI

Where the theoreticians above have been grouped according to their theories on the structure of the mind and man's relation to the cosmos, the following individuals, starting with Machiavelli, are covered because of their thoughts on the laws of history. Human action follows lawful principles. These great thinkers attempt to uncover specific psychological principles that direct the flow of human events.

An early forerunner to the field of psychohistory was the fifteenth-century Italian historian and political scientist Niccolo Machiavelli (1469–1527), who emphasized the role of *necessity* and its relationship to both chance and morality as crucial motivators to the historical process. Likening the understanding and control of history "to the taming of a mistress," Machiavelli stated that "it is necessary to keep her in obedience, to ruffle and force her," lest she rule you. For Machiavelli, knowledge of the past and of facts and the ability to visualize an obtainable future causes the prince to create policies that in themselves may be immoral, but within a larger context they protect the power structure of the leader and the state.

A recent leader who fits this bill is Vladimir Putin, prime minister of Russia. During Putin's reign (1999–2011), television shows satirizing the president were shut down, and more chillingly, upward of a hundred journalists were murdered.[2]

Although journalists are rarely murdered in America, oftentimes politicians are. Consider the assassinations that surround the rise and presidency of Richard Nixon. In 1960, he ran and lost against John Kennedy, who was assassinated before Kennedy was able to run for re-election. In 1968, when Nixon made a second bid for the presidency, his leading contender was JFK's brother, Robert Kennedy, who was assassinated during the primaries. And then, four years later, during Nixon's 1972 campaign against George McGovern, George Wallace, the third-party candidate who garnered forty-six electoral votes and almost 15 percent of the popular vote in 1968, was also shot and almost killed. Severely paralyzed, Wallace had to drop out of the race, and the votes that would have gone to him shifted to Nixon. Had Robert Kennedy not been killed, he might have beaten Nixon in 1968, and had Wallace not been shot in 1972, the race against McGovern would have been tight. The 1972 election has always been portrayed as a landslide victory for Nixon, which it was, but the outcome was skewed because Wallace was knocked out of the race. A similar scenario whereby a third-party candidate altered the outcome of a presidential election occurred twenty years later, when George Bush Sr., the sitting president, lost his 1992 race for reelection against Bill Clinton. A large percentage of potential Bush votes went instead to Ross Perot, who, much like Wallace before him, was a powerful third-party candidate. Had Perot not run, or had Perot been blocked from the presidential debates, it is likely that the sitting president, George Bush Sr., would have been reelected and Bill Clinton would have never become president.

Perhaps the ultimate Machiavellian in modern times was Adolf Hitler, who, five hundred years after Machiavelli, truly ran his empire under the credo "The end justifies the means." By his nature, Hitler was a serial liar who broke every treaty he ever signed. Ironically, Hitler formed the ultimate coup by demanding that his military swear an oath to God to protect the führer and the fatherland. Thus, when Hitler reversed himself by talking his high command into agreeing to invade Russia by breaking yet another treaty, this time one that he had with Stalin, Hitler caused enormous moral discomfort among his generals. Not only had Hitler forced his generals to become dishonorable, because they, too, would be breaking their word, the führer was also forcing the country into a two-front war, which was the key reason Germany lost the First World War. Ironically, Hitler's military men feared retribution from God Almighty for breaking a sworn oath, while at the same time they also apparently had little compunction about steamrolling through countries like Poland, Belgium, and the Balkans and killing tens of thousands of innocents along the way.

Using another Machiavellian credo, "It is better to be feared than to be loved," Hitler ruled his domain by sheer terror. Resurrecting the guillotine, and in special cases even an ax, during his reign, Hitler literally chopped off the heads of thousands of criminals and adversaries.

Hitler's view was a radical philosophical departure from generally accepted precepts of leadership, which before Machiavelli's time, at least overtly, aspired toward honor and virtue. In this new outlook, God would not punish corrupt or even depraved behavior, if, through this means, the state would survive and prosper. Hitler was fond of saying that "history was written by the victors." In this view, if deceitfulness and murder is necessary, it is just.

At its heart, the Machiavellian view opposed not only the church and an all-knowing God but also the Ten Commandments. There was no overriding deity watching over man, no day of judgment. Without consequence, man could do as he pleased.

GIAMBATTISTA VICO

A historian from the University of Naples, Giambattista Vico (1668–1744) had a view that seemed to combine a Machiavellian outlook, one based on selfishness, with an altruistic bent. Vico derived a cyclical theory of history, which suggested that "human nations pass through certain stages of development." The progress of civilization involved an interplay of divine providence and rationality, against a "strong impulsion of violent passions. . . . The first indubitable principle . . . posited is that this world of nations has certainly been made by men, and its guise must therefore be formed within the modifications of our human mind." Vico separated human history into three periods:

1. The age of gods and divine intervention
2. The age of heroes
3. The age of men

Undoubtedly Vico is trying to come to grips with man's supernatural origin as espoused by the Bible, a view still prevalent today. Vico's third period, the age of modern man, gave rise to "the first popular commonwealths and then the monarchies." Stating "All men recognized themselves as equal in human nature," these writings established a philosophical basis that fifty years later lay at the heart of both the American and French revolutions.

A realist, Vico stated that people are endowed with both free will and a "corrupted nature under the tyranny of self-love . . . seeking everything useful for themselves and nothing for their companions." Nevertheless, civilization evolved when the tendency to care for the immediate family was extended to the "local tribe, to nations and eventually to the whole human race." Thus, an innate quality of divine providence linked to self-preservation, causing selfishness on the one hand and a care for humanity on the other hand.[3] Certainly man's present concern about global warming corresponds to Vico's view, because this view places more concern for the fate of humanity at large, than it does for individuals, yet it does derive from a primal inclination toward self-love.

IMMANUEL KANT

Influenced in part by Vico's writings, Immanuel Kant (1724–1804) extended this idea of divine providence to suggest that so-called free will "is determined, like all other external events, by universal natural laws." For Kant, the universe was purposeful. To understand this teleological idea and thus also the "definite laws" that lay behind the historical process, Kant outlined nine propositions:

1. Inherent capacities are destined to unfold themselves.
2. Inherent reason in man is developed in the species rather than in the individual.
3. Humans, endowed with reason and free will, must produce out of themselves.
4. Humans are born with an internal antagonism, which, on the one hand can be a destroyer of society, yet on the other hand "drives them to overcome all his propensity to indolence."
5. Humanity is impelled to create a civil society.
6. The human being, as an animal, has an inherent need for a leader.
7. Humans need to create laws.
8. There is an inherent potential to develop and create a world community.

9. The fulfillment of these innate potentials is in accordance with the design in nature for a certain plan for the distant future.[4]

What Kant has done is uncover nine lawful tendencies that shape human behavior. He ascribes these to man's free will, which he links to reason, but he also recognizes that humans are driven by animal desires, and thus we are contradictory. This is a keen insight that will greatly influence one of his cohorts, Hegel. These ideas also lie at the basis of Freud's concepts of the ego (linked to reason), the superego (which Kant links to man's need to create a civil society), and the animalistic id (with its aggressive inclinations and death instinct). Kant also takes into account Aristotle's teleological principle, recognizing that there are larger forces than man's shaping human destiny. Like Aristotle and later Gurdjieff, for Kant the universe is purposeful. This view is a direct counterargument to the Darwinian notion that life evolved through a chance process. But more than that, the view also suggests that if indeed we do change our ways to care for the planet so as to reduce air pollution and derive our energy from renewable sources, this imperative derives from a realm that, in Kant's words, truly is "in accordance with the design in nature for a certain plan for the distant future."

A key question that comes to mind is whether or not man can consciously interact with this force, and the answer, so far, seems to be, "Unlikely." Here is where such themes as faith versus the existential loneliness of man come into play. Where most men yearn for a link to the force that created us, and in some way shapes our destiny, the harsh reality that many others suggest is that we are on our own, to do what we please, even if that means destroying the very world that gave birth to our species. This may seem like hyperbole, but man has indeed faced Armageddon several times during even this author's lifetime. The Berlin airlift comes to mind. This event, which took place in the late 1940s, placed man at the cusp of yet another world war. And even now, in 2011, we face similar challenges as countries like Iraq seek nuclear weapons with the stated purpose of using them, while rogue terrorists also aspire toward that same goal. There is no great hand from above that will stop the madness, and yet the majority of humanity still has faith in man's inherent reason.

ANTOINE-NICOLAS DE CONDORCET

For Antoine-Nicolas de Condorcet (1743–1794) "universal laws of history" were not only conceived in terms of intellectual and artistic advance; such goals as equality between the sexes, universal education, freedom of expression of thought, and redistribution of wealth were also laws of history. Eschewing the aggressive force in man, for Condorcet[5] humanity's aim was a search for truth. Humans evolve from barbaric existence to civilization and then to enlightenment. Our hopes for the future can be subsumed under three heads: (1) the abolition of inequality between nations; (2) the progress of equality within each nation; and (3) the true perfection of mankind. This is the propelling force for the historical process; it is, for Condorcet, a state of perfection. Man's wish to create a world community and advances in medicine and technology can be seen as expressions of this force. Certainly Condorcet has been prophetic with the advent two centuries later of the United Nations and a modern world with international free commerce and travel. Inspired by Vico and Kant, Condorcet as an idealist influenced Hegel and Marx, two theoreticians who ironically had a more complex view, with Marx's pragmatic, materialistic, and somewhat dark outlook as a counterpoint to Hegel's model, which still ascribed power to a friendly creator.

GEORG WILHELM FRIEDRICH HEGEL

Georg Wilhelm Friedrich Hegel (1770–1831) stands out as a seminal philosopher. Influenced by Kant, Condorcet, and Rousseau, Hegel expanded on Kant's fourth law of the historic process: that individuals are born with an internal antagonism that could be a destroyer of society, but which also leads humans to overcome their inertia. The *Hegelian dialectic* proposes that a concept generates its opposite "contradictory" idea. This antagonism, in turn, generates a synthesis, which contains the essence of both ideas, and this, in turn, generates its opposite, and so forth.

An excellent example of the Hegelian dialectic can be seen in the presidential election of 2008. Since America's foundings, white men had always ruled the roost. According to Hegel's theory, the very fact that white men were in power would stimulate an opposing force, which in 2008 resulted in the rise of a powerful woman, Hillary Clinton, a New York senator and wife of President Bill Clinton, and a powerful black man, Barack Obama, a senator from Illinois. These two Democrats were in a very close race against a third senator, John McCain, a white man and a Republican whose fate was determined by the Hegelian dialectical. On some level, realizing the need for an opposite spark, McCain shocked the nation when he chose a little-known female governor from the state of Alaska, Sarah Palin, to be his running mate. Seen from the Hegelian perspective, with the human tendency for history to shift through opposition, both Republicans and Democrats could be satisfied that their respective tickets had a dialectical component. As it turned out, of course, Senator Barack Obama beat Senator Hillary Clinton in the primaries and then, with his white running mate Joe Biden, Obama went on to beat John McCain and Sarah Palin for the presidency.

For Hegel, the mind/matter polarity can also be applied to dialectical law. The hard sciences adhere to the realm of matter, but history adheres to the "essence of spirit . . . the idea of freedom." Like Kant's teleological worldview, Hegel's history, although following a zig-zag pattern, is goal oriented. It proceeds in phases and according to the "needs of the age." Ideas inherent in Hegel's philosophy of history can also be found in psychohistorical paradigms as well as in both Freud's and Gurdjieff's theories. Hegel states that "world historical figures" operate from *nonconscious motives*. They may be creating history for their own pleasure, but also they are part of the "world spirit": God's will.

An interesting example of this would be John Kennedy's goal to place a man on the moon, which we actually achieved within ten years of his wish. One can't help but feel that although this achievement was a direct result of Kennedy's desire, he was also manifesting a need for the species, to fulfill our destiny by expanding out beyond the planet.

Manifestations of "individuals and peoples, in which they seek to satisfy their own purposes, are, at the same time, the means and instruments of a higher and broader purpose of which they know nothing, which they realize unconsciously. . . . Heroes of an epoch . . . are great men, because they willed and accomplished something great, not a mere fancy, a mere intention, but that which met the case and fell in with the needs of the age."[6]

Hegel's history operates according to God's will, either through devotion to the "One Aim" or through its "negation." In either case, and according to his dialectical principle, God's will prevails. Hegel's conceptualization credits world leaders with force of will, the ability to succeed and understand the needs of the time, but also with an unconscious mandate from a higher power. Mere mortals are actually instruments of "that spirit . . . [which] is the inmost soul of all individuals."[7]

JOHN STUART MILL

Looking at the forces that shape history in an entirely different way, John Stuart Mill (1806–1873) came to see that different cultures would operate with different sociological principles. In Gardiner's masterful compilation *Theories of History,* which was the major source for a good part of this chapter, Gardiner states, "Mill realized that social development can only be understood historically; it proceeds through different stages of civilization and cultural advance. . . . [However, social phenomena cannot be understood] without connecting them with the basic laws of human psychology."[8] These principles of human nature included social factors, morality of the subculture, technological advance, distribution of wealth, relationships between classes, cultural beliefs and ideals, and the form of government.

One must not only view the society as a whole in order to understand its history, but the history of the society that preceded it must be studied as well. Thus, causes and effects need to be analyzed. For Mill, social progress proceeds because of humanity's intellectual curiosity, care for the greater good, and pursuit of truth. "Advances in civilization are always accompanied by advancement in knowledge."[9] Mill therefore sees human progress as directly linked to increases in the intelligence of the masses.

Using once again the 2008 election of Barack Obama as a point of consideration, as Mill's theory suggests, there are many preceding events that led the way for a black man to become president of the United States in the early part of the twenty-first century. The seeds for this watershed moment started decades earlier, particularly with Martin Luther King's August 1963 "I Have a Dream" speech, whereby he envisioned that a person would not be measured by the "color of his skin, but by the content of his character." More recently, in the years 2000–2008, the last two secretaries of state, Colin Powell and Condoleezza Rice, were also African Americans. Further, there was a large movement in this country to get Colin Powell, who was a five-star general and former head of the Joint Chiefs of Staff, to run for president in 2000. So the country was already primed to accept the possibility that a black person could be president. In a major film, *Deep Impact* (1998), the president of the United States was the actor Morgan Freeman, another black man. These preceding sociological factors could correlate with how Mill would view the outcome of the election of Barack Obama.

In discussing whether or not history is created by individuals or by a people, Mill notes that, for instance, although murders are committed by individuals, the number of murders per year is a rather stable number. This principle extends to "illegitimate births, suicides, accidents, and all other social phenomena." Nevertheless, for Mill, history is not created by the local culture due to some statistical or evolutionary law. Innovative leaders and scientists may be ahead of their time; however, they do not merely see or create advancements before their inevitable appearance. *Individuals create the history* and are themselves causes for new effects. Citing a number of outstanding individuals such as Confucius and Julius Caesar, Mill supports his hypothesis. "Certain social improvements," Mill postulates, "can only follow and not precede others. . . . [For example] the whole stream of Grecian history is one of a series of examples how often events on which the whole destiny of subsequent civilization turned, were dependent on the personal character for good or evil of some one individual."[10]

A modern example of this would be the recent siege of Iraq in March of 2003. This war was caused, to a great extent, because of the personal desires of a single man, President George W. Bush. Some say the president went to war to complete the task started by his father, who fought a war in Iraq in 1990, and to avenge Saddam Hussein's inept attempt to assassinate George Bush, the father, several years after that war. President Bush's stated reasons for invasion were fourfold: (1) the possible (but virtually nonexistent) connection to bin Laden and al-Qaeda, the man and group responsible for the 9/11 Twin Towers attack in 2001; (2) Saddam Hussein's supposed stockpile of weapons of mass destruction; (3) Saddam Hussein's financial support to the families of Palestinian suicide bombers; and (4) Saddam Hussein's murderous regime, which was a crime against humanity.

President Bush gave Saddam Hussein ample time to comply with specific requests for dismantling his arsenal and for giving up power. In other words, although the invasion of Iraq took place essentially because of the desires of one powerful man (the event has been called a war of choice), another powerful man could have prevented the conflagration had he decided to capitulate. The end result is that the entire future history of the Middle East has had its course irreversibly altered because of the conflicting wills of two men. Tens of millions of people, if not the entire world, have been affected. This is clearly an example of Mill's supposition that *individuals* create the history. However, the exact way Iraq will go—if there will be civil war, if the Kurds will get their own state, if President Bush will ultimately gain or lose prestige because of the war, and so on—is no longer dependent on single individuals. The event may have been started because of the desire of one man, but like a wild fire born from a single match, the consequences, and thus the resulting history, will be caused by "the agitated wills of many."

In a more positive light, perhaps only Nelson Mandela could have helped South Africa transition from apartheid to a democratic regime in a peaceful fashion for the very reason that Mandela had been in a white man's jail for nearly thirty years. In South Africa, blacks outnumber whites approximately ten to one. When Mandela emerged from prison in 1990 and was elected president of South Africa in 1994, his attitude of forgiveness and his emphasis on a multiracial government and love of country were powerful instruments to ease extraordinarily difficult tribal tensions.

Mill calls for "great flexibility in [his] . . . generalizations," or laws of the historical process. Further, Mill notes that if one takes a sufficiently large cycle, say several thousand years, "individual contributions may be eliminated." Nevertheless, Mill is quite clearly on the side of the individual, for he concludes, "Great men and great actions . . . send forth a thousand unseen influences. . . . [Even] the whole destiny of subsequent civilization[s] . . . were dependent upon the personal character for good or evil of some one individual."[11]

HENRY BUCKLE

One of Mill's acolytes was businessman and scholar Henry Buckle (1821–1862), who reduced the philosophical discussion of the lawful nature of the historical process to two doctrines: *free will* and *predestination*. Buckle states that predestination cannot be proved or disproved, but free will "rests on the metaphysical dogma of the supremacy of human consciousness." Just as one can predict physical events when prerequisites have been established, "if I know a person's character, I can predict his behavior. If I am wrong," Buckle continues, "it would be honest because I lacked all of the important information."[12] Thus, Buckle formulated a law pertinent to the historical process: "The actions of men are determined solely by their antecedents." History, however, is still a complex affair. Unlike Machiavelli, Buckle recognized that a sense of morality did indeed influence the historical process. It is "the action of external phenomena upon the mind and the mind upon phenomena." Thus, for Buckle, one must understand the "mental laws," for they are the "ultimate basis for history."[13]

> People were coming out with completely new operating systems, but we had already captured the volume, so we could price it low and keep selling. . . . [And] believe me, it would have been a lot easier to write Windows so it wouldn't run DOS applications. But we knew we couldn't make that transition without that compatibility.
>
> BILL GATES, 1994

Buckle's theory has merit, but chance still plays a role. Thus, any attempt to truly uncover the laws of history must take this factor into account. For instance, in the 1890s J. Pierpont Morgan, who was destined to become the most powerful man in the world, almost died in a snowstorm. One hundred years later, Bill Gates became a billionaire ostensibly because Gary Kildall, an engineer with a better disk-operating system, missed a lunch meeting with IBM executives. Astonishingly, rather than research the difference in technologies, these same executives settled on the Microsoft slap-dash disk operating system, which lies at the heart of all IBM-compatible/Intel chip computer systems, and which even as late at the early twenty-first century still represents over 90 percent of all computers sold in the world. To give the reader an idea of how inferior this system is, as compared to the disk-operating system of the Apple Macintosh computer: since about 1995 and for the next fourteen years, I used an Apple Macintosh computer and my wife, Lois, used an IBM compatible. In 2005 we both purchased laptops, but by 2009, my wife's computer was not working well. When she brought it in to be fixed, she found that she had upward of a hundred viruses on it, whereas my Mac was virtually virus free. The entire development of our modern computer age and the inherent weakness of the IBM-compatible disk operation system can be traced back to this one lunch meeting Bill Gates had with the IBM people. Gates was actually unprepared to offer a secure disk-operating system; he bluffed his way through with an incomplete and thus inferior system, and he succeeded beyond anyone's wildest dreams, thereby becoming one of the richest men in the world. However, the fact of the matter is, as he states himself in the quote above, even after he realized the problem, he still refused to change the system to a better design. In that sense, the mental laws that Buckle alludes to (e.g., hubris) did indeed play a major role, but chance was the underlying trigger for this monumental event in the history of our computer age.

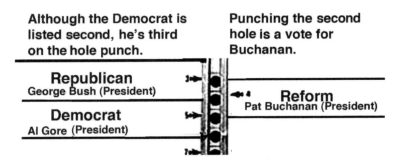

Fig. 3.1. The infamous "butterfly ballot" put out in southern Florida in the election of 2000 gave thousand of votes to Pat Buchanan that were meant to go to Al Gore.

In the year 2000, the choice for president of the United States was ultimately determined by a mistake in the way some ballot boxes were designed. The race was a dead heat between incumbent vice president Al Gore and Texas governor George W. Bush. Whoever won Florida would become the next president of the United States. Pat Buchanan, an arch-conservative Republican candidate, was listed on the so-called butterfly ballot in southern Florida in an incorrect fashion. Hundreds, if not thousands, of people who thought they were voting for Al Gore ended up voting for Buchanan. This simple truth was acknowledged by Buchanan himself when he realized that he could not have legitimately taken so many votes in this heavily Democratic district, enough votes to alter that outcome of the election. And so the entire direction that the U.S. took, and thus the world from that point on, was really linked to an innocent error that ended up having monumental consequences. For instance, it is well known that Al Gore would *not* have invaded Iraq in 2003. In fact, Gore gave a speech three months before the invasion advising specifically not to invade. Gore also would not have instituted the large tax cuts implemented by the Bush administration. All of this directly affected, on the international scale, not only the balance of power in the Middle East but also the lives and deaths of literally hundreds of thousands of people. And on the national level, these decisions affected the collective debt of the nation, and thus interest rates, the cost of housing, actions in the stock market, and so on.

KARL MARX

The most significant philosopher of this period, in terms of influencing the course of history by his philosophy, is Karl Marx (1818–1883), who was heavily influenced by Hegel and Ludwig Feuerbach. Echoing the Marxian view, Gardiner writes, "Many ideologies men create and believe in are explicable by reference to the material conditions in which they find themselves."[14] Stated simply, a poor person will have a different view of the world than a rich person. For instance, in the United States, the vast majority of men and women in the armed forces come from families from modest or poor incomes. The sons and daughters of wealthy individuals, in general, do not go to war. Working with colleagues Engels and Saint-Simon, Marx stressed the role of class conflict as an important criterion to the historical process.

In his article "The Materialist Conception of History," Marx criticizes Hegel's abstract concept of the absolute spirit as being a motive force to the historical process, a force "above and beyond" the real man.[15] For Marx, whose father was a convert from Judaism to Lutheranism, the first premise of all human history was "the existence of living human individuals."[16] Opposed to a religious or metaphysical formulation as the underpinning of history, Marx based his philosophy upon "the fundamental facts of material production and the conflicts between different economic interests."[17] In direct opposition to the religious views of philosophers like Leibniz and Hegel, Marx states that "men produce their own conceptions. . . . [They] are not in some imaginary condition." Their actions and situations can be observed "empirically . . . under determinate conditions."[18] Further, "the dominant material force in society is at the same time its dominant intellectual force. . . ."[19] It is not the consciousness of men that determines their being but, on the contrary, their social being determines their consciousness."[20]

This is a brilliant insight, as it ascribes a person's worldview not to some abstract spiritual influence or religious affiliation but to one's economic status, and in that sense to one's job. According to this view, a white-collar person does indeed think differently from a blue-collar person.

Marxian philosophy states that the worker is exploited because "he becomes an appendage of the machine,"[21] yet ironically, the advancing technology shall also serve to "obliterate all distinction of labor."[22] Thus, as the worker gains more freedom through advances in technology, he becomes an equal class and eventually seeks to overthrow the bourgeoisie (middle class). Marx predicts that the revolution will succeed because the bourgeoisie becomes "incompetent" in providing for the worker. Certainly this was the case in Russia in 1917, where peasants were suffering to a great degree. Oppressed, the proletariat overthrew the Russian nobility and ostensibly took on the philosophy of the man who predicted the revolution one-half century earlier.

As Marx's writings have clearly indicated, the historical process is vitally dependent upon economic criteria. And that is why revolution did not occur in the United States, because the worker, although exploited by the robber barons, was still earning enough money to support his needs and thus prevent any large-scale movement against the wealthy from taking place. The progression of history is a complex phenomenon involving science, philosophy, psychology, and political science. Also, and ironically, the historical process is sometimes shaped by the writers who sought merely to describe it.

The Russian writer Leo Tolstoy (1828–1910), who died before the Russian Revolution, also wrote on the philosophy of the historical process. In his classic book *War and Peace,* Tolstoy asks, "what is the power that moves people?" Tolstoy delineates three factors:

1. The role of the hero or ruler
2. The interaction of many persons connected with the event
3. The intellectual activity of the culture

These reduce down to "the sum of human wills."[23] Although Tolstoy emphasizes the potential for free will, he also realized the overriding importance of the role of necessity. What may seem free at the time of its occurrence may actually be inevitable, as so many historical occurrences appear inevitable when looked at from a perspective of extension in time (e.g., the collapse of the Berlin wall in 1989).

This theory, however, is countered by Mill's "great person" theory, because in Mill's theory the will of but a single person could override the will of millions. A good example of this occurred during World War II after Hitler invaded Russia. Although the initial invasion was tremendously successful, a number of key factors worked against the Third Reich. These included the incompatibility of railroad lines at the border of Russia, the rainy season of mud, which made it near impossible for the German army to advance their vehicles, the enormous size of Russia and Siberia, Stalin's institution of a scorched earth policy, and the incredibly harsh winters whereby the temperature could reach 30 and 40 degrees below zero. Hundreds of thousands of soldiers simply froze to death. Hitler's generals pleaded with the führer to retreat, but Hitler would hear none of it, and because of this one man's obstinate stand, the German army lost nearly four million men!

4

The Role of Technology

Certainly one of the most important reasons for human advance, aside from our large brain, was the advent of tool making. In the film *2001: A Space Odyssey,* primitive man discovers that if he uses a large bone as a weapon, he can control his adversaries. In a remarkable scene this ancient precursor to man takes this large bone and begins to crush not only his opponents but also the skulls of living and dead animals. In a moment of exalted fervor, this ape-man throws the bone up into the air, and as it rotates, it transforms into a spaceship. The writer and director team of Arthur C. Clark and Stanley Kubrick condensed several million years of human evolution and technological advance into one staggering take-your-breath-away scene.

As we reached the new millennium symbolized by the year 2000, *Time-Life* sought to come up with the *most important person* of the past one thousand years. Many well-known philosophers, scientists, explorers, political leaders, and inventors were on the list—Newton, Edison, da Vinci, Marco Polo, Columbus, Darwin, Freud—but the editors surprised the readership when they settled on a printer: Johannes Gutenberg (1398–1468). Why Gutenberg? Because the advent of moveable type allowed books to be mass-produced for the first time. Books became available to the masses, and so the general intelligence of the race could increase markedly. This would cause history to proceed in an entirely different way. Scientific development, medical discoveries, and so on would advance at a much more rapid rate.

NIKOLA TESLA

A concept initiated by Hegel and discussed by Marx was that humanity was "nothing but a mass"[1] following along the path of history. Whereas Hegel emphasized the role of an abstract world-spirit, Marx was a materialist who described history in direct relationship to humanity's connection to technological and economic production. Inventor extraordinaire Nikola Tesla (1856–1943) considered these concepts as he thought about easing man's physical burdens through the specific acts of his creations. Conceiving of humanity as a whole entity (e.g., a mass), Tesla employed principles of physics to explain the historical process.

> Though we may never be able to comprehend human life, we know certainly that it is movement of whatever nature it may be. The existence of a movement implies a body, which is being moved, and a force, which is moving it. Hence, wherever there is life, there is a mass moved by a force.[2]

If M = mass of humanity, Tesla suggested, and V = "a certain hypothetical velocity, which in the present state of science, we are unable exactly to define and determine," then the total human force would be equal to MV^2, the standard mathematical formula for calculating force.[3]

Where Marx proposed a world revolution in order to usurp the power of the ruling class, Tesla sought, as a humanitarian, to increase the amount of human energy as a whole by creating inventions that would reduce inertia while also serving to increase the mass. With such devices as his induction motor (1888), Tesla calculated that this invention ultimately saved the planet tens of thousands of man-hours of labor per year. Machines would do the work instead of humans. Tesla's telautomaton (1898), or remote-controlled robot, and his inventions in wireless and mass communications also worked to markedly advance the race. In the first two instances, machines were created to take over the more mundane levels of labor so that humanity's intellectual capacities could be harnessed more efficiently. In the third instance, Tesla understood that the elimination of borders through wireless telephones would effectively shrink the planet, and thus, world peace was more likely to ensue.

At the turn of the twentieth century, Tesla foresaw not only a global wireless network, but also the positive ramifications of this development. The quote below was written in 1904. Looked at a hundred years later, one cannot help but see a direct parallel to the onset of the age of the Internet, whereby the world truly has achieved a global communication scheme that has advanced the race at an astonishing pace. Just as an example from my own life, at the time of writing, January 2011, I live in Rhode Island and am presently involved in a project that puts me in daily contact through e-mail with individuals from England, China, Australia, and California. We are all interlinked essentially instantaneously. Most recently, even repressive regimes are being forced to alter their path for the simple reason that they can no longer control the masses because intercommunication is so advanced. Just this past year a bevy of revolutions were organized by e-mail, Facebook, and Twitter. One, in Iran, has been to date ultimately unsuccessful. However, other essentially nonviolent revolutions with help provided from Wikileaks on corruption in government were successful. In just a matter of days and weeks in January and February of 2011, governments in Tunisia and Egypt collapsed and rulers fled. And as this book goes into production, these Internet social networks are also helping to spark great change and other potential revolutions in Yemen, Syria, and Bahrain. As Tesla predicted in 1901 with his human force = MV^2 equation, human advance is occurring at such a rapid rate that the entrenched powers can no longer control and hide information from the youth. This presents a problem in many other nations as well, such as China and North Korea.

Note the sheer genius of the following quote from Tesla, which he wrote in 1904.

The results attained by me have made my scheme of "World Telegraphy" easily realizable. It constitutes a radical and fruitful departure from what has been done heretofore. It involve[s] the employment of a number of plants each of [which] will be preferably located near some important center of civilization and the news it receives through any channel will be flashed to all points of the globe. A cheap and simple [pocket-sized] device, may then be set up somewhere on sea or land, and it will record the world's news or such special messages as may be intended for it. Thus the *entire earth will be converted into a huge brain, as it were, capable of response in every one of its parts* [emphasis added]. Since a single plant of but one hundred horse-power can operate hundreds of millions of instruments, the system will have a virtually infinite working capacity . . .[4]

Mental energy (e.g., increase of mass education), when expressed in creative pursuit of goals, was, in Tesla's view, equivalent to "mass of higher velocity."[5]

Stated more to the point: if, for example, the children are of the same degree of enlightenment as the parents, that is, mass of the "same velocity," the energy will simply increase proportionately to the number added. If they are less intelligent or advanced, or mass of a "smaller velocity," there will be very slight gain in the energy; but if they are further advanced or a mass of "higher velocity," then the new generation will add very considerably to the sum total of human energy.[6] Conversely, it scarcely need be stated that everything that is against the teachings of religion and the laws of hygiene is tending to decrease the mass.[7]

Tesla's writings trace the role of technological development in shaping the evolution of culture in lawful ways. As he himself is the inventor of our hydroelectric power system, fluorescent lighting, wireless communication, and cell phone technology, Tesla also changed the world through his creations. Where Machiavelli studied the role of the iron-fisted prince as a shaper of the destiny of the species and Henry Buckle considered moral factors, Tesla discussed the part played by the inventor.

OTTO SPENGLER

We end this section with Otto Spengler (1880–1936), a German theoretician who was, without doubt, one of the most original theoreticians on the forces that shape history. In his book *The Decline of the West,* Spengler discusses his concept of *historical recurrence*. Heavily influenced by Goethe and Vico, Spengler was opposed to a linear conceptualization of history. Rather, he conjectured that human history followed dynamic processes inherent in nature. Just as animals and plants grow and die, so do cultures (e.g., Egypt, Greece, Rome, the Aztecs).

"I see world-history as a picture of endless formations and transformations, of the marvelous waxing and waning of organic forms. The professional historian, on the contrary, sees it as a sort of tapeworm industriously adding on to itself one epoch after another." Taking an approach in line with Darwin's view that evolution proceeds through the process of random mutation and survival of the fittest, Spengler dismally concludes that "mankind has no aim, no plan any more than the family of butterflies or orchids."[8]

Wikipedia notes that Spengler's book unleashed a firestorm in the intellectual community. Coming out at the time of Germany's humiliating defeat during the Great War and the corresponding Versailles Treaty, which further stripped the fatherland of any of its remaining manhood, many Germans took comfort in Spengler's view because it placed the destruction of their empire within a natural process of rises and falls of nations. Where critics like Karl Popper and Count Harry Graf Kessler saw Spengler's dismal view as "pointless," so-called neo-Kantians, who were really anti-Kantians, took comfort in a cyclical paradigm "that saw no meaning to history." On the other hand, Thomas Mann and Max Weber praised the work. As Hitler rose to power, Spengler, initially a supporter, came to criticize the Nazis. He had become a world figure and highly regarded, even if he was quite pessimistic; however, he died early in the Nazi story—he was only fifty-six—so there is no way of knowing how his thinking would have been reshaped had Spengler lived past the mid-1930s.

Seeing the time line as an artificial artifice that was misleading at best, Spengler's history was spiralized, or cyclical, and thus he would argue that human action was more in line with the pace and rhythm of natural processes. Unlike Aristotle, Kant, and later Bergson and Gurdjieff, Spengler saw no underlying purpose or élan to human action. Just like any other animal who had its day in the sun and is now extinct, humans would also follow that course.

5

Modern Psychohistory

Two key differences between the philosophical historians of the eighteenth and nineteenth centuries and the modern-day psychohistorians are (1) the emphasis on analysis of childhood experiences as major shapers of personality in world leaders, and (2) the realization of the impact of primal and unconscious factors in the historical process. Whereas the earlier philosophers tended to discuss the general forces, which initiated the historical process, the psychohistorian utilized psychoanalytic techniques developed mainly by Freud to explain various motivations responsible for historical movements. In an attempt to make sense out of any legacy from the past, analysis and usually psychoanalysis are essential. It is simply part of the human condition to want to know why, for instance, a man like George Washington led the rebellion against the British in the late 1700s when it would seem that he could have lived out his days easily as a successful and wealthy British subject.

Modern psychohistorians make greater use of psychological interpretations of the development of the individual's personality, unlike the philosophers from the past who tended to deal in more abstract and thus universal terms. Whereas traditional historians attempted to create a chronological account of historical events, the new psychohistorian attempts to understand psychodynamic motivation of the individual in question, as well as the psychology of the times in which the event took place.

WILHELM DILTHEY

Psychohistorians credit nineteenth-century European philosopher Wilhelm Dilthey (1833–1911) and, more recently, twentieth-century French thinker Lucien Febvre as important forerunners of this field. Commenting on Dilthey's contributions, Manuel wrote, "the history of man could best be presented as a series of psychological world outlooks. . . . [Dilthey] attempted to seize the essence of entire ages and to inter-relate economico-social philosophico-religious trends. . . . [He] seemed more comfortable with biographical studies of creative men in whom he saw the various psychic currents of an age criss-cross."[1] A twentieth-century world leader that fits that bill would be Mahatma Gandhi. Schooled in England to become a barrister, Gandhi survived great prejudice as a lawyer defending Indian rights in South Africa before he returned to India to lead his nation in a peaceful revolt against the ruling British.

Understanding "psychic currents" of an age would also help explain the unlikely rise of actor Ronald Reagan to become first governor of California and then president of the United States. At least in America, the very fact of being famous gives one an edge. The body-builder and actor Arnold Schwarzenegger is another case in point, as he, too, rose to become governor of California, and he, too, had been talked about as presidential material even though the Constitution ruled him out as a potential contender because he was not born in this country.

Dilthey emphasized inferential reasoning in the investigation of "human studies."[2] The analyst must do more than simply root out "the fundamental relationship between cause and effect. . . . [Understanding should be] directed toward the structure of the plot, the characterizations, the interplay of events."[3] In the case of Reagan, one would have to consider the very force of his personality and simply his likeability factor as key reasons why he was able to unseat Jimmy Carter, the sitting president, whose persona was simply more glum. Dilthey suggests that historical moments are intentional creations brought about by the demands of the situation as well as by the psyche of the individual in question. Through inductive reasoning and also a reliving of the event in imagination, a whole physical expression can be understood. Thus the outer manifestation of this expression can never be separated from "the world of the mind."[4]

Each historical moment, Dilthey states, can be understood on two levels: (1) the elementary level, which links sequential causes with effects; and (2) the higher level, which looks at the event as an interrelated whole. Outer actions may obscure hidden motivations. Only through higher understanding and empathy can a full picture emerge. Returning to the 1980 Reagan/Carter election, and seeing it in Dilthey's terms as a plot with outer action and hidden motivations, Carter's popularity and corresponding influence as a leader had taken a nosedive mainly for three reasons: (1) gasoline had almost doubled in price *overnight* in the midst of his administration; (2) because of this, great uncertainty as to oil reserves reached a peak and Carter handled the situation badly by giving a "crisis of confidence" speech—an American president should never show weakness, and one way or another, Carter did; and (3) fifty-two Americans were being held hostage in Iran. For these and other reasons, many Americans were looking for a new leader. The likeable California governor and former movie star Ronald Reagan, a man who always had a smile and a friendly story to tell, fit the bill. The day of Reagan's inauguration in January of 1980, all fifty-two hostages were released. Many people asked if this was a coincidence.

During Reagan's two terms as president, there were few scandals and, overall, the country prospered. The biggest black mark against him, however, did indeed involve Iran, whereby Reagan and his team secretly sold arms to the enemy nation and used the proceeds to fund the contras in a covert war in the Central American country of Nicaragua. This imbroglio, often billed as the "Arms for Hostages" scandal, suggests that before the election the Reagan team made a secret deal with the Ayatollah Khomeini, the new head of Iran, to supply him with arms (they were in the midst of a war against Iraq) in exchange for the hostages' release. If this scenario is correct, Iran purposely held the hostages throughout the presidential campaign for the Machiavellian reason of helping to insure Jimmy Carter's defeat so that they could obtain essential weapons from the new administration. Khomeini was no fan of Carter because Carter had helped the ousted Shah of Iran by providing sanctuary and medical attention, as he was dying of cancer and no other country would take him in. And Khomeini did indeed receive a secret shipment of arms from Reagan who also inscribed a Bible for the Ayatollah, which was given to him by Reagan's emissary, Oliver North.

Keep in mind that America was, at that time, backing Iraq in a long, costly ten-year war against the very country America was also secretly helping, Iran. In other words, America was playing both sides against the middle. At this time, Iraq was our ally and Iran was our enemy. Selling arms to the Iranian Khomeini was treasonous activity. And the funding of the overthrow of a neutral nation in Central America was also illegal. Although Reagan's people deny such a deal, Wikipedia notes that "former Iranian President Abolhassan Bani-Sadr, former naval intelligence officer and National Security Council member Gary Sick, and former Reagan/Bush campaign and White House staffer Barbara Honegger have stood by the allegation."

Dilthey suggests not only that history is complicated and personalities complex but that hidden aspects may involve the precise opposite picture than is created on the surface. For many reasons, including Richard Nixon's demise and the great success of such Democrats as FDR and John F. Kennedy, the Republicans want very much to portray Ronald Reagan as a great world leader. Events such as the one described above are often underplayed so as to keep Reagan's positive image in the foreground. In FDR's case, even though he won four presidential elections, the vast majority of the public had no idea that he was wheelchair bound. In JFK's case, his many affairs were also hidden from the public eye. The surface told us one thing; the true story was quite another. The human condition, by its nature, according to Dilthey, is contradictory; history proceeds on many levels and reality oftentimes is harsh.

Translating Lucien Febvre's[5] work from French, Manuel writes that Febvre (1878–1956) "cautioned against reading in other's epochs a psychology derived from contemporary sensibility. How would it be possible, he wondered, to apply psychological models of the comfortable twentieth century to ages [from ancient times]."[6] For Febvre, the ultimate goal of the historian was the "capturing of the unique sensibility of a past age."[7] Thus, each age needs to be understood from its own context.

A good example of this can be found in recent movements to abolish Columbus Day as a holiday because (1) Columbus was a racist and cruel to Native Americans; (2) he did not set out to discover a new land; he was really looking for another route to the Orient; and (3) America was not really discovered by Columbus—there were already people living there, and if any European discovered America, it was probably Leif Erikson who got there five hundred years earlier. These critics have chosen to measure Columbus's remarkable achievement from a twenty-first-century perspective, which is precisely what Febvre is arguing against.

Freud, too, can be considered a psychohistorian, although as Manuel indicates, "virtually no historian was aware of it at the time."[8] Freud's books *Totem and Taboo,*[9] *Civilization and Its Discontents,*[10] and *The Future of an Illusion,*[11] and his psychohistorical treatments of Leonardo da Vinci[12] and Woodrow Wilson,[13] are often cited as psychohistorical texts. They affirm Freud's theory of the dominance of our biological and primitive drives. In the biographical works, Freud applied his theories on psychosexual stages of development, repression, and sublimation to well-known individuals, whereas in his sociological treatises psychoanalysis is utilized to explain the history of human culture. On the collective level, determinants such as the incest taboo[14] promoted exogamy. As inbreeding most often proved disastrous from a biological perspective, the incest taboo insured natural selection, and from a sociological point of view it created a foundation for civilization to develop.

In *The Future of an Illusion,* Freud continued this theme by maintaining that the emergence of civilization was due specifically to the necessity for the "renunciation of instinct"[15] and also a denial of this sublimation. In other words, civilization proceeds when humans overpower their primitive and selfish instincts, yet ironically, they may not even be aware that they have done so. If anarchy truly ruled, no society could ever evolve. Rules had to be obeyed for a variety of reasons. Self-preservation was certainly a key factor. For instance, if a man's wife died, in general he could not murder his neighbor and take his wife because (1) the new wife might object and even kill him, and (2) the neighbor's brother, father, or first cousin could murder him. As Mick Jagger so eloquently stated, "You can't always get what you want, but if you try sometimes, you get what you need."[16]

Freud's view on how culture is formed combines biological imperatives (e.g., the incest taboo) with the mandatory need for self-control. This is not to say that murderers can't survive and prosper in society. Oftentimes they do. In fact, on a large scale, these kinds of individuals often succeed remarkably well. Many world leaders have been associated with mass murder. Hitler is an obvious example who, during just three or four years in the midst of World War II, exterminated about eleven million European citizens, about half of whom were Jews. But there is also Stalin, who ruled Russia for almost thirty-five years (ca. 1920–1953) and was responsible for the deaths of tens of millions, many of whom he starved to death or sent to die in Siberia, and as many as forty-thousand upper echelon military personnel whom he had executed because he feared someone in their ranks might overthrow him; Mao Zedong, who ruled China for about the same amount of time (1943–1976), was responsible for the deaths of as many as seventy-five million; and more recently, Pol Pot, who executed one and a half million Cambodians while he was in power (1970–1975), and Saddam Hussein, ruler of Iraq for twenty-five years (1979–2003), who gassed thousands of Kurds and wiped out tens of thousands of Shiites during his reign. Sometimes these kinds of leaders are overturned or taken out by a more powerful force, as in the case of Hitler, Pol Pot, and Saddam Hussein; other times they live to a ripe old age and die in office, as was the case with Stalin and Mao Zedong. Freud sees man as mostly a primitive being, and when looked at through this lens, great support for this view can be seen.

6

Sociology, Psychology, and History

As an officially separate discipline, psychohistory is generally considered to have begun in December of 1957, when William Langer, president of the American Historical Association, proposed at its annual conference that the principles of psychoanalysis be utilized to explain the historical process.[1]

World leaders can now be understood both from the individual and from a sociological point of view. Thus, the field has extended beyond analysis of personal motivations to encompass the interplay of psychoanalytic with sociological concerns. This division is clearly explained by Bruce Mazlish in his article "What Is Psychohistory?"[2]

Psychohistory, in my view, divides rather sharply into two categories: 1) the treating of individuals and 2) the treating of groups. . . . In life history, we are primarily concerned with the motives of an individual, suitably psychoanalyzed, of course, and the way in which these personal motives are shaped by the culture and society, as well as by his genetic factors, and so forth. We then seek to understand how the individual interrelates with and helps further to shape his surrounding culture and society. In what I shall now call group history, for want of a better term, we are concerned with groups driven or inspired by common motives. In both cases, individual and group, motives will be complicated, ambivalent, and so forth; in the case of groups, of course, the complications can be expected to be of a higher order.[3]

ERIK ERICKSON

It was really Erik Erikson (1902–1994) who popularized the idea of psychohistory in 1958, although the term itself evolved a few years afterward. Erikson's two great psychohistories concerned the lives of Martin Luther[4] and Gandhi.[5] In *Life History and the Historical Moment,*[6] Erikson discusses the role of the *identity crisis* in understanding how and why a person's life "interweaves" with history: "Every person harbors a *negative identity,* which the individual has to submerge in himself as undesirable or irreconcilable."[7] Regarding Luther and Gandhi, Erikson "found a motive drive to heroic action in the need for sons to outstrip their fathers and compensate for their failures."[8] By utilizing "disciplined subjectivity" and psychoanalytic investigations, Erikson isolated eight common characteristics of historical world figures of genius.[9]

1. A secret foreboding that a curse lies upon them
2. A tie to the father, which makes open rebellion impossible
3. A sense of being chosen and carrying a superior destiny
4. Feelings of weakness, shyness, and unworthiness
5. A precocious conscience in childhood
6. An early development of ultimate concerns
7. A brief attempt to cast off the burdens associated with their difficult fate
8. A final settling into the conviction that they have a responsibility for a segment of humankind

Erikson also applied Freud's psychoanalytic mechanisms of resistance and transference to his analyses of Luther and Gandhi. Resistances revealed the presence of regression and unconscious motivations and also "resolution only in indirect ways."[10] In the case of Gandhi, for example, his utilization of "militant nonviolent Satyagraha" in the 1918 labor strike against mill owners may have stemmed from a "suppressed sense of hate against a beloved person." Erikson maintains that Gandhi had much suppressed rage stemming from unpleasant childhood experiences with his father. Thus, Gandhi's nonviolent stand was a more complex phenomenon than simply his need to create a new country by peaceful means.[11]

Erikson defines transference as "a universal tendency active wherever beings enter a relationship to others in such a way that the other also stands for a person as perceived in the preadult past."[12] In the case of Martin Luther, who was suffering from an identity crisis, according to Erikson, Luther chose his church overseer and "spiritual mentor" Dr. Stampitz as a "fatherly sponsor" to make up for the inadequacies of his real father.[13]

Erikson concludes that historical figures have to be understood not only from the point of view of their developmental role in their family unit and in the community but also in their time and place in history. Sequencing is important for the person with regard to age and experience, and also in relationship to the particular moment in history. For the prominent individual *a wider identity* [emphasis added] is created . . . [which] survives the limitation of [the] person and of the historical moment. These are matters that the psychohistorian cannot approach without the help of the sociologist" and the political scientist.[14]

Essentially, Erikson is discussing famous individuals, who, because of their power and influence, are perceived as more than mere mortals. I personally witnessed some of this with a close college friend, Jim Walsh, who later became the well-known actor J. T. Walsh (1943–1998). Jim, as I knew him, was constantly struggling to maintain his normal identity, but as he had become so successful, having acted in such films as *Hoffa, Backdraft, Tequila Sunrise, A Few Good Men, The Negotiator,* and *Pleasantville,* it became more and more difficult. There were several reasons for this. From a personal point of view, his self-image was impacted through all this success mostly in a positive way, but where I think the greater challenge lay was in trying to deal with how others now perceived him. People want to touch fame. Except to his close friends and associates, on some level, he was no longer just Jim, he was also J. T. Walsh, a movie star on the rise, something much bigger. This same theme was brilliantly portrayed by Julia Roberts in the movie *Notting Hill,* where she plays essentially herself, a successful actress trying to live a normal life. The idea of a wider identity can also be seen every weekday night in the opening of the Jay Leno show, where twenty or thirty audience members try to touch the famous comedian's hand before his monologue.

Many highly successful entertainers have suffered with identity problems. Obvious examples include Marilyn Monroe, Michael Jackson, and Elvis Presley. But the odd thing about Erikson's theory as outlined above is that out of all the people it describes, it would be Erikson himself that best fits his model. The psychohistorian Wilhelm Dilthey notes that when reading such books as biographies, it is often important to know a bit about the biographer as well, as that writer may be framing someone else's life through a lens that has been biased by his or her own experiences. In referring to Erikson's general theory and eight-point list above, starting with the first point, namely that the person feels that there is a secret curse placed upon them, this exactly fits Erikson's life. Yes, one can see this in Michael Jackson who changed his skin color and had plastic surgery to remove any remnants of his African American features, or in Napoleon, who thought himself too short, but it would be hard to make this case for Ronald Reagan who, it seems, led a charmed existence.

A quick review of Erikson's life history reveals that Erikson's original last name was not Erikson at all, but rather it was Homberger. His mother, who was Jewish, had had an affair with a Christian from Denmark and then she married Mr. Homberger who was also Jewish. Thus little blonde-haired Scandinavian-looking Erik grew up in an odd way because he did not resemble at all his dark-haired Semetic-looking father. It wasn't until Erik was about twelve years old that it was revealed to him the man that he thought was his biological father, but who he suspected was really not, had actually adopted him. So the boy's identity crisis was to some extent solved, because he could now understand why his light Danish appearance in no way resembled the man who brought him up. It wasn't until the age of thirty-nine that he finally decided to shed his given last name and take on the artificial name Erikson, son of Erik. Once this is realized, one can easily see that most of the eight points of greatness listed above—what he sees as a universal need to "outstrip the father" and his ideas of identity crisis, resistance, and transference—were all really forms of projection. In other words, Erikson assumed that what happened to him were common themes found in the lives of many great men.

Erikson makes a great case that both Gandhi and Martin Luther harbored "suppressed hate towards the father." This may or may not be true, but it is certainly true in Erikson's case. But then the question arises, at which "father" was Erikson more mad: the one who brought him up but lied to him about his true heritage or the one who abandoned him before he was even born?

Was a man like Erikson truly blind to the psychoanalytic underpinnings to his theory? Given that his teacher was Sigmund Freud and that he was highly interested in psychoanalysis, it seems unlikely. Most importantly, given this information about this particular theoretician's childhood and upbringing, does his theory still bear merit? The fact is that Erikson is highly regarded for his many insights. He is a deserved leader in his field because of concrete contributions. However, much like Freud, who himself suffered from an Oedipal complex and therefore assumed everyone else also had to have one, Erikson's theory likewise derived from highly painful personal experiences. And yet, perhaps because of that, he did indeed uncover some universal truths. Erikson's uncertain beginnings may have been the catalyst that made him such a success in the field of theoretical psychology.

Certainly on some level everyone suffers an identity crisis at some point in his or her life: it is part of the natural process of growing up. Also many, if not most, adolescents do indeed experience a phase of having a negative or counter identity. Look at all the people who now have tattoos. One way or another, this desire to adorn the body certainly stems from a complex primal need to stand out from the crowd, rebel against conservative norms, and yet also be accepted into another crowd, one that has tattoos! In some kind of way, the need to adorn the body with indelible ink would also be linked to a primary form of narcissism, an unconscious wish for immortality.

Erikson ends his eight-point list with his supposition that as thinking people grow and develop, they turn their attention to wider concerns. This is also true on a group scale as society considers collectively the ramifications of polluting the air and sapping the earth of finite natural resources.

LLOYD DEMAUSE

Lloyd deMause (b. 1931), founder of the Institute of Psychohistory, outlines the scope of the field into three divisions:

> 1. History of childhood
> 2. Psychobiography
> 3. Group psychohistory

This threefold model, which is repeated in each generation, encompasses sociological, developmental, cultural, and psychoanalytic factors, all revolving around the central theme: *the understanding of historical motivation.*[15] Where psychohistory differs from history is in its "methodology of discovery."[16] Psychohistory has a "double burden of proof, for it has to conform not only to the usual standards of historical research, but it must also be psychologically sound."[17]

Echoing Dilthey's guidelines, deMause states that in order to accomplish a psychohistorical analysis, an exploration of one's *own* unconscious must also be undertaken: "Only if I can accomplish this inner act of discovery can I move back to new historical material to test patterns of motivation and group dynamics."[18] One of his most controversial themes involves mental experiences that occur before birth.[19]

This *fetal drama,* as he calls it, supercedes the Oedipal complex because it occurs earlier. DeMause maintains that the action, habits, psychology, and diet of the pregnant mother can all affect the growing embryo. Birth, for the child, is a double-bind situation because it is an escape from a womb that has been both a provider and also a constrainer.[20] DeMause suggests that the placenta can be perceived as poisonous, as it denies a liberating existence, and it may actually impede development of the fetus if the mother is disturbed. Also, of course, the placenta nurtures the baby. The birth experience is both a death of an old self and a liberation and birth of a new self. This experience is played out later in life as a rebirth fantasy, which can affect individuals or societies. In the case of going to war, for instance, the rebirth wish becomes "a group fantasy derived from a desire to end a severe collapse of confidence in the nation and its leader."[21] After the war, it is hoped, much like birth, that a new nation can be spawned.

Applying this idea to individuals, deMause suggests that President Jimmy Carter became the victim of a "ritual sacrifice,"[22] when this essentially good man lost the election to his untried opponent Ronald Reagan. This relationship to the symbolic death of the placenta (nurturing president) was now perceived as poisonous (need for birth). Thus the topsy-turvy attitudes of the public to their leaders are analyzed in relationship to the fetal drama of the rebirth fantasy. In this sense, de Mause has taken psychohistory full circle, from a discussion of individual childhood experiences to the explanation of the behavior of groups. He maintains that the goal of this new field of psychohistory should be interdisciplinary, as the findings of philosophy, history, sociology, and psychology all contribute significantly to the understanding of historical motivation.

7

Critical Theorists

In the early 1920s, a group of European philosophers began to gather at the newly formed Institute of Social Research in Germany in order to discuss social and historical problems from a new perspective. Although "Marxism was made the inspiration and theoretical basis of the Institute's program,"[1] and the ills of the worker placed at the foreground, nevertheless, the group, which came to be known as the critical theorists, also began to develop in an eclectic way.

Such members as Adorno,[2] Fromm,[3] Horkheimer,[4] and Marcuse,[5] like modern psychohistorians Runyan and deMause, combined precepts from psychology with historical analysis. Placing history at the center of their approach to philosophy and society rather than psychological precepts at the center of historical research, they called for an interdisciplinary science of historical analysis. Their views, however, were varied and by no means cohesive.[6] In general, they suggested that a new paradigm, which had not yet been called psychohistory, should combine a Marxian or neo-Marxian viewpoint, which stressed analysis of the overall structure of society (political and economic systems and modes of production) with Freudian findings about the structure of personality and the unconscious. Thus, for instance, they tried to discern the interface of an evolving personality of an individual with the laws that govern and operate in a given economy.[7]

The critical theorists maintained that an interdisciplinary approach, combined with a historical awareness, was essential for understanding the nature of individuals, society, and culture. These theorists wanted to redefine the "great philosophical question."[8] By using an eclectic approach, which specifically reinterpreted Marxist philosophy and integrated it with a Freudian or neo-Freudian doctrine, they attempted to marry economic and sociological theories of history with a psychology for the individual. In other words, they would look at historical events from both an outer and inner perspective. In essence, the critical theorists felt that in order to design a comprehensive view of *Homo sapiens,* such fields as psychology, sociology, anthropology, economics, history, philosophy, and political science would have to be combined. Fragmentation of the social sciences had resulted, and worse, the various disciplines had become mainly theoretical exercises in analytic thinking rather than actual vehicles for change. The critical theorists not only wanted to describe the human condition, they sought to change society by pointing out its ills and suggesting ways to alter conditions. Unfortunately most of them, writing in the 1920s and '30s, were forced to flee Nazi Europe, and so their attempts at transforming their local societies were thwarted.

Nonetheless, the critical theorists were brilliant in their criticisms of orthodox Marxism and classical Freudian doctrine. Just as Freud had basically forgotten or ignored history, Marx had overlooked the intricacies of the human psyche. Where Marx saw history as proceeding along the lines of continuing class struggle, Freud theorized that civilization developed due to the renunciation and/or repression of instinctual urges. Rather than supporting one philosophy over the other, the critical theorists sought to merge these two previously thought-to-be incompatible approaches. Therefore, the new philosophy of human nature must recognize the particular political and economic structure, which gives rise to historical change (e.g., sociology), while also recognizing the role of unconscious and libidinal urges (e.g., depth psychology) as drivers of both individuals (and world leaders) and mass movements (history).

Critical theorists embraced the ideas of *paradox, dialecticism, historical materialism, Eros,* and *Thanatos,* while also delineating the forces that activated social change. "No one method could, in this

[Horkheimer's] opinion, produce definitive results about any given object of inquiry. To take one type of approach is always to risk a distorted perspective on reality."[9] One needed varying theoretical ways as well as empirical analyses of actual historical events in order to construct a complete science of humankind.

An excellent example of this can be seen in the recent political arena on the one hand, the media's love of Sarah Palin, former governor of Alaska and Republican vice-presidential candidate, and the repudiation of congressman and perennial presidential-contender Dennis Kucinich. In a famous interview that Sarah Palin did with CBS news anchor Katie Couric, the Alaskan governor could not mention a single national newspaper or magazine that she read. This lack of intellectual curiosity for a vice-presidential candidate was stunning, given that she was close to being a heartbeat away from the most powerful position in the world. Palin became so famous and so much in national demand that she actually stepped down from being governor of Alaska, after serving only two years of her four-year term. Kucinich, on the other hand, former mayor of Cleveland and seven-term congressman from Ohio, got trounced in both of his bids to be president in 2004 and 2008, even though he displayed an adept grasp of many complex ideas. Where Sarah Palin continues to be the media darling, Kucinich constantly complains of lack of media coverage. From a Freudian point of view, one cannot escape the fact that paradox, contradiction, and Eros, and perhaps even Thanatos, play key roles. Sarah Palin is a striking, sexually attractive, confident woman, whereas Dennis Kucinich, although also confident, from a physical standpoint is short, has large ears, and for want of a better term is geeky looking. In this instance, it is painfully clear that physical characteristics trump competency in the political arena. From a psychohistorical perspective, the outer social/economic forces are no match to the inner libidinal forces that shape the psyche of the masses. In the case of presidents of the United States, fully thirty out of forty-four presidents were 5'10" or taller. Physical characteristics play a defining role in deciding who a leader will be.

Another important concept developed by the psychohistorians was that of *instrumental reason,* which was a "rationalization of the world" that developed due to the corresponding seeming logic inherent in the existing political and economic structure of the (capitalist) society. "The objective and impersonal character of technological rationality bestows upon the bureaucratic groups the universal dignity of reason. The rationality embodied in the giant enterprises makes it appear as if men, in obeying them, obey the dictum of objective rationality."[10] For Marcuse, this "delusive harmony" makes it appear as if the corporate structures that have been created are by their nature objective vehicles because they exist. "Freedom is willfully relinquished"[11] as society becomes conditioned by these structures. In turn, "the individual becomes mechanized."[12]

This position clearly and consciously opposes Marx's insistence that class struggle and the alienation of the worker from his product will lead to revolution. Opposition can be subsumed in part because humans by their nature may find revolution an unappealing alternative; also they may have been conditioned by the very structure of their ordered, regimented environment.

Certainly in the case of the United States, its history could be recorded as a history of class struggle. Yet as yesterday's radicals sell insurance on Wall Street, the lower classes seek not to overthrow the existing order so much as to somehow gain access to it. Marx knew nothing of the "American dream" whereby a penniless man one day becomes a millionaire.

The critical theorists are saying that the economic and political system we live in must also be understood when attempting to comprehend the life histories of significant world figures. Further, sometimes these economic and political systems may actually be irrational, but because they are pervasive, they are accepted as rational. An interesting example of instrumental reason can be seen in the collapse of so many local newspapers at the dawn of the twenty-first century. By 2008, the revenue stream of American newspapers was cut in half and many key papers simply folded. The reason is obvious. Because the Internet rose so rapidly, information became instantly and freely available. To keep pace, newspapers and magazines began posting their articles online and the subscription base to many newspapers plummeted. With less circulation (1) less could be charged, and (2) advertisers were less likely to spend money in a smaller market. If news is provided without charge, who is going to pay reporters to get the news? The answer is obvious. People should be paying to access news from the Internet, but because they don't, they shouldn't. That is instrumental reason. An irrational situation has arisen, but because it is the way of things, it is assumed to be rational.

Cell phones are another example. They evolved in such a way that only one cell phone exists per phone number. Phone companies could provide entire families, or, say, husbands and wives, with one single wireless phone line connected to two or more cell phones and a single bill, *if they wanted to.* That's how landlines are handled. But this option is not available. When I was a child in the 1950s, the homes in our neighborhood had party lines. In other words, three or four families had to share a single phone line! It is simply a matter of numbers. The phone companies make billions of dollars by making it seem that the only way to have a wireless line is to have one cell phone per person, but that is an arbitrary decision completely driven by the profit motive.

Adorno notes that the structure of capitalism by its nature involves "the domination of men over other men."[13] Capital becomes centralized, monopolies are created, and methods developed, which seek to maintain, secure, and reproduce these existing (and emerging) corporate conglomerates. In 2008, the helicopter company Sikorsky had a rebellion of sorts from their workers who were complaining that they were paying too much for medical coverage. The CEO, whose salary was $80 million dollars per year, showed no compassion and threatened layoffs to get the workers back in line. Eventually the workers ratified a contract, but what stood out to this observer was the great imbalance in pay. Perhaps if the CEO made less money, he could afford to lower the medical costs of his workers. Does he really need $80 million a year? Could he survive on, say, $5 million and use the residual funds to offset the medical costs for 7,500 of his workers? Occasionally, a CEO comes along who does not fit the mold because his wealth is so great to begin with. Two who come to mind are Steven Jobs, who runs Apple Computer, and Arnold Schwarzenegger, governor of California. Neither man takes a salary.

From a critical theorist's point of view, psychohistory can be seen not only as the science of historical motivation but also as an interdisciplinary genre, which combines formal teachings from psychology and its subdivisions (e.g., personality theory and psychoanalysis) with that of anthropology, economics, ethology, philosophy, political science, and sociology. It recognizes the multidimensionality and uniqueness of every event, the need for self-understanding as part of the methodological tools for analysis, but also that conclusions rest most soundly on the researched evidence from the case. The psychology stems from the history and not the reverse. Psychohistory seeks to describe not only what happened but also why it happened.

8

The Critics

A clear split exists between the disciplines of history and psychohistory. Not only do historians tend to shun psychohistorians, but also, as deMause informed me a number of years back, Erikson himself came to reject the International Psychohistory Society. Criticism of the field abounds, not only outside its ranks, but within as well. Comments fall into two major categories:

1. The viability of psychohistory as a separate discipline
2. Specific methodologies used

The historian Jacques Barzun, in his text *Clio and the Doctors: Psycho-History, Quanto-History and History,* suggests that psychohistory may not be a new field at all but really a subunit of history known as the special study.

Barzun states that simply because history tends to describe what happens and psychohistory tends to describe why it happens, this in and of itself is not a reason to create a separate delineation. If psychohistorians understood the fundamental questions inherent in historical inquiry, they would not need to create a separate discipline because the framework for such avenues of research already exists in the established field of history.

According to Capps,[1] this lack of knowledge of history's breadth and scope weakens the emerging field of psychohistory because psychohistorians tend to be long on analysis but short on narrative descriptions.

Historians therefore often tend to disagree with conclusions when they read psychohistories. The historical facts that are presented tend to be limited in scope and detail. Thus, when deMause states that psychohistorians "assume the history"[2] in favor of psychological analysis, this very assumption creates an antecedent premise, which fails the rigors set up by the historian. This is why Barzun's critique is so valuable, because it ties psychohistory to a branch of history and therefore forces the psychohistorian to subject his work to the rules and regulations of the more established field of history. This solves part of the problem inherent in psychohistory's relationship to conventional history; however, it still leaves unsolved the question of the viability of psychological analysis.

This brings us to the second major criticism, which concerns the specific methodologies used in psychohistorical investigations. Dilthey has been criticized by mainstream psychohistorians not only because his writings failed "to join history and psychology, the disciplines went in opposite directions,"[3] but also because his treatises were too theoretical and yet lacked the depth achieved by modern psychoanalytic investigators. "Economic and social reality may penetrate his [Dilthey's] narrative, but only as part of a worldview. . . . Political revolutions are quickly transformed into abstract ideas, and nothing below the navel was mentionable."[4]

Ironically, although Dilthey is judged harshly for not discussing sexuality or for not "seek[ing] the sources of adult behavior in early experiences,"[5] Freud was admonished for his overreliance on this mode of inquiry. David Stannard, in his text *Shrinking History,* not only condemns the entire field, e.g., "little, if any psychohistory is good history,"[6] he also lambastes Freudian psychoanalysis, which he describes as a "stupendous twentieth-century confidence trick."[7] He states that there is little if any scientific evidence to support the findings of psychoanalysis, and that it is a highly speculative field based upon faulty assumptions.

In a chapter entitled "The Failure of Psychohistory," Stannard suggests that the psychohistorian is too bound to classical psychoanalysis. Concerning Freud, who suggested in his psychobiography of da Vinci that the artist was a latent homosexual,[8] Stannard criticices a "cavalier attitude toward fact . . . a contorted view of logic . . . a myopic attitude toward culture . . . [and] an irresponsible attitude toward validation."[9] Freud's work, according to Stannard, is poorly supported by historical data, reductionistic, "crudely mechanistic," vulgar, trivial, and unfounded in its overdetermined reliance on the primacy of childhood experiences. Stannard boldly states, "The best modern research now firmly indicates that there are no psychological structures established in childhood that are sufficiently resilient to survive into adulthood without constant environmental support."[10]

This comment may or may not be valid, as Stannard offers no supporting evidence or even reference for this "best modern research." His book is thus flawed because of this tendency for unsupported generalizations. Stannard raises some important points, but his objectivity is questionable, as he staunchly supports a polarized point of view and is incapable of seeing any benefit in the field he is criticizing.

One-half century earlier, Freud anticipated Stannard's criticism by devoting his opening chapter and concluding statements to pointing out the restrictions of psychoanalysis and why he would be unable to supply a complete analysis of Leonardo's motivations. "Even if psychoanalysis does not explain to us the fact of Leonardo's artistic accomplishment," Freud wrote, "it still gives us an understanding of its experiences and limitations."[11]

Thus, if Stannard had been truly objective, he would have at least cited Freud's awareness that psychoanalysis is a limited tool for psychohistorical investigation and acknowledged that Freud's conclusions based upon sexuality were not made in ignorance.

Perhaps the most devastating critiques have been against Lloyd de Mause, an admittedly controversial and overtly Freudian psychohistorian. Having attended a number of his talks, my own criticism is that he is too political in his views and uses psychoanalysis and psychohistory to attack the power structure (e.g., Reagan is viewed as a warmonger due to a castration complex; Carter was viewed as a "poisonous placenta" discarded by the embryonic society). DeMause's lectures tend to preach or foresee doomsday, yet due to his astute observance of a growing number of militant magazine cover articles, he was also able to successfully predict the wish-fantasy need for a war, and he even accurately chose the area of the world (Latin America) about a year before the invasion of Grenada by the United States, and well before the 1984 mining of the harbor of Nicaragua.

Another intriguing critic of this emerging field was Karl Mannheim (1893–1947), founder of the concept of the "sociology of knowledge" and/ or the link between "human thought and the circumstances of existence." For Mannheim, the will of individuals "is deprived of its autonomy in favor of some basic reality. It is a relatively insignificant difference that for Hegel, the basic reality [God's plan] is mental, whereas [for] Marx the basic reality is an economic or social one."[12] Both these views, Mannheim suggests, reduce individuals to mere pawns enmeshed in a larger super-structure. Mannheim, like Mill, is really a proponent of the "great person" theory: individuals can alter the future; that is their greatest potential and their most important reason for being, as the masses simply follow along.

The analysis of history is a difficult assignment because the structure of the psyche is so complex. There are many theories that attempt to explain human motivation, yet none of these are all-inclusive, and none are correct in all instances. One of the greatest problems for the psycho-historian has to do with the role of subjectivity. Choices are made in all analyses for numerous reasons, including such a simple one as article-length constraints. Evidence is sifted through, decisions are made, some factors are enhanced, some ignored. Hidden political and/or religious agendas also make their way into various paradigms. It is the task of the reader to realize that some of the information lies between the lines on the page. As my mother often told me, "Just because it appears on the page doesn't make it so."

9

Nineteenth-Century Psychology

My supposed opponent and I are like two children who have looked through a keyhole at the first few moves in a game of chess. My companion states that since we have only seen pawns moved, it is probably that the game is played with the pawns alone. I reply that those pieces stand on the board like the pawns; and that since they are larger and more varied, it is probably that they are meant to play some even more important role in the game as it develops. We agree that we must wait and see whether the pieces are moved; and I now maintain that I have seen a piece move, although my companion has not noticed.

F. W. H. MYERS, 1901

AN OUT-OF-BED EXPERIENCE

I awoke one morning in the winter of 1972/73 while attending graduate school at the University of Chicago. I had a class in ego psychology, and I was late. I dressed, grabbed my coat and books, walked down the stairs, and began to cross the street on my way to campus. Suddenly I awoke. I could not believe it, for there I was, still rolled up in bed!

Four decades later, I remain astounded by the experience, for I had completely and unquestionably mistaken a dream for reality.

During an instance of recounting this story to one of my classes, I noticed that one student remained impassive, so I asked why. "Why?!" he remarked. "What's the big deal? You only went across the street. I drove half way to work, stopped for a coffee, and had a donut at a breakfast shop before I woke up!"

ERNST WEBER

Ernst Weber (1795–1878) is credited as being one of the first "modern" theoreticians to apply the *scientific method* to the investigation of mental processes. He was following in the footsteps of Descartes who, a few hundred years earlier, tried to find out if it were true that humans see everything upside down and somehow "right" the image in their minds. Descartes proved this astonishing finding by obtaining the eye of a cow and flashing an image into it. Lo and behold, the image projected through the eye onto the screen was upside down! That's how we see, and somehow our mind turns the object back right side up, at least in terms of how we perceive it. The more one reflects on this paradoxical situation, the more bizarre it really is. We all see the world upside down, but we *perceive* the world right side up. How this really occurs remains a complete mystery.

●   ●

Then there is the blind spot. Hold this book up with your left hand at arms length. Place your right hand over your right eye. Now, stare at the right dot and slowly bring the book toward your nose. At some point, if you are truly staring at the right dot, the left dot will disappear. Hold it there for a second and consider your blind spot. Now continue to move the book forward and the dot will reappear. Move the book back slowly and the left dot will disappear again and then reappear once you move past the blind spot.

All humans have a blind spot for each eye. It is the part of the retina where the optic nerve leaves the eye. Since there is no retina at that spot, that area is blind. Consider the philosophical implications of these two limitations in perception: (1) all humans physically see the world one way but mentally perceive it in a very different way; and (2) all humans have blind spots. From a mechanical point of view, we are simply unable to know the world as it is, and because of that, we make guesses and interpretations alter our perceptions.

I had a rude awakening to this fact last year. My wife and I were watching the movie *Paper Moon* (1973), starring Ryan O'Neal and his eight-year-old daughter Tatum as his possible daughter in the film. I had seen the film several times before, but it had been many years since my last viewing. At the end of the movie, the character played by Ryan drops the little girl off at her aunt's house. I had the distinct memory of the "father" accompanying the little girl into the house to meet the aunt to complete the hand-off. I was flat-out wrong. In entering the aunt's house, the little girl is alone; the father stays in the car. Had there not been the objective proof of the actual film to show my error, I would have continued in my false belief. At least in this instance, I could prove or verify the truth to the situation. But what about eyewitness testimony when there is no photographic backup, or emotional factors coloring one's perception? For instance, a significant segment of the population thinks that Barack Obama was born in Africa even though his parents met as students at the University of Hawaii, were married and living in Hawaii at the time, and the birth at a maternity hospital was announced in the local Waikiki papers. Obviously, if a voter would have preferred a different candidate to be president, that person may have a distorted view of the opposing candidate, which conforms to how he or she wants the situation to be. There is much truth to the term of "seeing the world through rose-colored glasses." Optimists and pessimists really do see the world differently.

Weber used the process of trained introspection; that is, he simply studied his own psyche through self-analysis in an orderly fashion to try and comprehend just how humans actually perceive the world. The term "just noticeable difference" was coined by Weber to denote various threshold differentials for perceiving subtle changes in visual brightness. The subject simply reported when he could distinguish a particular change in illumination or change in color, or, if he were studying hearing, a difference between the pitches of two notes. By studying the physical senses, Weber was able to bypass the question as to whether or not a "mind" existed. Weber also ignored the problem of the subjective nature of the perceiving entity so that specific mathematical measures in perceptual acuity could be ascertained. From these studies in perception, the branch of psychology known as psychophysics was born. This work was furthered by Gustav Fechner (who also had an interest in spiritualism), Hermann von Helmholtz, the famous electrical scientist, and Wilhelm Wundt, the founder, in 1878, of what is generally considered to be the first modern experimental psychology lab.

WILHELM WUNDT

The founder of structuralism, Wundt (1831–1920) was looking for the "structures of consciousness," and, like Weber, he also studied using trained introspection. Wundt assumed that the process of consciousness itself was the result of the combined action of three elements of consciousness, the so-called building blocks:

1. affects (emotions)
2. sensations (the five senses)
3. images (the ability to create mental pictures in the mind)

This work was furthered by Wundt's student Edward Titchner, who measured these three elements for their quality, intensity, and duration. It was believed that all higher mental processes derived from complex arrangements of these three key structures.

THE RISE OF FUNCTIONALISM

Whenever two people meet, there are really six people present. There is each man as he sees himself, each man as the other person sees him, and each man as he really is.

WILLIAM JAMES

Harvard professor William James, father of American psychology and brother to novelist Henry James, also used trained introspection, but he had difficulty finding the so-called building blocks that Wundt and Titchner discussed. Thus, James attacked the idea that the mind could be broken down into smaller components. James said that the mind was an active, ongoing stream, which is in a dynamic relationship with the environment. As Edwin Boring informs us, James felt that Wundt's structuralism was investigating "pseudo-problems . . . [arguing whether a feeling was] an attribute of a sensation or an element. . . . Whether it has attributes of its own is to learn nothing new about man," said James.[1] James had his eye on the bigger picture. He looked at the mind as containing teleological components, and also he was interested in its transcendent capabilities, which included creative expression, the importance of subjective perception, will psychology (change your attitude, change your life), and such parapsychological topics as telepathy and scientific study for the potential of life after death. Experimenting with nitrous oxide, James dabbled in altered states of consciousness where he had so-called out-of-body experiences. The reductionistic (structuralist) point of view, from James's perspective, avoided real inquiry into the nature and potential of the psyche. James was more interested in the mind's dynamic functions—one's sense of "I-ness" and the wonder of creative thought, the importance of the subjective experience, and the process of consciousness—not in its static structures.

This general trend became known as functionalism, a new aspect of the field, which studied the functions of consciousness. This branch emerged in the early 1900s, at first mostly under James's direction at

Harvard and also at the University of Chicago. The focus of the functionalists was to study mental processes such as learning, memory, evaluation, sensation, and organization. In particular, functionalists wanted to know how humans adapted to their environment, how they processed information, and what they did with it.

10

The Mystery of Hypnotism

The word *hypnotism* comes from *hypnos,* the Greek for sleep. It refers to the ability of an operator to artificially place someone else into a sleeplike state and then take over the will of that person. In 1814, Abbé Faria returned to France from a trip to India with the ability to induce sleep in subjects by means of suggestion.[1] He was thus the first major practitioner to separate himself from the highly popular Anton Mesmer (1735–1815), who also hypnotized people, but did so under the impression that a magnetic fluid or etheric *force* derived from the planets was somehow passed from Mesmer to his subjects when he put them under his spell.

As healer, Mesmer thought that this same substance could be transferred during this induction procedure from doctor to patient in order to precipitate a cure. Eventually this idea of an occult force responsible for healing and various suggestible states was eliminated from the theory, but the use of mesmeric trances to initiate various cures continued throughout the 1800s. Ironically, well over a century later, the concept of *therapeutic touch* has come into vogue, used not only by healers but by medical personnel as well. "The practice is based on the assumptions that human beings are complex fields of energy, and that the ability to enhance healing in another is a natural potential."[2] This force, which Mesmer called *animal magnetism,* fell out of favor to be replaced by the term hypnosis as more and more medical doctors studied and practiced the phenomena.

Ancient high priests in many cultures proclaimed supernatural powers with their ability to place subjects into trance by using "a few grotesque passes and weird incantations." In this way, they could direct their subjects to do strange and miraculous feats.[3] Since similar bizarre acts can be precipitated by modern hypnotists, this lends credence to the great power these shamans must have wielded. I refer the reader to any number of startling examples of people put in trance by hypnotists on YouTube on the Internet.

The term *hypnotism,* coined by James Braid in the early 1840s, soon replaced *mesmerism,* and thus the mystical aspect of the phenomena was slowly stripped from the topic, although medical doctor and author Robert Ellsworth insisted that hypnosis and mesmerism were two distinctly different states. Ellsworth denotes three stages to the hypnotic trance:

Stage One: *The Cataleptic Stage:* a state of "drowsiness" whereby the subject possesses no volition and "does not respond to mental or verbal instructions."

Stage Two: *The Lethargic Stage:* a state of "hypotaxy," whereby "the subject is a helpless lump of inanity [resembling] coma, drunkenness, or a dead faint. . . . Surgical operations can be performed in [this] stage without real or apparent pain to the subject."

Stage Three: *Somnambulism:* whereby "the subject acts as if in a dream—but he [also] acts the dream—such as may be suggested by the operator. . . . With good subjects, memory, reflection, and imagination can be intensified and exalted, [and] the past recalled to the present." This is the trance state.[4]

Hypnosis can be seen as a state whereby the hypnotist commandeers the dream mechanism and uses it to control his subjects who, rather than lying in bed dreaming, are physically active and walking about.

Ellsworth describes the traits of a good hypnotist. "The operator must believe in his own power or he will fail to inspire confidence in others. He must give his orders in a tone that will carry conviction if he expects to impress his subjects with his wishes."[5] The hypnotist uses various methods to suggest sleep in the subject and then takes that person to greater and greater depths.

A mesmerist, on the other hand, according to Ellsworth, achieves his goal by staring into the subject's eyes to bring on the trance with confidence by speaking and also *thinking* sleep-inducing commands. The subject must also trust the mesmerist, whose goal is to "do good." A mesmeric trance differs from a hypnotic state of suggestion, according to Ellsworth, because "intention" and "mind energy" is used to achieve the effect.[6] Ellsworth's goals as a mesmerist included healing physical diseases through realigning disturbed life forces,[7] "training psychic faculties" (e.g., thought transference, clairvoyance as in séances), and also inducing thoughts of "happiness, purity, love, contentment, and patience." In other words, instilling a sense of mental healing and peace of mind.[8]

Ellsworth's conclusion is that the field of hypnotism "recognizes to each finite body, the mind self and the matter self." The goal is for the mind self to "govern" the matter self. This can be done on one's own through self-hypnosis, or this can be done by the hypnotist.[9]

At the turn of the twentieth century, the French psychologist Alfred Binet began to use hypnosis. On several occasions Binet would be thinking of something to do, like opening a window, and his subject under trance would go over and perform this action. It became obvious to Binet that thought transference had occurred, because he had not given a verbal command, but he was too afraid to publish these studies because of the potential damage that might occur to his reputation. Possibly he was right, as his mainstream work at Stanford University led unimpeded to the development of the Stanford-Binet IQ test, which is still in use today.

Boris Sidis (1876–1923), a Harvard associate of William James and latter-day opponent of Sigmund Freud, emphasized the idea that the state of being in a hypnotic trance was based on the power of *suggestibility*. Sidis wrote a major treatise on the topic in 1898 titled *The Power of Suggestion*. In this text, he makes it clear that man has a dual mind, or "double self," consisting of a conscious mind and also an unconscious mind. He predates Freud in his realization that the "secondary self" that is susceptible to hypnotic states has its own consciousness, "a self in possession of memory and even intelligence."[10]

According to Sidis, this "subwaking self" can have full knowledge of the upper primary waking self, but the reverse is not true; the primary does not know the subconscious/secondary self. Yet at times the subwaking self, when it obtains consciousness, may lead a life completely independent from the primary waking "conscious self."[11] This can occur in a variety of ways. For instance, if a person is in trance, he or she can carry on as if awake, but this secondary self does not know or even interact with the primary conscious self, which is now, for all intents and purposes, "asleep." People can also, while awake, perform unconscious behaviors of which the awake self remains unaware.

Sidis notes that the subconscious self is highly susceptible to suggestion or trance, and during this state the senses can be enhanced. For instance, a blindfolded subject while in trance may traverse a room without knocking over objects because of extreme sensitivity of the skin to air pressure and temperature differentials. In other words, the subject in trance can detect objects through a hypersensitivity that in his normal state he could not access. At the same time, Sidis notes that this secondary self has no real personality and completely lacks critical ability. "You can [mold] the legs, hands, and limbs [any way] you like, [or mold them] perfectly rigid; you can make it eat pepper for sugar; you can make it drink water for wine; feel cold or warm, hear delightful music; feel pain or pleasure; see oranges where there is nothing; nay, you can even make them eat them and feel their taste. In short, you can do with the subwaking self anything you like."[12]

Sidis concludes that, in a sense, the subwaking self is "stupid." It completely lacks critical ability. And this realm lies in the hypnotist's power "like clay in the hands of the potter. The nature of its plasticity is revealed by its complete suggestibility." Yet this other self is also "extremely unstable, ephemeral, a shadowy outline."[13] Sidis has uncovered the primary mind beneath one's conscious personal self. "The subwaking self," Sidis concludes, "is devoid of personal character; it is

Fig. 10.1. Mesmer's animal magnetism

both subpersonal and impersonal. And when it attains the plane of self-consciousness and the conditions are favourable to its remaining there, it is always roaming about, passing through the most fantastic metamorphoses, assuming with equal ease all kinds of personalities without regard to time, station, sex, or age."[14]

My own belief is that Mesmer's idea of some type of energy transfer should not be so easily dismissed. This eighteenth- and nineteenth-century idea is probably linked to an early realization that trance states involve physical changes in the brain. In 1976, I was teaching a course in consciousness research at Rhode Island College in one of their non-credit branches called the Third Curriculum. Most of the students were freshman. However, one student, a man in his forties, was a hypnotist by trade. He made his living using hypnosis as a tool for weight reduction and to help people stop smoking. During his oral report he asked if anyone wanted to be hypnotized. One young lady raised her hand.

This man walked over, snapped his fingers in front of her face, told her to *sleep!* and into a trance she went. He told this girl that she would be Barbra Streisand, and the girl did her best impression of being that actor/singer. The hypnotist asked her for an autograph, and she gladly gave it. Then the hypnotist told the girl that he would count to five and then she would become Mary Tyler Moore, and shortly thereafter she began acting like the well-known TV star. He then asked for an autograph and the girl signed the name Mary Tyler Moore, but to my utter shock, she did so directly *over* the other signature. She was completely in trance, because she did something no one, to my knowledge, would ever do. (Normal people who are given a piece of paper to sign their name find an empty area on the page; they would not write where there was already writing.) And then he told her he would take her out of trance and she would have no memory of the experience.

After the girl took her seat, the hypnotist ended his little talk, everyone applauded, including this girl, and I continued my lecture. I spoke for about a minute and then asked this girl if she had any memory of what had just occurred. She said no. I said, "You don't remember getting up in front of the room and becoming Barbra Streisand?" "No," she said. "Mary Tyler Moore?" I asked. "No," she said again. But I did not stop there. I grilled her intensely, practically shouting at her for five more minutes, but she had no memory of it at all. After further intense prodding, she offered a vague recollection, which she barely conceded. It occurred to me it was like another person trying to recall a dream that had faded from memory. This student really did not remember what she had done five minutes earlier in front of everyone. She also had no explanation for the two signatures, even though she recognized her own handwriting.

During part of this procedure, the hypnotist tried to hypnotize me. He walked up to me and snapped his fingers across my face and shouted, *"Sleep!"* I remember having the distinct feeling of almost collapsing myself, but I decided (maybe it was a macho thing!) that I would not succumb. I did, however, feel as though he had an energy that he could transfer.

I have seen other performances by professional hypnotists as well, and they are all powerful reminders of the fact that we do indeed have two distinct states of consciousness, a *conscious* self that we live our world in and also a *subconscious* state, which is subject to very different rules. One writer called this subconscious *the horse without the rider.* The hypnotist is a rider who can replace his subject's conscious self and thereby ride that person's horse.

Hypnotists can also use posthypnotic suggestions to their advantage. In the late 1960s I came across a very successful hypnotist who appeared in Boston. He could pack a house with one thousand to two thousand people. He would use trigger words to get people to jump up from their seats. For instance, he would bring up a group of people and have one fellow become Tarzan when a trigger word like "Moon" was used, another fellow become the ape when the word "Stars" was said, and a girl become Jane when the "Sun" was mentioned. These people would then take their seats, and sometime later in the middle of some other aspect of his performance, the hypnotist would use these trigger words and the real show would begin. When he took these subjects out of hypnosis, when they were nowhere near their seats, you could see how dumbfounded they really were. I remember in particular the fellow who was the ape. He wasn't an actor playing an ape. He *was* Ape. There was no doubt whatever of his *total* belief at that moment in who he thought he was when he was pounding his chest as he made his way down an aisle. On some primal level, seeing this performance was one of the most astounding moments of my life.

I don't remember the hypnotist's name. However, I do remember that he would give additional *posthypnotic suggestions* to his best subjects so that they would make their way to his other shows around New England. Most of these people, there were maybe five of them, would go out and purchase tickets to his next shows in neighboring cities without knowing they were in some sense still under trance. His best subjects did imitations of Louis Armstrong and the comedian Phyllis Diller, and these people would show up in Boston, Hartford, New York, or wherever he performed, and they never knew the real reason why they kept going.

In Rhode Island, for many years, Frank Santos (recently deceased) was billed as the R-rated hypnotist. I remember one show in particular whereby he had several of my students up on stage, and lo and behold, they began to take their clothes off. Thankfully Frank stopped the action before things went too far, but a profound point was made. Since I had taught these students my course in psychology, I remember having the distinct feeling that I had failed them as their teacher somehow, because they had so easily succumbed to his trance. In one bit, Frank told one fellow that when he went to the bathroom he would find that his penis had disappeared. The audience got a big kick out the fellow when he returned and expressed extreme anxiety for what he could not find. I, instead, was flabbergasted.

In exploring the topic with other students, I recently (2008) had one girl who had been hypnotized by a stage hypnotist at her high school prom. As she told the class, she had absolutely no memory of the idiotic things she had done on stage, and she would not have believed it except for the fact that the show was taped. Clearly, if a stage hypnotist could easily hypnotize a dozen or more subjects in a matter of moments, imagine the power that really is available to certain individuals who might hypnotize people for reasons other than entertainment.

The movie *The Manchurian Candidate,* the original, which came out in 1962, was the story of a number of soldiers captured by the Communist Chinese during the Korean War. Taken back to China, they were then brainwashed with the goal, through a posthypnotic suggestion, of assassinating a presidential candidate. The American villain in the story was played by actress Angela Lansbury. She portrayed such a despicable character in the movie that it took me several years to warm back up to her. Coincidentally, as I once had a friendly encounter with her in an elevator, my feelings for her have changed. Thus, I am loathe to see that old movie again for fear of resurrecting the highly negative feelings that I finally overcame!

Serious study of posthypnotic suggestions can be traced back to the work of British psychologist Edmund Gurney, as reported in the United States by William James in popular articles published in the 1890s in *Scribners, Forum,* and *Science.* After putting a subject into trance, Gurney would give that person a posthypnotic suggestion, and when the subject came out of trance, he or she had no memory of it. However, if given a paper and pencil and asked to perform automatic writing, the subject's hand would "immediately" write out the command. James concludes that Gurney, along with two French psychologists, Pierre Janet and Alfred Binet, "share the credit of demonstrating the simultaneous existence of two different strata of consciousness, ignorant of each other in the same person."[15]

Janet breaks down consciousness into three major divisions:

1. Lower tendencies: elementary, personal, and intellectual reflexes
2. Middle tendencies: immediate and assertive actions and beliefs
3. Higher tendencies: rational, experimental, and progressive actions

Each of these nine centers, along with four key emotions, can take over and become conscious at the expense of the others, which become subconscious. Being one of the first to use the term "subconscious," Janet described thought as a form of inner language, but the implication was that some thought was conscious, some reflexive or automatic, and some subconscious.[16] Further, these tendencies were arranged in a shifting hierarchy where the tendency at the top could change, whereby the rest became subordinate.[17]

There is a huge secret here glossed over or generally ignored by mainstream psychological models of mind, when psychologists who use hypnosis say it is merely a form of suggestion. Under hypnosis I have seen people become as stiff as boards so that they can lie between two chairs supported only by their head and ankles, and I have seen a hypnotist thrust a needle into the cheek of a subject and pull the needle out through the mouth, and the subject felt no pain and did not bleed.

Sigmund Freud (1856–1939), like Binet, had studied with Charcot, the famous French hypnotist and medical doctor. Forced to leave the University of Vienna because of anti-Semitism, Freud used his time well in France. During this period of the late 1800s, a common ailment often found in women was hysterical paralysis, whereby a limb, such as an arm, was completely paralyzed. Freud had learned from his Austrian teachers that the cause of this disease was biogenic. There was something wrong with the brain or the arm. Charcot took a lady who had this malady and hypnotized her. While in trance, the lady was able to move her arm all about, but when she came out of trance, the arm was once again paralyzed. Through Charcot's demonstration, it became clear to Freud that many problems thought to be physical actually had a psychogenic underpinning. According to this new model, certain abnormal behaviors and physical symptoms were not caused by brain dysfunction. Rather, they were caused by a disturbed mind.

When Freud returned to Vienna, having abandoned the idea of becoming a professor, he started his own practice of treating psychologically disturbed patients. When he began this practice, he started by using hypnosis. Freud's goal was to get patients to recall early childhood events. However, Freud found that these subjects could not remember the recalled information once they came out of trance. Since self-understanding was crucial for helping his patients, Freud abandoned the use of hypnosis and replaced it with *free association* and *dream interpretation*. Patients would lie down with Freud sitting slightly behind them, and in that situation, the subjects would either describe their dreams or talk about anything they wanted. Once they got going, certain themes would arise, and from these Freud discovered resistance and defensive behavior in attempts to avoid discussing certain issues, and transference, that is, the tendency to project onto the analyst similar feelings that the patient felt toward corresponding significant others or loved ones. Transference often developed into a feeling of love that the patient began to have for the analyst. As the weeks went by, Freud began to compile a dossier of where the patients' problems lay, and from there, he would begin to help these individuals gain insight into their problems and thus into who they really were. It was Freud's goal to travel together with his patient on a "voyage of discovery," so that under his guidance, the person would begin to truly understand the root causes of his or her difficulty.

Hypnosis is one of the most perplexing topics in the field of psychology. If we can get a handle on the mechanism of hypnosis we will come a long way toward understanding some profound things about what it means to be human and how our conscious mind interacts with (for want of a better term) our brain-mind, what Sidis would call the subliminal self. The keys to figuring out what is truly occurring during hypnosis takes us into the architecture of the brain and also into the world of dreams.

11

The Brain

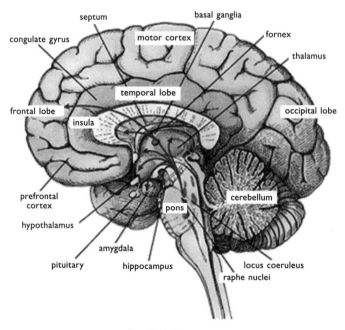

Fig. 11.1. The brain

One of the most difficult problems in discussing brain/mind interactions is how to correlate the two. One of the best ways to grasp how the brain is organized is to look at it from an evolutionary perspective. Biologist Paul MacLean coined the term the "triune brain" to suggest that there are three distinct levels, which would be associated with three major developments in evolution and three major corresponding changes in the brain's architecture and capabilities. With the caveat that this theory oversimplifies a highly complex organization, let us proceed.

REPTILE BRAIN (Brainstem and Spinal cord) **INSTINCTS**
MAMMAL BRAIN (Midbrain and limbic system) **EMOTION**
HUMAN BRAIN (Cerebral cortex) **INTELLECT**

The idea essentially is that the BRAINSTEM AREA, consisting of the spinal cord, medulla, pons, cerebellum, and reticular formation, is involved with *instinctual functions*. For instance, the spinal cord has input and output pathways for receiving impulses (e.g., sensations) and exercizing motor movements (e.g., running, moving, picking up an object). The medulla controls breathing and heartbeat; the pons controls the REM cycle; the cerebellum, which is involved with balance, contains automatisms (habits) and also related behavioral and social programs, which over time have been transferred there after learning; and the reticular formation brings information from the brainstem up to the higher centers via the thalamus located in the midbrain. It controls consciousness and unconsciousness.

The MAMMAL BRAIN is associated with *emotions*. MacLean is suggesting that as animals evolved from reptiles to mammals, one key change that occurred was that while reptiles lay eggs, mammals give birth to live young. Thus mammals, by necessity, would have a much closer relationship to their offspring, and this would correspond to the onset of an emotional connection. Thus the limbic system of a mammal is much more complex than that of a reptile. Take the turtle, for instance, as compared to the lioness. The mother turtle has no connection whatever to her offspring. Once she lays her eggs, she is out of the picture. The lioness, on the other hand, must raise her children and also protect them from predators. That's the emotional connection.

Inside the midbrain is the thalamus, which is the main switchboard, or Grand Central Station, to the brain. All information from the outside world first goes to the thalamus, which reroutes the information to the area of the brain set up to receive these impulses. For instance, visual input will go to the visual cortex, motor movements will be routed to the motor cortex, higher thought processes are sent to the frontal lobes, and so on. The thalamus has been found to be associated also with one's sense of identity.

Other parts of the midbrain include the hypothalamus, which regulates body temperature, thirst, the sex drive, and aggression. Clearly a big change in the evolutionary tree occurred when animals evolved from being cold-blooded to warm-blooded. This change occurred in the hypothalamus. Attached to the hypothalamus is the pituitary gland, the master gland that regulates hormone production of the endocrine system and also growth.

Close to the hypothalamus is the amygdala, which is a very complex part of the brain involved with temperament, forms of aggression such as rage, and also personality. Although one's sense of self is located in the thalamus, the amygdala plays a key role in the subjective feeling of being an individual. The hippocampus works very much like a reference librarian. Memories are not stored in the hippocampus, but this area gives access to the memories. The corpus callosum connects the two hemispheres of the brain together.

The third and most recent development is in the CEREBRAL CORTEX, which MacLean linked to the *intellect*. The most advanced part is in the frontal lobes of humans where abstract thinking, voluntary behavior, and other higher thought processes are located. The other four lobes are the motor cortex or, more correctly, the sensori-motor cortex, which receives impulses from the five senses and sends out impulses to control the skeletal muscles; the occipital lobe, which processes visual input; the temporal lobe, which is associated with hearing, language, and music; and the parietal lobe, which works to coordinate the other lobes. Eye-hand coordination is under the control of the parietal lobe, or more specifically, the angular gyrus, which lies in the parietal lobe.

There are also many other areas and subsections of the brain, for instance, the insula, which, as a center in and of itself, connects the frontal lobes (higher centers) to the limbic system (emotional center); the pituitary gland, which releases growth hormones and regulates the other endocrine glands; the pineal gland, which modulates the circadian rhythm by releasing serotonin and melatonin; and also additional pathways for different neurotransmitters (e.g., the dopamine pathway found in the substantia nigra), which affect the autonomic nervous system, fine motor control, and also different states of consciousness.

LEFT AND RIGHT HEMISPHERES

One of the key differences between humans and the other animals is hemispheric specialization of our brain, known as lateralization. This occurred as language developed. Anatomically, an area of the left temporal lobe known as Broca's area became specialized in speech production and Wernicke's area, also located in the temporal lobe, specialized in speech comprehension. Once this occurred, several other factors came into play. For instance, one hemisphere—the left—which processes language, became the dominant hemisphere, and since the brain connects to the body contralaterally, the right hand became the dominant hand in most people. This is not the case with the other primates who do not seem to favor one hand over the other.

In the early 1950s, Roger Sperry began working with severe epileptic patients. Sperry realized that these individuals, who could suffer as many as fourteen seizures an hour, were also suffering mirror-image brain damage in the hemisphere opposite to where the seizure occurred. In other words, if a subject had an electrical storm in the right parietal lobe, that damaging discharge would cross over to the left parietal lobe via the corpus callosum and cause corresponding brain damage there. Sperry therefore got the idea to cut the corpus callosum and thereby separate the two hemispheres. This stopped the seizures and also eliminated additional brain damage caused by these severe events.

Since these individuals now had, in essence, two separate brains, Sperry began to test each hemisphere individually. When Sperry performed the surgeries, he made sure not to cut the optic nerves, which, like the rest of the circuitry, crossed over to the opposite side. This meant that each eye continued to send information to each hemisphere. The far

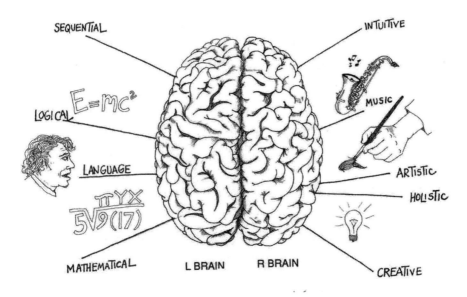

Fig. 11.2. The left brain thinks sequentially, whereas the right brain thinks intuitively. Drawing by Lynn Sevigny.

left side of the left eye sends information to the right brain, and the part of the left eye closest to the nose sends information to the same side, that is, to the left brain. Knowing this, Sperry could put a patch over one eye of such a subject and flash a picture card into the remaining eye. If he flashed the card right in front of the person, the information would go to the same side. If, on the other hand, Sperry flashed a picture in the peripheral vision of, say the left eye, that information would be sent to the opposite right brain and not sent to the left (same side) brain. In this way, Sperry could test each hemisphere independently.

As most people now know, Sperry discovered that each brain thinks differently. The LEFT BRAIN, which houses language, tends to think *sequentially* and tends to see the parts. The RIGHT BRAIN, which programs such things as music, pictures, and face recognition, thinks *intuitively* and tends to see the whole. Thus, a left-brain type person would lean toward more technical pursuits and generally prefer things to be in order. Such a person would also like to proceed step by step. For example, this book is set up somewhat chronologically. That stems from a left-brain tendency in the writer, me. On the other hand, a right-brain type person would think holistically, or to use Luria's term, *simultaneously,* and would be more visually or musically oriented. When I designed this book, I wanted to use illustrations. That reflects right-brain influence. I therefore would see myself as a mixed type.

HEMISPHERIC DOMINANCE:
A QUICK EXPERIMENT

To see which hemisphere of your brain predominates, perform this simple experiment. Take your right hand and make the "Okay" sign by creating a circle with your thumb and second finger allowing the other three fingers to stand upright. Now hold this circle out from your head and place it around a small object to look at, such as the corner where the ceiling meets two walls, a light fixture, or some object that you can see through a window. With both eyes open, place the chosen object right in the center of the small circle. *Now close one eye and see which eye you really used to line up the target item.* If you lined the object up with your left eye, you are a left-brained type, and if it was with the right eye, you are a right-brained type. Take a moment to see if your findings agree with your self-assessment. I always line it up with my

Fig 11.3. Experiment to test brain predominance.
Drawing by Lynn Sevigny.

left eye, which makes me a left-brain type. In my case, since I am also a visual thinker, I clearly see myself as a mixed type. You may find that you are more of a pure left- or right-brained type and there is also the possibility that your self-assessment will not match with the findings of this experiment.

If you find that neither eye dominates and you actually lined up the target in the center with both eyes, then neither eye dominates. This is known as "counterdominance," and such a person is often ambidextrous. Both hemispheres essentially have equal power.

If we are discussing dreams and hypnosis, the idea would be that conscious activity is more under left-brain control, and dreams and hypnotic trances are more under right-brain control.

12
Brainwaves and Dreams

A brainwave is an electrical oscillation of the brain as it changes its polarity from positive to negative at a rapid rate. For instance, in the case of being awake, we are in a state known as beta whereby the brain oscillates at 14–60 cps. Take a moment to watch the second hand of a clock traverse the dial. When the second hand covers a distance corresponding to one second, your brain has shifted its polarity somewhere around twenty times. This is fascinating for a variety of reasons, one being that we remain unaware that our brain is oscillating, or in a sense, flickering, as we perceive the world in continuous, uninterrupted fashion.

When one falls asleep, the brain goes through four stages. Essentially it slows down to a very slow beat, and at that moment the person becomes unconscious. Then the brain speeds up and returns to the beta state. This is the REM state of dreams. The term REM, rapid eye movement, refers to the eyeballs actually following the action in a dream. This state is called paradoxical sleep because the brainwave state of the dreaming person greatly resembles the brainwave state of being totally awake. The REM state also suggests synchronization between the retina in the eye in the front of the brain and the visual cortex/ occipital lobe in the back of the brain.

The brain is under the influence of two dominant rhythms, the circadian rhythm, or day/night cycle modulated by the pineal gland in the midbrain, and the ultradian rhythm, or ninety-minute REM cycle, modulated by the pons in the brainstem. Everyone falls asleep every night and awakens every morning. That is the circadian rhythm. Some people are day people; others are night people. If you enjoy getting up at 6:00 in the morning, you can consider yourself a day person. If you love to stay up to 1:00 or 2:00 in the morning, you are a night person. This diurnal cycle most likely influences the ultradian rhythm, which continues subliminally during the day. This means that even after you wake up, you still go through subtle highs and lows every ninety minutes.

Studies have been done linking the circadian rhythm to life-threatening toxicity levels. In one experiment, a lethal dose of a poison was given to a set of rats, some during their high point and others during their low point. Researchers found that a larger percentage of rats died when given the dose when they were at their low point.[1] Similar findings suggest that delicate operations should be done when a person is at his or her high point in the circadian rhythm.

Naptime occurs when the subliminal daytime ultradian rhythm and circadian rhythm are at their low points. Here, around 4 p.m.

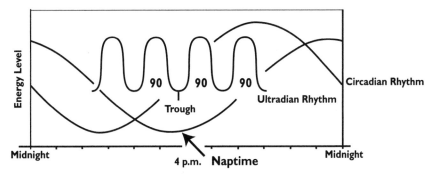

Fig 12.1. Ultradian and circadian rhythms. This image shows how circadian rhythm may influence ultradian rhythm.

This overarching day/night rhythm involves the production of certain neurotransmitters such as melatonin, which increases in sleep production, and serotonin, which is associated with dreams and an uplifted mood, and these neurotransmitters may also modulate the ultradian rhythm. This may be the reason why dreams tend to get longer toward the morning. Even though we dream every ninety minutes, the *length* of each dream *within* the cycle tends to increase as the morning approaches. When a person hits a low point in late afternoon and feels a strong urge to take a nap, this may be caused by the combination effect of two low points, in both the circadian and subliminal ultradian rhythm.

TABLE 12.1. STAGES OF SLEEP AND DREAMS

	STATE		CPS	BRAINWAVE	
B	Beta	Awake	14–60+	very rapid	CONSCIOUS
A	Alpha	Relaxed	7–14	a bit slower, regular	LESS CONSCIOUS
			Twilight Zone		
T	Theta	Drowsy	3–7	slower	SUBCONSCIOUS
D	Delta	Out cold	1–3	very slow waves	UNCONSCIOUS
B	REM	Dreaming	14–60	very rapid	
A	NREM	Thinking dreams	7–14		
T	NREM	Thinking dreams	3–7		
D	NREM	Thinking dreams	1–3		
B	REM	Dreaming	14–60	spike potentials linked to shift in dreams	

There are many things to consider about this chart. First of all, one can see there is a correlation between the rate that a brain is oscillating and the person's state of consciousness. (CPS in the chart above represents cycles per second.) In general, if the brain is oscillating in beta at a rapid, somewhat desynchronized rate, the person is either wide-awake or in the dream state. Secondly, the ninety-minute REM cycle is actually one form of dreaming, the more bizarre form, whereas in the NREM state a person may also be dreaming, but these dreams are much more realistic and resemble normal conscious thinking. They are not elaborate fantastical trips like REM dreams. This suggests that REM dreams are most likely under right-brain control, whereas NREM is more under left-brain control. In a sense, once the person drops into delta, that is, becomes unconscious, a switch takes place. During the day, the left brain, which houses language, dominates. We think in words and therefore structure our world in words. The right brain, which processes pictures, is more in the background during the day. And at night a reversal takes place. The "active" left brain becomes "inactive" or "asleep," and the subordinate right brain, which had been "inactive," becomes "active" or "awake." This model, of course, oversimplifies the situation because the right brain is quite active during the day and the left brain is active at night, but in terms of dominance, the left dominates during the day and the right dominates at night.

Another aspect of this chart suggests that as the person falls asleep,

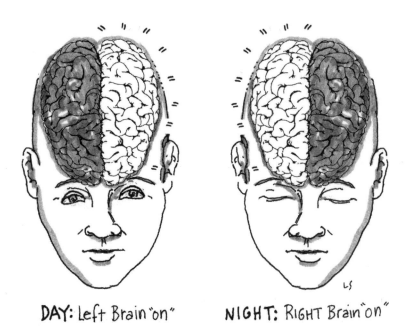

DAY: Left Brain "on"   NIGHT: Right Brain "on"

Fig. 12.2. During the day, left image, the left brain is "on" and the right brain is "off," and during the night a reversal takes place and the right brain is on and the left is "off." Drawing by Lynn Sevigny.

beta and alpha are more associated with being CONSCIOUS and theta and delta with being UNCONSCIOUS. As one falls asleep, one switches from being CONSCIOUS to being UNCONSCIOUS. The in-between state is called the *twilight zone,* which is essentially located in the theta state. We could liken these states to DAY-SUNSET-DUSK-NIGHT (e.g., beta, alpha, theta, delta), and upon awakening, NIGHT-DAWN-DAY (e.g., REM, theta, beta). The DAWN/theta state upon awakening sometimes involves a split in consciousness, as the person can be both dreaming and awake at the same time. The person is conscious but also experiencing or watching his dreams. This is the realm of *hypnogogic imagery.* Technically, the hypnogogic state is the extreme state of drowsiness as one falls asleep, and the hypnopompic state occurs when one awakens. For simplicity's sake, the term "hypnopompic" is rarely used and the word "hypnogogic" is used for both theta states upon falling asleep and upon awakening. Since this state is in-between waking and sleeping, it hovers between the CONSCIOUS and the UNCONSCIOUS. It is a complex fragile state associated with clairvoyance, trance states, and reverie.

In the early 1970s, when I began these studies, I was working with a neurophysiologist at a laboratory at the University of Rhode Island. I myself was hooked up to an EEG machine with the goal of getting into the relaxed state of alpha. As I watched my brain produce rapid desynchronized beta waves with no clue as to how to change them to slower, highly synchronous alpha waves, the professor began to get impatient. So he said in a loud voice, "Relax!" and suddenly my brain generated a burst of the regular rhythmic alpha waves! Here before my own eyes was a dramatic instance of *entrainment,* that is, the locking in of a particular brainwave state. We can look at this event in a variety of ways. One can easily see the parallels to the hypnotist commanding his subject to sleep! and have that person literally drop before him. Assuming these two situations to be closely linked, it would seem that the command to sleep! causes the subject to produce a particular brainwave associated with sleep, most likely delta waves, literally at the drop of a hat. The hypnotist has entrained the subject to drop into unconsciousness or trance state. Simultaneously, what is probably also occurring is a corresponding change in the neurochemistry, resulting in the release of specific neurotransmitters that correlate to this particular brainwave state.

What is so astonishing about hypnosis is that the hypnotist has not only essentially taken over the mind of the subject, he has also taken over certain brain centers associated with somnambulism, such as in: (a) the brainstem area, the pons, which regulates REM and is associated with dreams and sleepwalking, and the reticular formation, which controls conscious and unconscious activity; (b) the midbrain, the thalamus, which is not only the main switchboard center where all impulses are directed, but also appears to be the locus of one's identity; and (c) the higher centers, the occipital lobe where visual images are processed, the temporal lobe where the language center is located, the motor cortex, as the person acts out various commands, the frontal lobes for interpreting and acting upon the data, and the parietal lobe for integrating all of this information.

During the REM dream state, occasionally there will be a spike potential. This is a rapid burst of electrical energy above the already rapid desynchronized beta waves. When this spike potential occurs, the person makes a major change in the scenes of his or her dreams.[2] This was discovered by simply waking up a subject hooked to an EEG machine in a sleep laboratory shortly after such a spike potential was seen. One wonders if similar spike potentials would be seen in brainwave activity as the hypnotized subject changes from one action to another at the whim of the hypnotist.

13

Memory, Engrams,
and mRNA

A number of studies suggest that one of the functions of dreams is to put the person to sleep so that the day's events can be catalogued. Specifically, information accumulated during the day is held in a holding tank, or short-term memory container, associated with the base count sequencing of mRNA (messenger RNA) held in the neurons in the brain.[1]

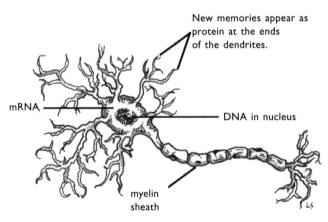

Fig 13.1. A neuron in the brain

If one looks at the neuron one sees the cell body with the nucleus in the center and also the long tail, which corresponds to the axon with its axon terminals. Surrounding the cell body are the dendrites.

Information enters the dendrites, goes through the cell body, travels down the axon, and then, through the release of a neurotransmitter, jumps over the synapse, or gap between neurons to get to the dendrites of the next neuron in the sequence, and so on. Thus, when someone learns something—say, how to shoot a bow and arrow—we know that this information is stored in the neurons of the brain. But the question remains as to whether or not this new information is also processed by the nucleus, or more precisely, the DNA inside the nucleus. The general consensus is that the nucleus is sacrosanct and, for the most part, impenetrable. It needs to be protected so that the integrity of the genetic code is conserved. If every time someone learned something that information was processed by the DNA, then certainly that information would be passed down to the next generation. And we know that this is not true, nor should it be true, because the integrity of the genetic code must be preserved for the sake of the stability of the animal. So where is this new information processed? That is the topic we are discussing here.

The liaison to the rest of the cell, and to that extent to the outside world, is mRNA (messenger RNA), which is structured much like DNA: mRNA holds the key to where new information is processed and stored.

DNA has four molecular bases: adenine, thymine, cytosine, and guanine, or ATGC. These four bases pair in a special way. **A** only pairs with **T,** and **G** only pairs with **C.** It is the sequencing of these four bases in the zygote (fertilized egg) that accounts for every living organism from virus to man. The difference between every species of life can be reduced down to the base sequencing of AT and GC with the realization that AT can pair also as TA and GC can pair also as CG. Each form of life has its own particular code. If a zygote or fertilized egg has an ATGC code in the DNA to build a squirrel, the zygote forms into a squirrel. If the code is set up to construct a wooly mammoth or a saber-toothed tiger, then that respective animal will be constructed. If the code says to build a fern, virus, or fish, then that is what will be built. Finer refinements distinguish an ape from a human, or a sparrow from a hawk.

Messenger RNA, or mRNA, also has four bases, but thymine is replaced with uracil. The four bases of mRNA are **AUGC** with **A** pairing with **U** and **G** pairing with **C**. Holger Hyden found that after learning takes place, the specific percentages and arrangement of AU and GC combinations in the mRNA in the neurons are altered. However, the original sequence is restored the following day. In a sense, mRNA works like a computer screen. Information is placed on the screen during the day and then transferred to the hard drive at night, and the screen is blank again the next morning. So, for arguments sake, say Hyden trained a mouse to walk a tightrope. (He actually did an experiment very much along these lines.) Before the experiment, Hyden sacrificed a control group of mice to see what their mRNA base counts were before learning took place, that is, to use an analogy, when they were in the *tabula rasa* state. After the experiment, that is, once information has been placed onto this so-called *blank slate,* Hyden would sacrifice the mouse and extract the mRNA from the balance area of its brain and measure the percentages of AU and GC. Before learning, the mouse's mRNA base count in the balance area of its brain had a particular set of percentages. The following figures are given for illustrative purposes and do not represent the actual percentages Hyden found.

ORIGINAL mRNA BASE COUNTS BEFORE LEARNING
15% adenine and 15% uracil
35% guanine and 35% cytosine

After learning, these percentages changed. In other words, the configuration of the mRNA sequencing changed. To continue this exercise, for argument's sake, say adenine and uracil percentages were raised by 5 percent after learning. This would therefore mean that the guanine and cytosine percentages would be reduced to compensate.

AFTER LEARNING
20% adenine and 20% uracil
30% guanine and 30% cytosine

After learning, Hyden found that the base count sequencing of mRNA changed, but a day later, it returned to its original state. So what happened to the information? Hyden further found that after learning to walk a tightrope, dendrites in the balance area of the brain grew. This all suggests that mRNA held the information for the day and *transferred these new engrams to protein chains at the ends of the dendrites* at night. This most likely occurs during the REM state.[2] I am suggesting that, essentially, animals have to be asleep for this transfer to occur. That is why babies spend so much time in REM. It is because they are processing and storing a great deal of new information. It is probably why people also tend to sleep in the library or become exhausted after traveling to a new and exciting place. Information overload has to be dumped from the mRNA so that new information can be obtained the following day.

Information is transferred to protein chains at the ends of the dendrites in the specific areas of the brain where new learning has taken place. Motor memory will be placed in the motor cortex, visual memory in the occipital lobe, abstract information in the frontal lobes, and so on.[3] Because this process is complicated, the brain must be in a passive state, so it makes sense that it would occur while sleeping. This theory also explains why Einstein's brain has a larger math area than the normal brain. Like any other muscle, the area that is used the most in the brain during life will literally have more protein than other areas. In other words, all mathematicians would have an enlarged part of the brain associated with mathematical calculations, musicians would have an enlarged musical area, and so forth.

Keep in mind that what we are witnessing here is the area of crossover from a mental world to a physical one. A boy reads the novel *Moby Dick* and remembers the story his whole life. A mental event causes particular molecules (mRNA) in his brain to be rearranged, and these, in turn, cause other molecules on his dendrites to be altered. If we go a step further, we can see that the elements involved in this process are hydrogen, carbon, oxygen, and nitrogen, which comprise the four bases, and also phosphorous, which is the fifth element that lies along the backbone that holds the bases. In some sense, we are witnessing some form of psychokinesis, or mind over matter, as a pure thought directly changes the physical world. Simplistically stated, dendrites grow after learning takes place.

To add to the complexity of this process, take the dream state. We know that the pons, which is in the brainstem, regulates the REM cycle. Thus a thought, which begins as some kind of impulse from the pons, travels up the reticular fomation and sends a signal to the thalamus, which is the Grand Central Station of the brain, and from there this information can be rerouted to whatever part of the brain the information is tagged for, including the occipital lobe or visual cortex and the retina. The prevailing neurological theory of dreams is that while the person is asleep, the frontal lobe sees these supposed random discharges from the pons and tries to interpret them, and that is what dreams are. Assuming dreams are logged somewhere in the brain, it follows that the dream engrams, like any kind of new information, also end up at the ends of the dendrites. Accessing this new information, however, appears to be state specific. In other words, in order to "download" or revisit most dreams, the person must again be dreaming. Certainly we are able to remember many of our dreams, but percentage-wise the vast majority of our dreams remain unnoticed or unremembered by the conscious mind.

During REM, from a physical point of view, impulses to the voluntary nervous system are inhibited. In other words, the neurons to the spinal cord are shut off and the person is somewhat paralyzed during this state. Men also often get erections during REM. If, however, the pons has been interfered with during REM, the person may act out his or her dreams.

We know that somnambulism occurs in the delta state. The person may also be dreaming, that is, in REM, but obviously, his or her access to the voluntary nervous system has not been interfered with, so delta (deep unconsciousness) and beta (REM) would somehow have to be interlinked. It is known that during hypnosis, "bilateral recording disclosed an asymmetry in the amplitude or orienting responses favouring [*sic*] the right hand in hypnosis in high susceptibles."[4] This suggests hemispheric asymmetry in trance states as well.

One of the problems with the EEG research is that due to the complexity of the architecture of the brain, discussions of brainwave states by necessity tend to be oversimplified. In point of fact, Michael Jouvet found that when a dreamer is producing beta in the REM state, that measure corresponds to the cerebral cortex, which relates to the *exterior* of the brain. The hippocampus, which is *inside* the brain, associated with memory, is producing theta. So during REM the outer brain is producing beta and the inner brain is producing theta. During the NREM state, the outer brain (cerebral cortex) is producing delta, and the brain stem where the reticular formation is located is producing alpha.[5] So what we see is a reciprocal relationship of brainwave states.

REM has beta on the outside and theta on the inside.
NREM, has delta on the outside and alpha on the inside.

But the left hemisphere and right hemisphere are also involved, as well as the pons. What I'm suggesting here is that *during sleepwalking and during trance states, there are complex alternative rhythms that are being produced, which differ from the normal REM state* where we see beta on the cerebral cortex and theta on the interior (hippocampus) of the brain. Further, these various and complex combination brainwave states are also linked to the release of specific neurotransmitters. For instance, during sleep and dreams there is increased melatonin production, and serotonin is also linked to active dream production. During addictive states, such as in cocaine addiction, large amounts of dopamine are released. To fully understand such states as REM, sleepwalking, and hypnotic trance, we not only need to know what brainwave states are occurring on the exterior and interior of the brain but also what neurotransmitters are being released and which hemisphere is predominating.

John Gruzeiler found "changes in EEG coherence in the left frontal lobe" during hypnotic trance[6] as well as inhibition of the frontal/

limbic system and a general disconnection between the hemispheres. Suggestive states of induced sleep or trance involve a closing off of the intellectual center (left frontal lobe), a corresponding arousal of certain areas of the midbrain, and also arousal of particular right-brain activities, which control executive functions of the midbrain, pons, and medulla, that is to say, control of unconscious emotional and instinctive centers and the center that controls dreams.[7] When a hypnotist places a person in trance, either slowly or through a rapid induction, such as presenting the word *sleep* in a special way, there is a shift in brainwave states equivalent to what happens in natural sleep when delta waves are produced and the person drops off into slumber. The shift into a hypnotic trance will involve the production of specific neurochemicals that change the brain state to simulate a somnambulistic state whereby the brain of that person is primed to take direction, and that would be associated more with theta waves. The person first drops off by producing Delta, and then the brain speeds up to take the person into a more active state of theta. In dreaming, when the person is back in beta, the captain of this journey, or "author" of the dream, is the subconscious. Neurologically, this mechanism stems from the pons. The conscious self gives itself over to an unconscious commander. Every person surrenders to this unconscious commander every night. We have no choice. There is no choice involved. This is a neurological mandate, part of the deal of being the animal human.

All humans are primed to take direction every night from some part of the self that the conscious self *cannot* control, and frankly, does not really even know. An analogous example occurs during narcolepsy, which could be caused by a misfiring of the pons, and a corresponding trigger of the pineal gland, which releases melatonin, which switches the person into a catalyptic state. A similar event, which just about all of us have experienced, is falling asleep at the wheel. A neurochemical (melatonin) is released and, even against one's will, one can't stop from falling asleep while driving. A similar switching mechanism occurs during sleep and during REM, and there are corresponding neurochemical changes. Hypnosis is directly linked to this process. In hypnosis, the unconscious commander that puts us to sleep and choreographs our dreams is replaced by the mind and will of the hypnotist. Neurologically, one way or another, the hypnotist has caused the left brain to become inhibited, awakened some aspect of the right brain, and taken over the lower centers as well, including the limbic system in the midbrain and the pons in the brainstem.

During the dream state, the conscious self is asleep but also in some way "awake" in the dream. However—and this is the crucial point—this conscious self is not the author of the dream. There is another self, which Freud calls the unconscious and Rampa calls the oversoul, which choreographs, designs, or creates the dream. When we dream, we are participants in the bizarre and oftentimes impossible world of the dream. In hypnosis, this choreographer has been replaced by the hypnotist who essentially has the same power that this other inner self has over us every night when we dream. Just as we can encounter absurd situations in a dream state *and believe it at that moment,* the same thing is true in a hypnotic trance state. The only difference is that the person's physical body is awake and active and the controlling agent is the hypnotist rather than the unconscious or oversoul. The hypnotized person truly is asleep or somnambulistic, but his or her physical body and subliminal mental functions are awake. And so, in the same sense, just as a dream disappears before our eyes while we awaken, the same is true when a person comes out of a hypnotic trance. The subject can have as much conscious memory of the ridiculous and sometimes demeaning things that he or she did in trance as you or I do when we awaken from a long, involved dream that we simply can't recall. This is the situation that we face every morning when we are fooled once again by our dreams, and it is the mechanism that the hypnotist has commandeered to control the many subjects he comes in contact with.

There are several important harsh truths to consider here. First of all, every one of us has to surrender to the night, give up total control to a primal self that not only puts us to sleep but designs our dreams. We have a CONSCIOUS self that thinks and controls our actions during the day, but we also have an UNCONSCIOUS self that thinks and controls our actions at night. This unconscious controller is mental for most of us, but the controller can also take over the physical body as in the case of sleepwalking.

If we look at the nervous system, we see that we actually have two separate systems: the voluntary nervous system, which controls skeletal muscles and voluntary behavior, and the autonomic nervous system (previously called the involuntary nervous system), which controls the release of hormones, smooth muscles, respiration, and such events as the heart-beat rate, sweating, and the opening and closing of the pupil in the eye.

Each nervous system has two parts:

1. **VOLUNTARY NERVOUS SYSTEM—VNS**
   Pyramidal Nervous System: controls fine motor control (e.g., picking up objects, self-feeding, handwriting)
   Extrapyramidal Nervous System: controls gross motor control (e.g., walking, climbing stairs)
2. **AUTONOMIC NERVOUS SYSTEM—ANS**
   Sympathetic Nervous System: active, speeds up heartbeat, gets body ready for flight
   Parasympathetic Nervous System: passive, slows heartbeat down, gets body ready for repose

Oversimplifying to make the point, one can see that the voluntary nervous system (VNS) has a CONSCIOUS and an UNCONSCIOUS and so does the autonomic nervous system (ANS). If we consider the two hemispheres of the brain, this model suggests that the VNS is more under the control of the left brain and the ANS more under the control of the right brain. Each hemisphere would have essentially two parts, a CONSCIOUS and an UNCONSCIOUS, so we would have four overall subsectors and two overarching divisions (left and right brain).

TABLE 13.1. FOUR QUADRANTS OF THE BRAIN

LEFT BRAIN *Voluntary NS*	RIGHT BRAIN *Autonomic (Involuntary) NS*
State I CONSCIOUS *Pyramidal*	State II CONSCIOUS *Sympathetic*
State III UNCONSCIOUS *Extrapyramidal*	State IV UNCONSCIOUS *Parasympathetic*

Thus, we see the possibility of four distinctly different states of consciousness.

State I: left brain/conscious quadrant (pyramidal)
State II: right brain/conscious quadrant (sympathetic)
State III: left brain/unconscious quadrant (extrapyramidal)
State IV: right brain/unconscious quadrant (parasympathetic)

There would also be in-between states and combination states, neurologically linked to (a) the corpus callosum, which connects the two hemispheres; (b) interior and exterior brainwave states discussed above, and states dominated by particular functional centers in different parts of the brain, e.g., frontal lobes, amygdala, thalamus, pons, and so forth; and (c) states under the control of the neurochemistry. For instance, when a person falls asleep, he or she is producing melatonin. If he or she is euphoric, serotonin would be involved. Ready for flight or fight, adrenaline takes over. Runner's high is associated with the release of endorphins, addictive states correspond to the release of dopamine, and so on.

Neurologically, we could also look to additional lobes and centers of the brain to find other ways to isolate states of consciousness. For instance, the frontal lobes are associated with voluntary behavior and abstract thinking, and the amygdala controls emotional states. Aggressive and sexual states have been linked to parts of the hypothalamus, speaking (Broca's area) and listening (Wernicke's area) are found in the left temporal lobe, singing in a corresponding center in the right temporal lobe, sporting events would greatly involve the motor cortex. Luria tells us that what we are really talking about here are functional complexes associated with each brain structure and a coordination of "concertedly working zones"[8] of these structures to achieve any activity. Take, for example, the act of playing a game of tennis. As stated, the motor cortex, which controls muscles, would have a dominant role, but other parts of the brain would also be keenly involved:

NEUROPHYSIOLOGY OF PLAYING TENNIS

Motor Cortex for muscle control

Frontal Lobes involve strategy and initiating behaviors

Occipital Lobe for vision

Temporal Lobe for keeping score and also for hearing

Parietal Lobe to coordinate the lobes

Hypothalamus is associated with emotions and aggression

Amygdala controls personality factors, temperament, and rage

Substantia Nigra produces dopamine to enhance fine motor control

Other Neurotransmitters (e.g., adrenaline, endorphins, serotonin) to modulate other factors

Cerebellum and **Hippocampus** to supply motor memories, automatisms (habits), and key subroutines

Thalamus for integrating all these different parts of the brain

Much of the rote part of this activity ends up in the cerebellum, but as you can see, trying to isolate a single lobe for a single feature is oversimplifying, as the brain needs to coordinate all these areas for just about any task.

One's sense of identity is apparently associated with the thalamus, the Grand Central Station of the brain, the main switching station; but the frontal lobes, insula, and amygdala would also be involved in the neurological correlate to one's sense of identity. Dreams are closely associated with the pons, the visual projection area of the occipital lobe, and the frontal lobes. A question that arises is whether or not some centralizing sense of self-awareness can shift from one part of the brain to another. Different emotional states will have different cerebral centers, but then these centers associated with one's sense of self can be switched off. Where is the center for the unconscious thinking self as compared to the conscious thinking self? Thus, we have two issues here, one neurological involving the actual BRAIN, which we can see is multileveled and quite complicated, and the other is psychological, which corresponds to the MIND, where we don't face the problem of localization of functions.

When we are talking about localization of specific functions within the brain, to some extent we know where to look, e.g., Broca's area for speech production, the reticular formation for controlling consciousness and unconsciousness, the frontal lobes for abstract thought. But we also realize that even this is oversimplified. For instance, if I do learn to shoot a bow and arrow, has my motor cortex become "conscious" when I undertake this activity? And how would that differ from punting a football? What specific centers in the brain become "conscious" for each activity? What part of the brain becomes "conscious" when I look at a tree? In the case of punting a football, the goal of where to place the ball will involve both the frontal lobes (for goal orientation) and the occipital lobes (visual cortex), the temporal lobe for thinking the words "punt this football," and the motor cortex for energizing the muscles used in the operation. In the case of looking at the tree, we have the physical tree, which is seen or processed in the occipital lobe, but the word *tree* has also been activated somewhere in the language center of the temporal lobe. However, if I am thinking about how pretty the tree is, that would involve the frontal lobe for abstract thought, the limbic area for emotions, and also, perhaps, the hippocampus for any other memories I may have about trees. The very acts of either punting a football or simply looking at a tree involve many lobes of the brain. To explain this process, the great Russian neurologist Alexander Luria coined the term "kinetic melody" to stand for the coordinated effort of "concertedly working zones" during these kinds of operations. Luria here is drawing an anology between a conductor in an orchestra bringing together all the different players, for example, the violins, horn section, percussion, wind instruments, and so on, with the ability of the brain to coordinate all the lobes involved in any single task.[9]

Freud, on the other hand, is not dealing with the physical location of these activities. Yet he has constructed a detailed conceptual map, which does lay out where, in a purely mental sense, similar kinds of activities take place. The issue I am raising here is that Freud has indeed created an extraordinary model for how the invisible mind works. But clearly we are a long ways away from correlating this mental map with the neurological map introduced in this chapter. For instance, we will be discussing Freud's ego (a person's sense of identity or self-image), superego (conscience), and id (primitive drives, particulary sex drive and aggression). Simplistically stated, the ego would be associated with the thalamus, the superego with the frontal lobes and insula, and the sexual or aggressive drives of the id with parts of the hypothalamus and amygdala. These correlations, however, are not exact; they are oversimplified, and, as Luria suggests, the localization of any function usually really involves many different coordinated areas of the brain. Nevertheless, this is a first step for uncovering the neurological correlates of Freud's model, which will be discussed in detail starting in chapter 15.

14

Chi Energy

Is Kundalini energy simply a theoretical construct, or is it a real energy? Certainly the body runs on energy. Freud called it "libido," Wilhelm Reich called it "orgone energy," Henri Bergson named it the "élan vitale," yogis call it "prana." One difference here is that prana involves an extra component from the air beyond the four main elements, particularly oxygen. Prana, *pneuma* in Greek, *mana* in Polynesian, and *ruah* in Hebrew, means the "breath of life." According to Choa Kok Sui, author of *The Ancient Practice of Pranic Healing,* there are three forms: prana derived from the sun, obtained through sunlight; prana derived from the earth, obtained through the soles of the feet; and prana from the atmosphere, obtained through breathing. A very easy way to feel enriched is to take some deep breaths. Concentrating on breathing is also an excellent way to meditate. Think of nothing but incoming and outgoing breath.

Is there really something beyond hydrogen, carbon, nitrogen, and oxygen (and some other trace elements) that is obtained through breathing? One fact that always intrigued me was the reality that people who lived near the sea did not get goiter (a swelling up of the throat), whereas people who lived far inland could contract the disease. The difference was the iodine in the atmosphere, which is breathed in by those near the sea. That is why iodine was added to salt, to help people who lived inland obtain an important trace element that they could not get from the atmosphere.

As is well known, the body uses many or maybe all trace elements such as copper, iron, magnesium, chromium, and so forth. Just check the contents of a multivitamin to see how important all of these are. Is prana the compilation of all or many of these components, or is it something else, the primal ether, the breath of life? An interesting theory of astrology suggests that the baby's first breath is what sets the horoscope. This would suggest that energy from the planets, sun, moon, and stars may also play a role. In any event, when prana is breathed in by a master, such as a karate expert, this is called chi energy, and it can be directed.

From 1975 until 1990, I taught four different courses on consciousness research at Providence College night school. A prestigious Catholic school, it was an interesting venue for discussing the link between science and such things as so-called miracles, spontaneous healing, and so on. My premise has always been that the universe operates lawfully, so anything that does occur must follow some natural law. It is man's task to uncover the underlying law. Thus, I never saw a conflict between religion and science. If God has set up a universe, he has done so following certain principles. Man may have free will, but that does not mean that there will not be consequences if he follows a path that is "ungodly."

As a rule, I assign oral reports in every class. The report must be succinct and in the person's own words, although the student can certainly use quotes and of course references. Through the years I have seen some truly amazing reports. In one instance, I had a fellow named Bob take all four of my classes at Providence College on the higher states of consciousness, and during the last class he asked if he could demonstrate karate. The next week Bob came in with a stack of patio bricks, which were all rectangular shaped, perhaps 6" x 10" and 1.5" thick. He placed one brick between two tables and put his fist through it after doing some breathing routines and directing what he said was chi energy out his hand.

One fellow thought this was easy to do, so the expert set up another brick and this fellow created a fist. Using a roundhouse method, the fellow put his fist through the brick. The following week, this second fellow came to class with his arm in a sling. He had broken the bones in his hand under his pinky finger.

Back to the demonstration, Bob then took out a stack of popsicle sticks and placed two per layer, one on each side, in between about eight bricks. They were stacked like a small high-rise building. Bob then went through another breathing exercise and then put the heel of his hand through the entire stack. As a finale, he had a girl hold up one last brick and Bob split it in two by directing chi energy out his forehead and putting it through the center of the brick. *"Heee yah!"* It was truly amazing, and we all applauded.

After school, Bob had essentially graduated from my classes, and he told me about karate masters who could put the palms of their hands through two-foot-thick blocks of ice. He had *seen* masters do this. He then asked if it would be all right if he were to return to class the following semester to give another demonstration. I said sure.

"But this time I want to bring two large cement blocks to put on my chest," he said, "and I will bring a sledgehammer and have one of your students break the blocks on my chest."

"No, Bob," I said. "Just do the patio brick thing. You can put your head through a few bricks if you like, but please do *not* bring large cement blocks and a sledgehammer."

"All right," he agreed.

Well, sure enough, the following semester, Bob showed up with his bricks. However, he also dragged in a garbage can containing two large cement blocks and a sledgehammer, which he placed by the first row of students near the doorway. "Bob," I said, "I just want you to do the first part of the performance. The rest is too dangerous."

"Okay," he seemed to motion. "Don't worry." He went through the entire performance and ended by putting his forehead through a patio brick held up by a strong and willing girl. He then gave me a gorilla stare and said that he would now direct the chi energy out his chest and demonstrate the power of chi by placing two cement blocks there. Then he would ask a student, and he motioned to the boy sitting by the sledgehammer, to come up and pound the cement.

I happened to be sitting behind the student, and I whispered, "Whatever he says, *don't* do it." And the student nodded agreement.

Bob then started a rapid and intense breathing exercise. By this time he had taken out the two large cement blocks. They were about 14" square and about 6" thick. He then lay on the ground in the front of the class and when his breathing had reached a maximum, he was humming like a freight train. He placed one block on his chest and then placed the other on top of the first one. "Okay," he motioned under his breath to the student, bringing his arm forward in a "come-on" motion.

I shook my head, "No," to the student and the student stayed put. Bob was directing a tremendous amount of energy out from his chest region, and he motioned with his arm once more. The moment was too intense, and I was fearful as to what would happen if we did not comply, so I said, "Go ahead."

The student picked up the sledgehammer and began pounding on the top block. When it would break, Bob would take a broken piece and place it back on top and the student would pound away again and pulverize the broken piece. The entire finale lasted perhaps three or four endless minutes. And then it was over.

After the top block was completely pulverized, Bob stood up and we all applauded.

After class, he asked if he could do this again at my next class. "But this time," he said, "I want to get a coke bottle and break it and put it on the floor and then take off my shirt, lie on the broken glass, and then put the blocks on my chest, and have the guy pound away."

"No," I said. "Do *not* come again. Do not. I will not allow it. I appreciate all that you have done, and having you in class, but please do *not* come again."

He put all the pieces of cement and the sledgehammer into the garbage can and dragged it down the hall. And that was the last I saw of Bob the karate expert.

15

A Psychoanalytic
Model of Mind

Freud began his epic work *The Interpretation of Dreams* with a presentation of the ancients' relationship to the Divine through their world of dreams. "The pre-scientific conception of the dream . . . was in perfect keeping with their general conception of the Universe [as they were] accustomed to project as an external reality that which possessed reality only in the life of the psyche."[1] Freud recognized the reason for the supernatural origin of dreams because they appear as if they come "from another world." However, Freud rejected this idea in favor of his belief that dreams were prompted by libidinal concerns directly stemming from the personal life of the dreamer. It was for this reason that his relationship with Carl Jung was doomed, as Jung always held out the possibility that dreams were a gateway to another place. Jung recalls in his autobiography:

> I can still recall vividly how Freud said to me, "My dear Jung, promise me never to abandon the sexual theory. This is the most essential thing of all. You see: we must make a dogma of it, an unshakable bulwark." He said that to me with great emotion. In some astonishment I asked him, "A bulwark against what?" To which he replied, "Against the black tide of mud," and here he hesitated a moment, then added "of Occultism." This was the thing that struck at the heart of our friendship.[2]

Although Freud saw dreams as biologically determined, he basically avoided the metaphysical or divine component to biology. The content derived completely from instinctual needs and one's personal experiences.

Freud's great gift to modern society was his model of mind, a theory so carefully constructed that it transcends his own bias, for the basic Freudian configuration can easily subsume Jungian and parapsychological theories. Although Freud said that the unconscious had infinite layers, he simply stopped exploring at the level of the personal unconscious. His reason for doing this was pragmatic, for he *was* interested in psychic phenomena, and he was quoted as saying later in life that if

Fig. 15.1. Sigmund Freud

he had it to live over, he would have devoted more time to the study of extrasensory perception.

The reason why Freud came out so strongly against Jung's mysticism was because most problems that people have in this world deal with libidinal concerns, personal relationships, the conflict between the ego, superego, and id, repressions, and traumas stemming from childhood. One need only look at such pop culture figures as Jimmy Swaggart, Michael Jackson, Elizabeth Taylor, or Woody Allen; or politicians such as President Bill Clinton, Senator John Edwards, or Governors Eliott Spitzer or Arnold Schwartzenegger; or go back to such ancient predecessors as Cain and Abel, Cleopatra and Mark Anthony, David and Bathsheba; to see that Freud was right. People have great trouble reconciling their id with their superego, but this does not deny the spiritual question. There is room for both in psychoanalytic theory.

Fig. 15.2. The ego (man in the middle) is surrounded by
the superego (angel/conscience) on one shoulder and
the id (devil/temptation) on the other shoulder.
Drawing by Lynn Sevigny.

EGO, SUPEREGO, ID

Freud identified a self as the main character that has to battle between instinctual forces and the conscience. This threefold model of the ego, superego, and id has been graphically represented in Bugs Bunny cartoons whereby Elmer Fudd (ego) wants to shoot "the cwazy wabbit." Just as he is about to, up on his shoulders pop two small characters, an angel standing for good on his right shoulder and the devil on his left. This model is an excellent beginning point for describing Sigmund Freud's personality model.

Ego: The *organizer* of the personality. Your name, your self-image, the "executive" of the personality. Who you think you are, that is your ego. The part of the personality that interacts with the world at large, that tries to make a go of it, is your ego. With access to awareness and self-awareness, the ego can split and observe itself. Because it deals with the everyday world, it oftentimes mediates between the superego and the id. The ego is ruled by the *reality principle,* which is the part of the personality that is willing to delay gratification in order to achieve a desired end. Any form of planning or goal-directed behavior would be classified as ego activity.

Superego: The *conscience.* The superego has within it the traditional values of society and also parental concerns. If one goes against the superego, he or she suffers the pain of guilt. This is a powerful mechanism that keeps a person in line with civil values. Note that the superego can change from generation to generation as the mores of society are changed. For instance, young women for the first three quarters of the twentieth century would feel shame if they were to give birth to a child out of wedlock. Some girls would even commit suicide. Sometime in the 1980s the stigma associated with having a child out of wedlock changed radically, and now it is quite common, even the norm. So the same event to the same person at different points in history would affect the superego in different ways.

An important subdivision of the superego is the *Ego Ideal,* which is associated with the person's best self-image. A chef cooks a dinner, a painter paints a building, a neurosurgeon operates on a patient. All of these individuals are generally motivated to do the very best they can. This is the ego ideal. It is also, for Freud, the spiritual component. The wish to do good has religious connotations: to do God's work. In eastern philosophy this is called dharma, right living.

Where "the superego punishes a person by making him feel guilty, the ego ideal rewards the person by making him feel proud of himself."[3] One of the most difficult features of the superego is to realize that it is not rational. Its main function "is to inhibit the impulses of the id" because these impulses "are condemned by society." The superego also seeks to convert the ego by having the ego replace realistic goals with moralistic ones. "The superego is inclined to oppose both the id and the ego and to make the world over into its own image."[4] That is why it can be so powerful, and that is also why overly aggressive people with strong moral convictions (e.g., religious zealots) can do terrible things in the name of religion. The only check to the superego is the ego, but if reality testing is weak, the superego will win and irrational behavior results. Examples of this include the recent wish by a deacon to burn the Koran because of misplaced anger over the events of 9/11, the bombing of abortion clinics, and the tendency for certain leaders in the Middle East to blame Israel for all that is wrong with the world.

Id: The seat of our *instincts.* The primitive self or primal urges. In particular, Freud identified two overpowering id forces, the sexual and aggressive drives. Where the ego is ruled by the reality principle, and is willing to delay gratification, the id is ruled by the *pleasure principle.* It wants immediate gratification. One can experience the id late at night when the refrigerator is raided, or on the beach when a sexy guy or gal catches the eye. The feeling of lust can be immediate, but it is checked, in normal people, by the ego (demands of reality) and the superego (conscience). Another place where this principle applies is out on the highway when some idiot cuts you off and you have the urge to smash him with your car. Road rage is a clear manifestation of the expression of the aggressive side of the id and also how it can come on so rapidly.

A person with a powerful id is often said to have a powerful libido. The *libido* is simply the life energy available to the body. Since much of the life energy is expressed sexually, the term libido is often used interchangeably with the term "sex drive." However, the libido is really a broader term.

In discussing Freud one must guard against oversimplification. What does he really mean by the sex drive or the aggressive drive? Does a one-month-old baby have a sex drive? Obviously not. Sexual expression is only one aspect of the sex drive. It is a complex drive that involves the body's need for pleasure, for instance, the need of an infant to be held or the need of an adult or a youth whose body has sexually matured to procreate. The wish to have sex is a powerful urge that can bring immediate pleasure to the person, even in the form of an orgasm. When looking at it from the long view, one realizes that the reason to have sexual orgasms has more to do with the species. The need to procreate is a biological imperative. In modern society the id, and the corresponding narcissistic need for self-validation, reveals itself often in derivative form, demonstrated by such practices as breast augmentation, short skirts, tattoos, odd hairdos, excessively long hair in men, and nipple piercing. Yet ultimately the desire springs from a more primeval realm.

Similarly, the aggressive drive can show up simply as the competitive spirit in moderate form, in more primitive form as road rage, or at the extreme as violence or murder. But the origin of the drive is self-preservation. Simplistically stated, Freud delineates a sex drive and an aggressive drive, but in the deeper sense, he is talking about the urge to seek warmth, pleasure, and to procreate (eros) and the drive to survive.

Some people's motivation tends to be dominated by one of these components over the other two. For instance, Billy Graham, Mother Teresa, and the Pope would all represent superego types. Mike Tyson or Steven Segal would be motivated by the aggressive side of the id. Marilyn Monroe and Lady Gaga symbolize eros, or the sexual side, whereas Madonna, who has a hard edge to her sexuality, tends to emphasize both sex and aggression. An ego character would be a well-balanced and clear thinker. Albert Einstein, Walter Cronkite, and Barbara Bush are three individuals who would symbolize predominance of the ego.

Note that having a big "ego" in the psychoanalytic sense is quite different from the common-day sense of "that person has a big ego." The pianist Elton John comes to mind. Vain and self-involved, but also with a sense of humor about himself, Elton John can be described as ego-centric, but in actuality, he is really an id character, ruled by the pleasure principle. His ability to learn piano, however, involved ego energies. In many cases, the ego is very vulnerable to the almighty id. Intelligence and even well-balanced thinking oftentimes may be no match for overpowering biological urges from the id. Governor Arnold Schwartzenegger's and presidential candidate Senator John Edwards' fall from grace, their giving in to the demands of the sex drive over all else, shows the power of the id. Modern-day society is bombarded with sexual symbols through the world of advertising and mass media. Sex is used to sell the vast majority of products, from beer and cars and blue jeans to toothpaste, cat litter, and magazines. Not only is sex a difficult energy to handle in any event, it is even more of a challenge to control in our sex-crazed society.

16

Kundalini and the Fall of Man

In the Book of Genesis, according to legend, humans had early on been in God's graces, but because of sin—Eve's biting of the apple—humans fell and lost their easy link to the Godhead. In Gurdjieff's ponderous book *Beetzebub's Tales to His Grandson,* Gurdjieff introduces the idea of the *kundabuffer,* which is essentially a block at the base of the spine that God has placed on the human's Kundalini energy to restrict access to higher powers.

There are a number of key issues in this story of Eve being enticed by the snake. According to P. D. Ouspensky's view, the snake does not represent evil but rather temptation. Eve is tempted. As she has *free will,* she can do whatever she wants. She can disobey God and eat from the tree of knowledge, or she can continue to live in paradise naively and not risk disobeying Him.

Kundalini energy is often depicted as two intertwined coiled serpents, yin and yang, positive and negative, male and female, lying at the base of the spine. When Kundalini is unleashed, energy shoots up the spine and triggers the seven chakras on the way to enlightenment. These chakras, or wheels of energy, correspond in a biological sense to seven (actually nine) endocrine glands and corresponding levels of consciousness:

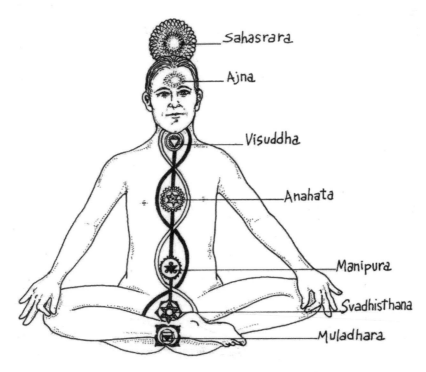

Fig. 16.1. The seven chakras. Drawing by Lynn Sevigny.

CHAKRA/GLAND	STATE OF CONSCIOUSNESS
1. Root – base of spine	Material world
2. Sex – gonads	Procreation
3. Navel – adrenal glands	Meditation
4. Heart – thymus gland	Love
5. Throat – thyroid gland	Truth
6. Third eye – pituitary	Wisdom
7. Crown – pineal	Spirituality
8. Higher octave of 6	Psychic abilities
9. Higher octave of 7	Enlightenment

Freud's theory of consciousness centers on the first and second chakras, survival and psychosexuality, and essentially ignores higher states, although it does touch on the fourth, fifth, and sixth chakras through the ideas of self-observation, insight, and wisdom. Sex, for Freud, expressed through the all-powerful id in all its multifacets, is the driving force of the personality. Certainly, as we have seen from the discussion above, Freud was right in that the sex chakra is mighty. Our id is our tempter. Just as President Clinton had the free will to choose whether or not to bend to the temptation of Monica Lewinsky, Eve had the choice whether or not to eat the forbidden fruit.

A simplistic understanding sees the serpent as the personification of the devil. According to Ouspensky's analysis, the devil, which appears in the New Testament, was actually a mistranslation from the original Greek. The word should have been translated as "the sly one." So who is this sly one? Certainly our id is not the devil, but it can be devilish if it is expressed in a way that goes against the moral grain of society.

We see a similar set-up in the construction of the hierarchy of the angels: with God at the top, Michael to his right, and Lucifer to his left. Lucifer is most often depicted as the dark force or evil. However, if we consider that Lucifer is really the id or Kundalini serpent, he is not evil per se, but he is rather the sly one, or what Jung calls the shadow. As one of my elder students, Philip Brownell, once pointed out in class, the Latin derivative of the word Lucifer means *light* or light-giver (lucidity). If the second chakra (sex) is expressed in a correct way, such as combined with the fourth chakra of love, a child results. This is the miracle of birth and the miracle of our existence. It is the misuse of the serpent that leads to evil. The serpent, in this analysis, stands for the driving procreative force inside us and also stands for our free will. If we adhere to higher law, difficult energies can be expressed in positive ways. However, if we yield to temptation and violate law, we risk destruction. President Clinton's decision to be tempted by the siren not only caused him to be impeached, it also caused him to lose a tremendous amount of prestige, so much so that when his vice president, Al Gore, ran in the next presidential election, Gore was unable to take Arkansas, Clinton's state. Gore also did not take his own state of Tennessee even though he took California, Pennsylvania, New York, and New Jersey. Clinton's peccadillo, no doubt, cost Gore the election, and so the entire direction that world history took from that point on was essentially caused by a real life reenactment of the Book of Genesis. The Democrats fell from grace. We truly do live in biblical times. One need only recognize the signs.

For Gurdjieff, the conscience is an objective force. According to this view, there are certain practices that are objectively evil, such as murder. What would happen if a person committed murder and felt no guilt? According to Gurdjieff, that person would have to avoid knowledge of his or her own conscience and therefore, by definition, would not be fully conscious. When looked at in this way, we see that such an event as the Nazi drive to create a master race, from a Gurdjieffian point of view, was actually a manifestation of *unconscious* activity! If a person were fully conscious, and therefore in touch with his conscience, he could not build a society based upon mass killing. For Gurdjieff, there is an objective level to what Freud calls the superego. The problem arises when people disagree as to what is a sin and what is not. Abortion, prostitution, open marriages, and war are cases in point.

17

Freud's Psychosexual
Stages of Development

As the twig is bent, so grows the tree.

Barbara Cloninger uses the above quote to begin her chapter on Freud's psychosexual stages of development. "Personality development involves a series of conflicts between the individual who wants to satisfy instinctual impulses," which include hedonistic needs and taboo desires, and restrictions imposed by "the social world (especially the family), which constrains these desires. . . . These adaption strategies constitute the personality."[1]

From a physical standpoint, as the child graduates from stage to stage, such as breastfeeding to toilet training, different parts of the body (e.g., mouth, anus) become the focus of erogenous attention whereby biological needs are either frustrated or gratified. "Conflicts, inadequate satisfaction, or excessive pleasure at any point during these stages can lead to a fixation." Sexual energy remains attached to that particular part of the body, and a fixation, such as an oral fixation, occurs.[2] Freud notes that because these events happen in early childhood, on a conscious level they are forgotten and repressed. Nevertheless, "they leave the deepest traces in our psychic life, and act as determinants for our whole future development."[3] Each stage is a critical stage for certain processes to unfold naturally. And if for some reason a process is thwarted, weighty repercussions can ensue.

Freud coined the term *libido* to refer to biological or sexualized energy available to the growing child. This libido, in a sense, changes its point of focus as it travels from one area of the body to another as the child grows and develops. The libido also has the capability to transform from physical to mental energy and vice versa—fixations can cause anxiety and anxiety can cause physical maladies. But the reverse is also possible. Through sublimation, physical exercise, or psychotherapy, mental problems can be alleviated and corresponding physical symptoms can disappear. In general, the way the child is raised and the way he goes through each stage will have a profound effect on his later personality.

Freud outlined five stages—oral, anal, phallic, latent, and genital— with the idea being that at the final genital stage, which is one of sexual maturity, the libido is no longer focused on one or another area of the body, but rather it now flows unimpeded through the entire body. So by the age of fifteen the five stages have been completed.

ORAL STAGE

The ages of 0 to 1.5 years, or the period of infancy, constitutes the first stage. For Freud, the most important occurrence at this stage is breast-feeding, and the site of the libido is the mouth. If a child is not totally satisfied at this stage, oral needs are left ungratified. Later in life the person may develop an oral fixation: smoking, drinking, overeating, talking too much. Norm on the TV program *Cheers* was a typical oral-dependent person. Overweight, an alcoholic, and overly dependent on Sam the bartender, Norm is a prototype for the oral-dependent type. Abused housewives unable to leave their husbands would be another dependent type stemming from this first stage.

On the other hand, oral aggressive types correspond to the child biting down on the nipple. Sarcastic and mean-spirited people fall into this category. Many AM talk-show radio hosts who constantly gripe about politics are good examples of this type.

One question that comes to mind involves the use of a pacifier. "Oh, I would never use a pacifier," said one mother, whose son, now well past fifty years of age, is a compulsive two-pack-a-day smoker. He is also orally aggressive to such an extreme that his biting comments can tear his opponents to shreds.

I remember watching *Good Morning America* one day, and the interviewer asked if it was the mother's fault in a similar instance. "It's always the mother's fault," came the psychologist's reply. I don't agree with that blanket statement, but there is great truth to it. Freud was a firm believer in causality. The way the child is raised greatly determines his psychological state later on.

The oral stage is by far the most important stage of development. This period was studied by Freud's student Erik Erikson, who renamed this stage TRUST vs. MISTRUST. Where Freud is emphasizing such traits as optimism, passivity, and dependency,[4] Erikson was emphasizing the *bonding* process that occurs between mother and child during the breastfeeding period. Is the mother warm, nurturing, reliable, affectionate, and loving during this period, or is she cold, indifferent, harsh, uncaring, mean, and punishing?

The animal psychologist Harry Harlow also studied this stage in his famous experiments with monkeys on the cause of schizophrenia. Harlow was trying to answer the question as to whether or not schizophrenia was caused by nature/genetics or nurture/environment. Stated simply, Harlow found that monkeys raised with surrogate dummy mothers made out of terry cloth were later able to socialize with other monkeys and even raise children, whereas monkeys raised in the harsh environment of having a surrogate mother made out of chicken wire developed schizophrenia. After a year in this situation, these monkeys would not socialize, female monkeys could not get pregnant, nor would they show any mothering tendencies toward a young baby monkey if one were placed in the cage. Harlow further found that if a monkey was raised with two surrogate mothers, one made out of terry cloth and the other made out of chicken wire, even if the chicken wire mother held the bottle, the baby monkey still preferred to spend all of its time clinging to the terry cloth mother. When it wanted to eat, it left its "mom" and fed on the chicken wire surrogate and then returned to the warmth of the other more comforting mother doll.

In an animal cage at the University of Wisconsin, Harlow found out that the most well-adjusted monkeys were the ones raised with siblings, followed by a baby raised by the actual biological mother. Out in a jungle, there is no doubt that the baby monkey would be legions better off with his adult mother. Nevertheless, Harlow has discovered something very important, particularly for parents who may end up having only one child. The best situation would be for that child to have playmates around his or her age on a regular basis.

The implication is clear. If a child does not receive sufficient love, attention, and affection in the first few weeks and months of life, that child will suffer psychological damage and corresponding detrimental neurological changes and/or chemical imbalances in the brain. The child may become overly suspicious, mistrustful, and tend toward isolation. At the extreme, he or she may also develop schizophrenia. On the other hand, if a child receives love, attention, and affection, proper hormones are released and the child will develop normally. This theory suggests a psychoanalytic cause for schizophrenia supported by Harlow's iconic monkey studies. It is well known that schizophrenia can also be caused by genetic factors completely unrelated to upbringing. This topic will be explored further below in the discussion of autism.

ANAL STAGE

Spanning 1.5 to 3 years, this is the time of toilet training. The whole key to understanding this stage is to be able to answer the question, "Why can't a six-month-old baby be toilet trained?" The answer is that the muscles that control elimination, the sphincter muscles, are simply not developed enough in early infancy. Just about the same time that the child is learning to walk, the sphincter muscles are also gaining the ability to manage bowel movements. Thus we see at polar opposites the two opposing positions of HOLDING IN vs. LETTING GO. Tense vs. relaxed, control vs. no control, neat vs. sloppy, clean vs. dirty, discipline vs. no discipline. These are the polarities. Corresponding personality characteristics that stem from the anal stage at the extremes include orderliness, extreme cleanliness, hoarding, obstinacy, parsimony, and extreme interest in time management on the one hand, and laziness, lack of discipline, disorderliness, poor hygiene, and a tendency to spend too much money on the other hand.

What is important to realize here is that at this stage there is no controversy whatsoever about interpretation when understood from a mechanical viewpoint. The child wears a diaper because he has no control over the function of elimination. At about the age of two, control becomes possible. Criticism of Freud enters into the argument when one discusses the PSYCHOLOGICAL RAMIFICATIONS of that stage. Is there a link, for instance, between parsimony and miserliness and constipation? Is a neatness or cleanliness freak that way because of how that person was raised during the toilet-training stage?

Ironically, anorexia—the eating disorder whereby a person, often an adolescent girl, simply refuses to eat—stems not from the oral but rather from the anal stage. Although the oral process of eating is involved, actually, the dominating theme is one of control or overcontrol. Much like the terrible twos, whereby the toddler learns to say the word "No!" the anorexic is also saying no to food and, in some sense, no to life, even if another part of that person is actively engaged in the social scene.

Several years ago I had a student tell the class about an anal-compulsive person obsessed with cleanliness. This individual washed his car every day and then garaged it and covered it with a giant car-cover. When this fellow showered, he felt the compulsive need to wipe down the shower stall so that germs would not accrue. His wish to have a germ-free bathroom grew so strong that he decided to shower at the local YMCA instead so he wouldn't infect his own bathroom! As a disclaimer, I have nothing against the Y. In fact, I am a member of the Y and frequently shower there. However, is it clear that if this person were so concerned about germs, he would have to be a bit nutty to choose to shower at the Y instead of his own house. My point is simple. People do irrational things, and oftentimes a person at one extreme of the polar chart is secretly interested in the opposite side. A control freak wants very much to lose control, someone overly interested in cleanliness is possibly quite interested in "dirt." As another example of this, I knew an individual who was also very strict on hygiene and lived an extremely orderly life. However, when drunk (the person was a binge drinker) he tended to literally wreck his apartment by tossing things about and smashing the furniture. In other words, his actions when his guard was down were the exact opposite of his lifestyle when sober.

Some theoreticians have found a link between bed-wetting and receiving physical punishment during the toilet-training stage. One day, after lecturing on this topic, a student came up and told me that her eight-year-old child wet the bed. "Did you punish him when he was being toilet trained?" I asked. "Yes," she said. "What should I do now?"

I wanted to tell her to go back six years and take away the hitting. Clearly the way she raised her child during this crucial period played a major role in his physical and psychological development. If he wets the bed at the age of eight, will he be able to go to sleep-away camp in the summer two or three years later? Will he be able to spend the night with a girl when he is old enough? Here we see that a problem in one stage can lead to a series of problems in later stages, such as in social interactions, self-confidence, and sexual maturity.

A famous individual who wet the bed was Michael Landon, the TV producer who gained his first success playing Little Joe on the highly popular 1960s cowboy show *Bonanza*. Landon went on to produce *Highway to Heaven, Father Murphy,* and *Little House on the Prairie.* In 1976, Landon produced the movie *The Loneliest Runner,* which was a semiautobiographical account of his years as a bed wetter. As Landon revealed on *The Johnny Carson Show,* when he was a boy, when his mother discovered the wet sheets, she would hang them out on the line for all the neighbors to see. Fearing that his friends would find out, young Michael would run home right after school and gather the sheets before the other kids arrived on the block. Because he ran so fast, Michael Landon actually became a long-distance runner and gained a scholarship to college for his athletic ability. He died at the age of fifty-four due to pancreatic cancer.

Michael Landon's situation presents an argument for a psychoanalytic cause for the onset of cancer. Due to the shame his mother inflicted on him for a problem he had with his bladder, one could argue that a tremendous amount of tension was focused on that area of his body and weakened it. There is some evidence to support the idea of the cancer-prone personality, that is, one that represses emotions. This is still a controversial topic (and I realize, in this instance, that the pancreas is different from the bladder). More study is required. However, it is known for sure that personality factors are responsible for other ailments, such as migraine headaches, ulcers, and heart disease. One way or another, the problem of bed-wetting and its psychological implications created a series of profound consequences in the life of Michael Landon and may have been a factor in his death.

PHALLIC STAGE

This stage covers the years 3 to 6. The theme is sexual identification. According to Freud, at about the age when the child enters kindergarten, sexual feelings arise. This is because the genitals are now growing and thus they become the focus of the libido even though the child is too young and has no idea what sexual intercourse is. Freud hypothesized that all male children encounter the Oedipal complex, which is set up as a triangle, whereby the boy has excessive or libidinal love for the mother and corresponding feelings of jealousy and hate for the father. In competition for the affections of the mother, the boy fears that the father will castrate him. And, according to Freud, the girl at this stage wonders why she does not have a penis. In that sense, for her, she is missing a vital part.

Through the years, a new term for the girl arose, which is called the Electra complex, whereby the girl has libidinal feelings for the father and corresponding feelings of competition and jealousy toward the mother.

There are many variations of these themes and a variety of psychological ramifications. The boy may also be attracted to any female that is in his sphere, such as an older sister or female teacher. The same thing is true for the girl, who may show interest in a next-door neighbor, older brother, uncle, and so on. If the girl supposedly suffers from penis envy, what about womb envy in the case of the boy? It seems to me that in the total scheme of things it is the female, in some symbolic sense, who ultimately carries more power for the simple reason that only the female can give birth. This magical act must seem even more so to the male, who, although capable of impregnating the female, ultimately is not capable of creating life.

When looked at from this point of view, it becomes more understandable why certain cultures would seek to strip the female of any power, because, in some deep sense, the male feels inferior for the reason cited above. In certain African countries, the woman's power is severely limited because the clitoris is surgically removed. In some Middle Eastern countries, females are stripped of all rights, including the right to vote, drive, or even work, and also they must cover their entire face when walking out in public. Why else would men go to such extremes to suppress the females in their culture? In some deep psychoanalytic way, these men fear women because of their inherent magical power to control men through their sexual prowess, ability to create life, and outlive men in the process! Best to keep them at bay.

Returning to the idea of the Oedipal complex and the rationale for its existence, similar dynamics can be seen in other animals. Male lions often kill the cubs of the females to force the females into estrus so they will mate again. In a similar sense, the female bear must protect her children from roaming males. In the case of deer, young bucks seek to drive out the head male so that they can replace him as leader of the pack and new breeder.

Add to this the tendency in many instances for mothers to favor their sons over their daughters and also over their husbands. Some mothers put their sons on pedestals. And no matter what, their sons can do no wrong. In this instance, we see not only that the son may start to feel close to the mother; the mother, in turn, is overly connected to her son. How does the father react to this situation? In one instance, a student came to me with a problem. Her five-year-old son was afraid at night, so every night he climbed into bed with his parents. The father was creeped out by this, and so he slept in the living room. Here we see the mother and son sleeping together and the father sleeping in a separate room.

"What should I do?" this young mother asked.

"Obviously, you have to get your son back into his own room," I said. "Sure, it is okay for him to occasionally sleep with the two of you, but not as a rule. He must learn that as a child, he has to sleep in his own room, and that later, when he grows up and marries, he can sleep with his wife."

"But he's afraid," she maintained.

Clearly this woman was overly protective of her son to the detriment of her marriage. Another suggestion was to sit at the son's bed and read to him until he falls asleep. One way or another, this son must learn to sleep in his own room.

But let us say that the mother continues to allow the son to sleep with her. And it seemed like this was going to be the case in this instance. The father may disappear altogether and possibly find another lady to sleep with. Now how will the son develop? The Freudian view suggests two opposite possibilities. Since this youngster sleeps with an older woman, he may become a very successful ladies' man. That is to say, later in life he may have many conquests and perhaps be unable to stay monogamous. On the other hand, if he overidentifies with his mother, he may, instead, become more feminine himself.

I had another student come up to me after class to ask about his son, who was dressing up in his wife's clothes. "What should I do?" he asked, concerned that the boy might grow up to become homosexual.

Ultimately, there is little that can be done concerning a person's sexual proclivity. However, in the early stages, according to psychoanalytic theory, tendencies toward heterosexuality or homosexuality can be environmentally determined. Either way, *the solution for the Oedipal complex, and for the Electra complex* (discussed below) *is for the child to identify with the same-sex parent.* In the case of the Oedipal complex, the best situation is for the boy to spend quality time with his dad so he will identify with dad. Thus, I suggested to this man that he do things with his son; go to ball games, go biking, fishing, or camping together. The boy may grow up to be homosexual in any case, but no matter, it is still most important that the father and son spend time together, and this certainly was the right advice.

The most classic instance of the Oedipal complex from my files concerns a lady whose five-year-old son liked to hug her when she did the dishes. At about 5 p.m. the father would come home from work, put his briefcase down, and try to kiss his wife. However, the son would continue to hug his mom and kick out with a foot to ward off his father, thus preventing the dad from having an affectionate moment with his wife. If ever there were a classic Oedipal triangle, it was here.

The key to understanding the full implications of the Oedipal complex revolves around how the dad handles this situation. At the extreme, there are two types of dads. The first is the MALE-CHAUVINIST type, or what I call the "macho-jerk" dad. This would be a Robert De Niro–type masculine dad who sees the son as a threat and therefore must impose his manhood so as to reclaim the position of dominance. Such a husband would grab the boy, throw him to the side, take his wife, and plant a powerful kiss on her lips, thereby proving to the son that he, the father, was the central character in the life of the wife.

This type of man continually feels the need to assert his masculinity. When meeting such a person, even in a business situation, the male counterpart must be careful during the handshake, lest it devolve rapidly into a macho competition. This exact situation happened when I once applied to a high school for a teaching position. Having been introduced to the assistant vice-principal, I was caught unawares when he proceeded to grab my fingers during the handshake and crunch them together. When shaking hands with a powerful person, the key to success is to reach as far forward as possible, so as to imbed one's own thumb as close to the thumb of the other person as possible. However, in this instance I was not quick enough, and thus I suffered the consequences. As I stood there during the handshake, I had the distinct feeling that I should kick the guy in the shins. I truly was amazed that a potential boss would try to inflict such pain on a new employee.

This type of dynamic appears quite frequently in a variety of situations, for instance when fathers and sons can never get along. Always in competition, they constantly feel the need to outdo each other. An interesting variation of this kind of relationship could be seen between President George H. W. Bush Sr. and his son, of the same name, President George W. Bush Jr. First of all, if we compare their resumes before their presidential runs we find that George Sr. was a fighter pilot during World War II with over fifty combat missions. Shot down over one of the islands off of Japan and rescued, Bush Sr. was a member of the House of Representatives, head of the CIA, and a vice president in two administrations. George Bush, the son, was a pilot during the Vietnam War who allowed his pilot's license to lapse while serving in the Texas Air National Guard. A reformed alcoholic at the age of forty who found religion, George Jr. ran a number of unsuccessful businesses, headed up a baseball team, and was governor of the state of Texas.

If we look at their relationship in terms of the Oedipal triangle, Barbara Bush, wife of the George Sr. and mother of George Jr., comes into play. Unfortunately for George Sr., he was perceived by many to be a failure as president for the simple reason that he was not reelected to a second term. Further, he left the dictator of Iraq, Saddam Hussein, in power after beating that country in a war over Kuwait in 1990. When George Jr. took office, from a psychoanalytic point of view, in order to outdo the father (for the symbolic affections of the mother), George Jr. needed to accomplish two things: (1) get reelected and (2) take out Saddam Hussein. And that is precisely what George Jr. achieved. He took the country to war in 2003 by attacking Iraq, and a few years later, he captured Saddam Hussein and also won reelection. A masculine figure, George Bush Jr. typifies, by his action, the playing out of the Oedipal triangle. By outdoing the father in two major ways, George Jr. remains an attractive figure to his mother.

If we return to the story of the young lady washing the dishes while her son clings to her as he wards off his father when the father tries to kiss his wife, we come to the second type of dad, the ENLIGHTENED DAD. In point of fact, this is precisely the kind of dad that was part of this story. When he approached his wife and his son began to kick him, the dad reached down and began to tickle the son and declare, "I'm going to kiss Mom! I'm going to kiss Mom!" By tickling, the boy's stronghold on his mother was breached. Once he let go, the father wriggled between his son and wife, held her in his arms, gave her a kiss, and gave his son a wink.

Here we see the full implications and resolution of the Oedipal complex. As much as the son is jealous of his dad and fears his retribution, the son also loves his dad. In other words, the boy is ambivalent. He has both feelings of love and hate. If the dad is a macho jerk and tosses the son to the side as he kisses his wife, such a son may indeed grow up in conflict with the father. Any love he has for such a father is thwarted, and so the best way to compete is to outdo the old man.

In the case of the enlightened dad, how could a son dislike that kind of father? With an enlightened dad, the son will grow up able to more easily pass through the Oedipal phase. He will have a better relationship with his father and be more likely to identify with such a man.

In the case of the Electra complex, everything is reversed. There are two essential problems: (1) how will the girl resolve her feelings of jealousy and competition toward the mother? and (2) how intense is the underlying sexual tension between the father and daughter?

In general, it is easier for girls to resolve their differences with their mothers as compared to boys with their fathers because mothers, for the most part, spend more time bringing up their children. Therefore, mothers have more opportunities to override the jealous feelings that their daughters might harbor.

A number of years ago, the actress Joan Collins was asked by Barbara Walters why she had so many husbands (eight). Collins responded, "Because I am always looking for Dad." Based upon what she said, it becomes clear that Collins' promiscuous and provocative lifestyle was sparked by her libidinal need to fill the void left by the missing father.

Another famous case is that of the comedian and talk-show host Rosie O'Donnell. Before she rocketed to success, Rosie revealed in her monologue that her father (a true macho jerk!) made Rosie, the young girl, feel embarrassed on the onset of her period. In Rosie's case, her mother had passed away at this crucial time of her sexual development. Unable to find comfort from her obtuse father, she took out her anger in a variety of ways, one being through the biting comments in her comedy routine. An outspoken lesbian, one wonders if her sexual orientation was influenced by her particular upbringing, whereby she was unable to gain affection from an insensitive dolt of a father. Mistrustful of men, Rosie found more comfort through the love of women, perhaps also filling a void left in her by the early death of her mother.

LATENCY PERIOD

Ages 7 to 11. The word latent means under the surface. Freud is suggesting here that the sexual turmoil that the child has experienced during the phallic stage is in abeyance, and the child, now at around the fourth and fifth grade, shifts his interests to school and schoolwork and also to socializing mostly with children of the same sex. Erikson called this stage INDUSTRY vs. INFERIORITY. This is the time when the growing child gets involved with personal interests, such as hobbies, science projects, and also physical activities, particularly sports. According to Erikson, if the child is actively engaged with others and the world, he or she becomes industrious. If, on the other hand, the child has had a poor relationship with the parents in the first stage, and had difficulty either by being physically punished or embarrassed during the toilet-training stage and made to feel guilty about his or her own body image and sexuality during the phallic stage, such a child is more likely to grow up with feelings of inferiority. Later in life, people who repress their sexuality and plow all of their life into their work (workaholics) would be considered fixated at the latent stage.

An interesting example of someone trapped in the latent stage would be the actress Grace Kelly. A highly successful movie star and Oscar winner, Grace Kelly gave up her exciting acting career to literally become a princess by marrying Rainier III, the prince of Monoco. Much later, in an interview, Princess Grace revealed a hidden sadness because she did not truly realize when she got married that she would never be able to act again. Yes, she could continue to meet with her old Hollywood friends like Frank Sinatra and Cary Grant, but in the process of literally becoming a princess, she sacrificed a creative part of herself that left her, in this way, empty.

GENITAL STAGE

Ages 11 to 15+. This is a very difficult stage for the growing adolescent. From a biological point of view, the child is now physically mature. Males are able to produce sperm and females are able to get pregnant. However, in most cultures these individuals are still too young to act on these impulses. From a psychodynamic point of view, in theory, the libido is no longer focused in one area of the body or another but now is flowing unimpeded throughout the entire body. The individual is now sexually mature. Psychologically, however, it is an entirely different situation.

Erikson called this stage EGO IDENTITY vs. ROLE CONFUSION. Either the youngster has a strong sense of self or he or she may become a conformist or a follower. Many children at the onset of adolescence have a rebellious period. They may take on a counter- or negative identity. Obtaining tattoos, eyebrow piercings, or nose rings, or becoming part of a peer group such as punks, rockers, goths, or hippies, individuals at this age are seeking an identity.

Due to various pressures, adolescents may suffer from an identity crisis, whereby the individual may have difficulty seeing how he or she will proceed in the world, and how in the future to make a living. Some people try out various identities. This time is recognized as a MORATORIUM period whereby youngsters try out different identities. For instance, a girl may dye her hair day-glow orange. A male may grow a long beard or give himself an odd hairdo, such as a mohawk. Society accepts and allows adolescents this time to experiment. However, it is understood that once that individual reaches the age of about eighteen or twenty, the moratorium period has ended. It is highly unlikely that a girl with day-glow orange hair will obtain a decent job. The constraints of society and the need to try and fit in usually work to guide the adolescent through this tumultuous period.

TABLE 17.1. FREUD'S PSYCHOSEXUAL STAGES OF DEVELOPMENT

AGE	STAGE	SITE OF LIBIDO	MAIN THEME	PSYCHOLOGICAL RAMIFICATIONS
0–1.5	ORAL	Mouth	Breast-feeding	Fixations: e.g., overeating, alcoholism, cigarette smoking, too much talking, sarcastic
	TRUST vs. MISTRUST (Erikson)			
1.5–3	ANAL	Anus	Toilet training	Control vs. no control—tense vs. relaxed; neat vs. sloppy—clean vs. dirty
	AUTONOMY vs. SHAME AND DOUBT (Erikson)			
3–6	PHALLIC	Genitals	Sexual identity	Oedipal and Electra complexes
	INITIATIVE vs. GUILT (Erikson)			
7–11	LATENT	Under surface	Friends/ Schoolwork	Later in life: Self-actualized vs. workaholic
	INDUSTRY vs. INFERIORITY (Erikson)			
11–15+	GENITAL	Entire body	Sexual maturity	Follower or conformist
	EGO IDENTITY vs. ROLE CONFUSION (Erikson)			

AGE	STAGE	SITE OF LIBIDO	MAIN THEME	PSYCHOLOGICAL RAMIFICATIONS
15–30	*INTIMACY vs. ISOLATION* (Erikson)			People either get married and find a mate or they have difficulty maintaining relationships
30–55	*GENERATIVITY vs. STAGNATION* (Erikson)			Either people have made something of themselves or they fritter away their time.
55–110	*EGO INTEGRITY vs. DESPAIR* (Erikson)			How does one reconcile old age? Are people happy with their choices or have they chosen poorly and become bitter?

Table 17.1. Freud outlined 5 stages of development starting at birth (oral stage) and ending in adolescence (genital stage). His student Erik Erikson renamed the stages and added three more, suggesting that stages of development continue on into old age.

Erikson makes the case that human development does not stop at the age of 15. He therefore proposes three more stages after the genital/ Ego Identity vs. Role Confusion stage. The next stage, INTIMACY vs. ISOLATION, covers the years 15 to about 30. The idea is that many people get married during this time. But those who don't may become isolated.

In astrology there is something called the Saturn return. It is the time, 29.5 years, that it takes for Saturn to go once around the Sun. Saturn, in this typology, represents the father or father image. As the young adult turns 30, symbolically, the prototype of the father image becomes more pronounced as the person asks whether or not he or she is headed in the right direction. Erikson called this stage GENERATIVITY vs. STAGNATION, covering the years 30 to 55. Is the individual actively engaged in the world, earning a living, "working" in the good sense of the word, or is the person stagnating? Now that the person has reached the age of 30, there is a realization that the clock is ticking and this is often one of the key reasons that prompts the person to work harder to find a proper path to success.

Erikson's final stage is called EGO INTEGRITY vs. DESPAIR and covers the years 55 through old age. Is the person happy in his or her life's path? Is he or she self-actualized, or is the person bitter because of poor upbringing and poor choices made along the way?

In looking at this chart of development, it seems that Erikson's last three stages are a rebirth of Freud's oral, latent, and genital stages, experienced as a second cycle. If the person bonded with the mother during the first stage, he or she will have the tools to become intimate with a mate at around the time of ages 18 to 30. And, just as the latent stage involves the child becoming industrious, this kind of energy reemerges after, in theory, the young adult has settled down and now concerns him or herself more with career.

The final stage involves self-reflection, a continual need to contribute to society and also a realization that life is short. One way or another, old age involves some reconciliation with one's mortality. What kind of stamp does one want to leave on the world? How does one live a full life and still be true to friends, relatives, and one's mate? Should a person retire at age 66 or 70, or should that person continue to engage in some type of work? What kind of wisdom can an older person impart to the upcoming generations? These are some of the questions that people in Erikson's final stage often face. With life spans increasing, it would seem to me that the final stage could be broken down by decades. That is to say, there is a difference in one's outlook, spiritual view, sense of mortality, and focus on one's legacy in one's 50s, 60s, 70s, 80s, and 90s.

18

Conscious, Preconscious, and Unconscious

Freud delineated three parts to the personality: the ego, superego, and id, and he also described three ways in which each of these parts can *think,* that is, consciously, preconsciously, or unconsciously. Likening the mind pictorially to an iceberg, with 10 percent above the surface and 90 percent below, Freud added an in-between realm, right below the surface of the water, which he called the preconscious. To fully understand these three components, it should first be realized that according to Freud the unconscious is first and foremost the repository for all psychic processes. In other words, the unconscious is the *entire* iceberg. The part of the unconscious that is above the surface of the water he called the conscious, but again, that is really part of the unconscious. Humans, according to this hypothesis, are essentially unconscious beings.

An interesting model Freud used to explain the conscious (CS), preconscious (PCS), and unconscious (UCS) was the "mystic writing pad." This is the child's tablet that has a plastic sheet lying on top of the slate. For Freud, the slate corresponds to the unconscious and the plastic to the conscious. As we can see from this model, there is nothing "in" the clear plastic. We can only read information from the plastic when it is bound or *cathected* to the slate. Everything is in the slate. The conscious, in this instance, can be seen as a moveable window, as it were, only becoming activated when it binds to the almighty slate. It is Freud's:

> unshakable conviction that the most complicated and the most accurate operations of thought . . . may take place without arousing consciousness. . . . As Lipps said, the unconscious may be accepted as the general basis of life. The unconscious is the larger circle which includes the smaller circle of the conscious; everything conscious has a preliminary unconscious stage.
> . . . The unconscious is the true psychic reality. In its inner nature, it is just as much unknown to us as the reality of the external world.[1]

This idea of a thinking unconscious can be traced all the way back to Descartes, who stated that "the soul must always think because its whole essence is thinking."[2] Leibniz also supported the concept of innate ideas, that is, that the soul of the infant came into the world with some type of preknowledge. This got transformed into the concept of instincts, and the idea/concept of a soul was essentially abandoned. According to my recollection, my teacher Bruno Bettelheim told our class in psychoanalysis that Freud did, in fact, link the soul to the unconscious, but when American psychologists such as A. A. Brill translated his work, this potentially religious connotation was removed. It is interesting to note that in the 1938 *Collected Writings of Sigmund Freud,* which is a thousand-page tome produced by Basic Books, the word "soul" does not even appear in the index.

THE CONSCIOUS

According to Freud, the conscious is simply an organ of perception. One of the reasons for this is that the conscious perception system has no memory. For "if the memories remained permanently in consciousness, they would very soon limit the fitness of the system for registration of new excitations. . . . [Only what] is present in our consciousness and [of] which we are aware" is termed conscious. Thus, this mechanism that is our consciousness only operates when we are awake or aware during the ongoing now. The conscious apparatus can be made to trigger an unconscious configuration due to goal-directed behavior or to the energy bound to an unconscious percept, for example, to a memory.

The conscious is also an apparatus that gives the being access to motility. A person could be "unconscious" but use the "conscious" apparatus. Sleepwalking would be an example of such behavior. In a way, both Freud and Gurdjieff are in some form of agreement here, as Gurdjieff states that humans exist in a waking sleep state, which is essentially a robotic existence. They go through the motions of life thinking they are awake, when really they are operating much like automatic machines. Freud says that humans are essentially unconscious beings. Psychoanalysis makes it abundantly clear that a large percentage of human behavior is actually dictated by unconscious needs. How else can one explain how Sylvester Stallone continues to make his exceedingly violent movies and to make a profit on them? The world of advertising is also well aware that most buying decisions are made for unconscious reasons. Just go into a drugstore some day and look at the ingredients in name brands as compared to generic brands. Most often they are identical, yet people prefer to pay more for a name they recognize, even when the drug is exactly the same as the uninteresting looking bottle sitting right beside it.

THE PRECONSCIOUS

All memories that a person can recall are located by definition in the preconscious. Symbolic or prelogical behaviors and automatisms, or repetitive psychomotor patterns, that is, *habits,* are also located in the preconscious. Once a task is learned, it becomes an automatism or habit, and thereby operates preconsciously. Touch typing, driving, and handwriting are all examples of preconscious activity. In these instances, the conscious apparatus is used, but awareness is not activated. When such activity has symbolic meaning, such as cigarette smoking, twitches, or constant anger, then this behavior is also called *prelogical.* It has symbolic value, which suggests that the habit is some type of converted expression from a repressed source.

The preconscious houses the *censor,* a very powerful part of the psychic apparatus used to protect the self-image. It therefore modifies unconscious conflicts by creating prelogical automatisms (nonconscious or symbolic behavior patterns) through the *defense mechanisms,* which are located there. The censor is ruled by the superego, which in turn is ruled by the demands of the parents and society.

THE UNCONSCIOUS

Anything that a person cannot remember is located by definition in the unconscious. There are generally two reasons for forgetting: (1) the memory has simply faded and cannot be retrieved, or (2) the memory is too painful to remember. In this second instance, the memory is *repressed,* that is to say, it is pushed into the unconscious or buried there on purpose. The true psychic self, or what a person really wants to be, is also part of the unconscious. So the unconscious houses our deepest desires and our soul or essence as well as our repressions. Again, the unconscious is everything. Part of the unconscious is preconscious and part is conscious. As Freud said:

> It is indeed an outstanding peculiarity of the unconscious processes that they are indestructible. Nothing can be brought to an end in the unconscious; nothing is past or forgotten.[3]

DEFENSE MECHANISMS

The term "defense mechanisms" was conceived by Freud's daughter, Anna Freud. The purpose of defense mechanisms is to protect the self-image from the demands of the id. The defense mechanisms are all located in the *censor,* so it is the role of the censor to keep unwanted thoughts unconscious. The main mechanism for this procedure is repression. Before we discuss the defense mechanisms, let us first take a look schematically at what is occurring.

There are three parts of the personality the ego, superego, and id, and each of these has three ways of thinking, consciously, preconsciously, and unconsciously.

TABLE 18.1. WAYS OF THINKING FOR EGO, SUPEREGO, AND ID

EGO	CS PCS UCS	The most **Conscious** part because of association with the awareness function
SUPEREGO	CS PCS UCS	The most **Preconscious** because of its association with the censor
ID	CS PCS UCS	The most **Unconscious** part because it is the most primitive

The ego is the most conscious of the three personality parts, although it also has preconscious and unconscious aspects to it. The superego is the most preconscious, and the id is the most unconscious, but these can also think in the two other ways.

Joe is attending a sermon in a chapel. It is around dinnertime and Joe has become hungry. If the id, which seeks immediate gratification, takes hold, Joe may get up in the middle of the sermon and exit the room to find something to eat. In this case the id has attained use of the conscious apparatus to gain access to motility (movement). If Joe feels that he might insult the chaplain by interrupting the sermon in this way, then a battle has erupted between his id and the superego. Joe may stay seated because he realizes that it would be better to wait for reasons of propriety, or because the planned meal at a restaurant, which will take place in two hours, will be more beneficial than any food obtained in the hallway where the candy machine is located. Here we see that the ego and/or superego win the fight.

On the other hand, say Joe has a candy bar after the sermon but before dinner. The id wish was still too strong, so the id obtained access to the conscious apparatus and caused the person to ruin dinner by snacking before the meal.

THE ID OPERATING IN THE GUISE OF THE SUPEREGO OR EGO

Sometimes the id can express itself by fooling the ego, as it probably did in the situation outlined above. Joe eats the candy bar and rationalizes, "Well, at least I didn't embarrass myself by getting up in the middle of the pastor's sermon." In fact, what really happened was the id got its way, although it took a little longer than the id had wanted.

A more serious situation would be an act such as the bombing of an abortion clinic. A person may in all sincerity be against abortion, and argue persuasively that abortion is immoral because it is a form of murder. This would express superego concerns. However, if this person resorts to violence to win the argument, one can see that this is not superego activity, but really it is the id operating in the guise of the superego. Many wars are fought for similar reasons. They appear on the surface to be motivated by moral concerns, when in fact they are rerouted aggressive expressions from the id. The suicide bombers who were promised martyrdom and scores of virgins in heaven are another ghastly example of the id operating in the guise of the superego.

From [our arguments] I learned that the crucial element of conversation is the unspoken, the deftly avoided chuckhole that words swerve around—which dictates by denial, deception, and omission the path and shape of human conflict. . . . [My mother] taught me that nobody is who they appear to be, and nobody says what they really mean, especially if they love you.[4]

REPRESSION

All of the defense mechanisms, more of which are listed below, are forms of repression. Repression occurs when an unwanted or painful thought is pushed into the unconscious. Most repressions start with *denial*. Bob's fiancé has moved to a distant location. Because of this, Bob's phone bill skyrockets. At the beginning of the next month a phone bill of many hundreds of dollars comes in. Angry at himself for making so many calls, Bob places the bill down and looks through his other mail. As the weeks go by, Bob continues to add more mail to the pile. Along the way, other debts such as gasoline and credit card bills are paid. Why does Bob forget to pay the phone bill?

Let's take it a step further. Why *should* Bob pay such a large bill just because he made a few phone calls to his girlfriend, especially when he considers that the phone company is so wealthy? The reason is obvious. The phone company will shut off Bob's phone if he does not honor the debt. In other words, the phone company is powerful enough to force Bob to dig into the developing repression and deal with the pain of the debt. Suppose, however, that the phone company had no leverage. In that instance, Bob may never pay the bill and eventually forget that he owes it. Further, he may become extremely angry and defensive if someone tries to remind him that he welched on a phone bill. Unless a person is forced to deal with the discomfort of uncovering the unpleasant material in a timely and optimum fashion, the person will most likely deny the situation's existence. This is the power of repression. People do indeed forget painful memories. It is easier to forget than to deal with the pain. Further, if such painful memories stem from many years ago, or early childhood, the corresponding repression will be more deeply buried and ingrained.

RATIONALIZATION

Making up a good excuse, Joe thinks, "Since I sat through the sermon, I deserve to have the candy bar." The point is that this seems to be a good reason, but it is not the real reason. Joe was actually at the mercy of his hungry id, and because of this, he could not follow through on the ego's wish to delay eating until food was ordered at the restaurant.

INTELLECTUALIZATION

This means removing the affect, or emotion, from an ardent event. A married man goes out for lunch with his secretary, who is also married. They talk about the sex life of the president or the recent risqué movie that is making the rounds. They each may really want to go to the nearest motel, but they don't for all the reasons why they can't. Talking about the sex allows them to discharge their own pent up sexual feelings in a way that can be tolerated by the ego and superego.

There are many forms of intellectualization. It can be used to ward off the pain of dealing with an emotionally charged event. A young debutante carries deep resentment for her stolid parents, because they shipped her off to boarding school when she was an adolescent but let her younger sister go to school at home. Having grown up in a somewhat artificial environment, she never shows her anger toward her parents, but instead she tells people that she's simply bored with them. If she allows her real feelings to surface, she may be overwhelmed by them, so she intellectualizes.

When the military makes a mistake in a war and kills its own men, they call it "friendly fire." Through a terrible blunder, they slaughter their own men but call it a friendly act. The killing fields where battles take place, where humans are maimed, incinerated, and massacred, are called the "theaters of operations."

PROJECTION

This is a very common defense mechanism whereby a person attributes his or her own neurosis to another. For instance, a shoplifter may accuse a friend of thievery. A husband who is cheating on his wife may accuse her of sleeping with other men.

Projection is not just a defense but also a way of life, as people tend to project their worldview onto others and the world. An atheist cannot understand how his friend can believe in God; a Republican cannot understand how a Democrat could vote the way he does—and vice versa. An adult has difficulty understanding how an adolescent can get her nose pierced. Is the glass half empty or half full? The person's attitude is projected onto the world, and that becomes his or her other reality.

DISPLACEMENT

Taboo forms of satiation are exchanged for different forms of gratification. A man is angry at his boss; he comes home and yells at his wife. A female employee named Cloris dresses daily in spiked heels and provocative clothes, so much so that she resembles a high-class hooker. She is married, has children and grandchildren, and is a faithful wife. She frequents gambling casinos, her forté being the slot machine. This lady has displaced libidinal desires for buying clothes and for gambling.

REACTION FORMATION

The real wish is denied and converted to its opposite. Further review of Cloris, above, finds that she was appalled when it was discovered that President Bill Clinton was having an improper tryst with a twenty-one-year-old White House intern. Cloris's outrage is disproportionate to the sorry affair. From a psychoanalytic point of view, it is blatantly obvious that Cloris is secretly envious of the young intern, who is able to act out her sexual fantasies with the powerful boss. Cloris has changed her feelings of lust to disgust and displaced them onto the president, because her censor will not allow her self-image to admit to her own tawdry underpinnings. This is reaction formation.

Alice's mother, Henrietta, is overly nice. She is cheerful, considerate, and kind, but too much so. One senses this is a mask. Alice tends to be sarcastic and does not date. After college, as a graduation present, she is given fare to Hawaii and she goes with a friend. Shortly after landing, she has an anxiety attack followed by a psychotic break. Institutionalized, she is never the same. Alice has become schizophrenic.

A further analysis of the family reveals that the Alice's grandmother, Mrs. Danvers, is a dreadful woman, and that she treated her daughter, Henrietta, horribly as the child grew up. Fearing retribution from the wicked mother, Henrietta submerges her feelings of revilement and converts them into kindness. Henrietta becomes the perfect daughter so that she can never be punished by her mother. And when she has a child herself, she becomes the perfect mother. But what does Henrietta do with the hate that she has repressed?

One way or another, she covertly inflicts cruelty to her daughter, Alice, under a cloak of kindness. Alice realizes that there is another side to her mother, and this shows up in Alice's sarcasm. But why does her mind snap? I asked this question of my teacher Bruno Bettelheim. He took a book and placed it on the table and slowly pushed it toward the edge. At one moment the book is still safe, but after one more nudge, it crashes to the ground. Alice had taken so much for so long, but because of the nature of the neurosis, most of the battle was occurring unconsciously. Perhaps it was a comment made by Henrietta before she left on the trip—said in all sincerity, "Now, don't come home pregnant, honey"—one will never know. In any event, the final straw was placed on Alice's back, the neurochemistry of her brain shifted permanently in a negative way, and she broke, never to be completely healed. As Bettelheim stated in class, it can take three generations to create a schizophrenic.

19
Jung and Freud

In the dream I was in this meadow [near Laufen castle]. Suddenly I discovered a dark, rectangular, stone-lined hole in the ground . . . [with] a stone stairway leading down. Hesitantly . . . I descended. At the bottom was a doorway with a round arch, closed off by a green curtain . . . Push[ing] it aside, I saw before me . . . a rectangular chamber about thirty feet long . . . and in the center a red carpet ran from the entrance to a low platform. On this stood a wonderfully rich golden throne . . . a real king's throne in a fairy tale. Something was standing on it which I thought at first was a tree trunk twelve to fifteen feet high and about one and a half to two feet thick. It was . . . of a curious composition . . . made of skin and naked flesh, and on top there was something like a rounded head with no face and no hair . . . [just] a single eye, gazing motionlessly upward. Above the head . . . was an aura of brightness. The thing did not move, yet I had the feeling that it might at any moment crawl off the throne like a worm and creep toward me. I was paralyzed with terror. At that moment I heard from outside and above me my mother's voice. She called out, "Yes, just look at him. That is the man-eater!" That intensified my terror still more, and I awoke sweating and scared to death. For many nights after, I was afraid to go to sleep, because I feared I might have another dream like that.

CARL JUNG

Jung explains in his autobiography that this dream "haunted me for years."[1] Only later did he realize that the large tree-trunk-like figure made out of "skin and naked flesh" was a ritual phallus, an erect penis. In analyzing the dream, Jung clearly wants to avoid the potential Oedipal nature of the dream. Instead, he suggests that the hole in the ground suggests a grave, the red cushion corresponds to blood, and the phallus stands for God himself, for that is the man-eater, both the creator of life, through the production of sperm, and the taker of life, that is to say, the force or entity that takes all of our lives and places our dead bodies in the ground.

Jung makes it clear that he distrusts God or Christ, because this entity, although giving him life, will also later on take it. Having seen a dead man floating down the river around the time of the dream, Jung grew up with a certain uneasiness about religion.

Dreams are multidimensional. One must credit Jung for the idea of extending the meaning of dreams beyond the more limiting constraints of a Freudian interpretation. For if his dream is simply a manifestation of the Oedipal complex, then the game is over. Jung is overly attached to his mother. His father, who is a preacher, threatens to castrate him and even kill him (or eat him) should Carl's penis become attractive to his father's wife, Carl's mother. When one studies Jung's life, one finds, much to the consternation of Carl Jung, that this kind of interpretation rings true. Carl was indeed much closer to his mother, to whom he ascribed psychic powers. Further, not only was he bored with his father, who tended to drone on during his sermons, Jung tells the reader that he felt much closer to God, or whatever this spiritual energy might be, when he was sitting alone in the woods watching a stream, as compared to suffering through yet another tedious sermon. In one dream, also covered in his autobiography, Jung has God defecate on the roof of his father's church. Thus the dynamics of the Oedipal triangle are present. Jung wishes (symbolically) to slay the father, not only to become closer to the mother (and show his mother his erect penis) but also to distance himself from the organized religion that his father espoused.

Jung may want to suggest that in his dream the large tree trunk made of flesh was a ritual phallus, but if one studies Jung's later life, one finds that he was quite enamored with his own phallus. Not only did Jung have a well-documented affair with one of his patients, Sabina Spielrein, Jung also had a longstanding affair with Anna Wolff, a young psychoanalyst who became so important to him that he actually talked his wife into allowing the liaison. On a regular basis, for several decades, Jung would spend one day a week with Anna and then invite her to Sunday dinner where she would sit at the dinner table with Emma (Jung's wife) and his children. According to several sources, after Jung's break with Freud, it was Anna more than Emma who saw Jung through his darkest period. Jung also supposedly wrote a chapter on Anna for *Memories, Dreams, Reflections,* but this chapter was apparently removed by Jung's children, lest the affair be broadcast in such an overt way.[2]

What is important to realize here is that, from a religious point of view, Jung is an adulterer and thus a sinner. When looked at in this light, the dream that haunted Jung his entire life becomes even more understandable. Staying with the Oedipal theme, not only must Jung slay the father to attain the affections of his mother, he must also slay God himself so that he can enjoy a lifestyle frowned upon by religious teachings.

> Freud was the first man of real importance I had encountered. . . . There was nothing the least trivial in his attitude. I found him extremely intelligent, shrewd and altogether remarkable. And yet my first impressions of him remained somewhat tangled. I could not make him out.[3]
>
> CARL JUNG

In 1909, both Carl Jung and Sigmund Freud were invited to speak at Clark University in Worcester, Massachusetts. By coordinating their trip, they traveled together across the Atlantic and spent the time analyzing each other's dreams. For reasons difficult to understand, Jung, writing fully twenty years after Freud's death in his autobiography, mentions that he analyzed one of Freud's dreams, but Jung "would not think it right to air the problem involved."[4]

Why ever not?

Jung, on the other hand, quite freely discusses his own dream. It concerned a house with four floors. On the top floor, which would correspond to the attic, Jung found some "precious old paintings," and he wondered if this were his house. On the ground floor "the furnishings were medieval," and in the basement he found stonework dating from ancient Roman times. Looking more closely at the floor, Jung discovered a ring. Lifting it, he realized it was a trap door that led to a subbasement. "I descended," Jung wrote, "and entered a low cave cut into the rock. Thick dust lay on the floor, and in the dust were scattered

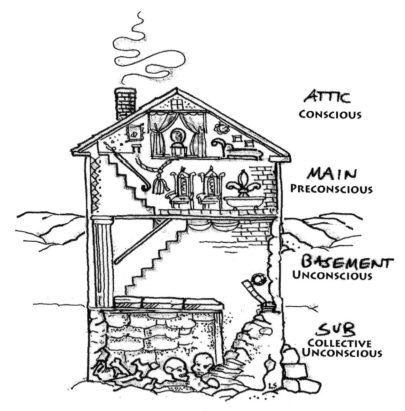

Fig. 19.1. Jung's dream of a house with
four levels to it, as told to Freud. Drawing by Lynn Sevigny.

bones and broken pottery, like remains of a primitive culture. I discovered two human skulls, obviously very old and half disintegrated. Then I awoke. What chiefly interested Freud were the two skulls."[5]

Jung realizes that Freud thinks that the two skulls must stand for Freud and Jung and that this is an Oedipal dream. According to this view, Jung, who is about twenty years younger than Freud, needs to knock off his mentor so that Jung's newer theory will come into vogue. Jung resists this idea. He does not feel that the dream is about the Oedipal complex. Jung also realizes that for Freud the Oedipal complex is central to his (Freud's) theory. Further, Jung knows that Freud himself suffers from the Oedipal complex, so much so that on two occasions Freud fainted!

In one of these instances, which took place in front of several other colleagues, Jung, who was a much larger and taller man than Freud, reached down and lifted Freud into his arms and carried Freud into another room so he could be comfortably placed on a couch. "As I was carrying him," Jung writes in his autobiography, "he half came to, and I shall never forget the look he cast at me. In his weakness, he looked at me as if I were his father. Whatever other causes may have contributed to this faint—the atmosphere was very tense—the fantasy of father-murder was common to both cases."[6]

Why would Freud faint when the topic of father-murder was discussed? The answer of course is obvious. Freud suffered from the Oedipal complex to such an extent that he could not face the full ramifications of what this complex revealed to him. Clearly Freud had intense and overt sexual feelings for his mother and corresponding jealousy toward his father. Given the extent of Freud's neurosis, it is quite possible that Freud's mother had sexual feelings toward him as well, and it is also possible that when he was a boy some type of sexual activity took place between the mother and the child. Freud had a primal memory that was so taboo, to come even close to realizing what it was, was too much of a threat, so he blanked out. Further, Freud projected. That is to say, because he suffered from the Oedipal complex, he assumed that everyone else did as well. Whether or not this is true, clearly very few people are hiding such an intense kind of libidinal secret as that which plagued Freud.

None of this was talked about between Freud and Jung. Thus, when Freud asked Jung who those two skulls were at the bottom of the sub-basement, Jung knew that Freud wanted him to say, "You and me." But at the same time, Jung also knew that should he state something along these lines, he would most likely rupture his relationship with Freud. And that was something he dared not do.

To fully understand the dynamics of this situation, I would like you, the reader, to consider your own relationships. Have you ever had an argument with somebody and never spoken to that person again? Do you have any topics with particular friends or relatives that you cannot discuss, because to do so would threaten the very integrity of the relationship? We are talking here about Pandora's box. In many instances it is best to keep this box shut, and that is what Jung did. "And so I told him a lie," Jung writes. The two skulls, Jung said, may symbolize "my wife and my mother-in-law."

"In fact, Freud seemed greatly relieved by my reply. I saw from this that he was completely helpless in dealing with certain kinds of dreams and had to take refuge in his doctrine. I realized that it was up to me to find out the real meaning of the dream."[7]

This was the year 1909. The duo landed in New York, toured the city, went up to Niagara Falls, and took a train to Worcester to give their respective lectures. To this day, the meeting of Freud and Jung at Clark University remains the highlight of the history of the school.

It would be six more years more before their relationship would really fall apart, but before that time, Freud and Jung would meet and converse on a regular basis. The *Freud Jung Letters* is a book over six hundred pages long! But once the relationship did rupture, Jung nearly lost his mind. It took him at least a year to recover, and it was at this time that he finally solved the meaning of the house dream to his satisfaction; this is when Jung crystallized his ideas about the archetypes and the collective unconscious.

The pre-scientific conception of the dream . . . obtained among the ancients was, of course, in perfect keeping with their general conception of the universe, which was accustomed to project as an external reality that which possessed reality only in the life of the psyche. Further, it accounted for the main impression made upon the waking life by the morning memory of the dream; for in this memory the dream, as compared with the rest of the psychic content, seems to be something alien, coming, as it were, from another world. It would be an error to suppose that the theory of the supernatural origin of dreams lacks followers even in our own times; for quite apart from pietistic and mystical writers . . . we not infrequently find that quite intelligent persons, who in other respects are averse to anything of a romantic nature, go so far as to base their religious belief in the existence and co-operation of superhuman spiritual powers on the inexplicable nature of the phenomena of dreams.[8]

SIGMUND FREUD

In 1909, Jung began to plunge into his study of ancient legends. Freud, trying to take the high ground, replied, "I'm glad you share my belief that we must conquer the whole field of mythology."[9] Jung was trying to reconcile in himself the problem of the spiritual element as another source of conflict beyond the psychosexual one. The following year, Jung had a breakthrough concerning the incest taboo. He realized that the individual must, on the one hand, renounce the sexual urge, yet the urge must also resurrect itself "to reach its propagative goals," that is, to perpetuate the species. Jung suggested that incest, and thus the Oedipal complex, "signified a personal complication only in the rarest cases." Instead, Jung hypothesized that the incest theme played an important role in the construction of worldviews, ancient legends, and world religions. "It was a mistake to take the literal interpretations of incest when it clearly had spiritual significance as a symbol. This to Freud was explosive thinking."[10] In fact, this is what lay at the heart of their disagreement. Where Freud emphasized the all-powerful id and its primitive instincts as drivers of personality and the source of human conflict, Jung was drawn to the psyche's spiritual concerns as a significant additional source.

This created an unusual theoretical dilemma for Freud, because he had already covered this argument in depth in his book *The Interpretation of Dreams,* which he wrote at the turn of the century, well before he met Jung. Paraphrasing Aristotle, Freud wrote that although most ancient cultures see dreams as messages from the gods, "the dream is not god-sent, and it is not divine but of daimonic origin. For nature is really daimonic, not divine; that is to say, the dream is not a supernatural revelation, but is subject to the laws of the human spirit, which has, of course, a kinship with the divine. The dream is defined as the psychic activity of the sleeper." And Aristotle was well aware of this, for instance, how physical sensations or instances from the day influenced the dream.[11] So, what Freud worked so hard to achieve—that is, to remove the supernatural component to dream interpretation—Jung was working to undo.

What Jung was beginning to realize is that Freud had oversimplified the underpinnings of the human psyche by focusing too much on the Oedipal complex and the primitive instincts. Both Freud and Jung were fully aware of the biological reason for the incest taboo. Inbreeding increases greatly the likelihood that the progeny will be defective. Where Freud would see the need for repression as biologically determined, as he wrote in his book *Civilization and Its Discontents,*[12] Jung would consider the spiritual connotations. God had made man not only as a predator but also as a species that, by necessity, had to repress the sexual urge in family situations, or the species itself would suffer. How did such a situation help spawn the various religions? This is the kind of question Jung would ask.

> The unconscious is never quiescent in the sense of being inactive, but is ceaselessly engaged in grouping and regrouping its contents.[13]
>
> CARL JUNG

The COLLECTIVE UNCONSCIOUS began to crystallize as a fully formed idea in 1915, after Jung's split with Freud. Lying beneath the personal unconscious, like the sub-basement in Jung's dream, was the collective unconscious, which for Jung became the foundation of the psyche common to all humans. It was composed of "latent memory traces inherited from man's ancestral past. . . . The psychic residue of man's evolutionary development, a residue that accumulates as a consequence of repeated experiences over many generations." A "transpersonal" aspect of the human psyche, the collective unconscious is the very basis of the human mind, the primal mind that the child is born with. And upon this psychic template, or in Jung's words, "virtual image" of the world, the child's sense of self, personality, and experiences are erected.[14]

Let us start with the zygote, the fertilized egg, which carries within it the DNA from both the mother and father. Nine months later, a fully formed child will be born. This child will have two arms, two legs, ten fingers and toes, toenails, eyebrows, a nose, lips, and so on. In other words, present in that first fertilized cell is a map of the human body. Is there also a map of the human mind? What does that map look like? What information is already present in the child's psyche at day one? That is what the collective unconscious is made up of. It contains all of our instincts and inborn patterns of behavior that come to the surface as the child goes through life.

ARCHETYPES

Jung coins the term "archetypes" for the building blocks of the collective psyche. The archetypes are dominant motifs, formative patterns, prototypical images, primordial symbols, or predispositions. Jung sees the archetypes as "thought forms" that have been created through common repetitive thoughts and actions through the millennia by our ancestors. These archetypes (inborn behavior patterns and images) are charged with energy and drive us to action.[15] If we used a computer analogy, the archetypes would be the software or preprogramming; they are essentially our instincts.

EMOTIONS

All our emotions are prewired, and all of them cause us to act in common ways. All humans since the time of the caveman have experienced the same panoply of emotions: love, hate, jealousy, fear, hostility, embarrassment, joy, sadness, anxiety, terror, regret. Take grief, for instance. If a key person in your life dies, you mourn. You do not have a choice. Jung points out that the archetypes are *autonomous*. They have their own energy. At the appropriate times, they take over, or in Jung's terms they "seize you," whether you want them to or not. They stem from a more primal place.

Concerning primordial symbols, many things in our environment are archetypes: the sun, moon, stars, the ocean, mountains, waterfalls, streams, animals, the forest, the mystery of nature. Anything that promotes awe is most likely an archetypal event. Watching a bird in flight, a campfire, or a lightning storm—these are all good instances of archetypal experiences. We are fascinated by lightning because something deep inside us, stemming from our ancient past, is awakened.

Many events are also archetypal; weddings, funerals, parades, dreams, initiation ceremonies, and major sporting events fall into this category. One of the reasons why football is so attractive to so many people is because, in one way, it is a form of organized war. Two armies meet on the battlefield. A boxing match is a resurrection of the fights of the gladiators. The strongest man in the world is an archetype. Rock stars, Hollywood celebrities, and great leaders trigger archetypal responses in the crowds that follow them.

All of the great myths also revolved around archetypal themes: Book of Job (suffering), David and Bathsheba (lust and jealousy), King Solomon (splitting the baby in half), Icarus (hubris—flying too close to the sun), Achilles' heel, Samson's hair, and so on. All of these motifs lay deeply imbedded in our DNA, at least as predispositions. The sinking of the Titanic, the plunging of America into a deep recession caused by the excesses of Wall Street, Bill Clinton's fall from grace due to a wrongheaded sexual affair—all these events can be seen from an archetypal point of view.

Jung would come to isolate five archetypes—the self, the persona, the anima, the animus, and the shadow—but he certainly realized that all of the realms discussed above were archetypal as well, and any one of them could have just as profound an impact on a person as an Oedipal complex. That is why his theory so threatened Sigmund Freud.

THE SELF

The ego, for Jung, is that part of the psyche that has access to conscious material. As stated above, it is also the organizer of the personality. Jung states that the ego is a subset of the self, which, in itself, is both the totality and also the center of the personality. Striving for wholeness, the self lies midway between the conscious and the unconscious. Jung argues that the self is more than the ego because "the most decisive qualities in a person are often unconscious." The symbol for the self is the mandala, the rich circular symbol, which contains the "total expression of the self."

THE PERSONA

The persona is the social mask "adopted by the person in response to the demands of social convention and tradition."[16] In itself, it "is nothing real: it is a compromise between individual and society as to what a man should appear to be. He takes a name, earns a title, exercises a function. He is this or that."[17] The persona or social mask is a necessity for getting along in society. When we visit the doctor, we want to call the physician "doctor." That is his or her appellation. It has a surface reality, but underneath it is really a "self" who at that moment is taking on the assignment of being the "doctor." When that person goes home, the appellation may change to father or mother, husband or wife, brother or sister, son or daughter, couch potato or bridge partner. Social masks can change all the time. They allow us to get along in social interactions.

In the negative, some people become their personas, and they feel like phonies who have lost their connection to their real selves. The typical bureaucrat would fit this category. Persona types often hide behind the mask of their job, and through that strategy they may initiate actions that are annoying, that further hide their true nature, and that are even antisocial or sociopathic. For instance, a salesman who cheats customers, the hypocrite, or the politician who lie to get into office—they all use the vehicle of the persona to achieve recreant goals.

THE ANIMA AND THE ANIMUS

These are the female and male archetypes, yin and yang. The way to remember the difference is to see that the word "ma" appears in the female archetype. Features of the anima on the positive side include emotional, receptive, intuitive, nurturing, and motherly, and on the negative side, submissive, passive, weak, and timid. Features of the animus on the positive side include assertive, ambitious, rational, analytical, strong, active, and competitive, and on the negative side, mean-spirited, aggressive, insensitive, hard, and cold.

Every male has a bit of the female in him and every female has a bit of the male in her. To be a complete "man," a male should be in touch with his feminine side, and to be a total "woman," a female must be in touch with her masculine side. However, these archetypes are more than these traits; they are also the image that the man carries in him of the perfect female and the image that the woman carries in her of the perfect male. We can look to certain Hollywood stars as typifying prototypes for the male and female archetypes, for instance, John Wayne for the archetypal male and Grace Kelly for the idealized or perfect woman.

Jung points out that these archetypes are complicated. For example, the anima may appear in a dream as a mother figure, perfect mate, or siren. The same is true for the animus. Male figures in the dream may be protective or scary. And sometimes these archetypes battle themselves out in the individual. The singer Michael Jackson comes to mind.

In his music videos he liked to portray a strong masculine figure, yet his voice when he spoke was meek and quite feminine. He clearly was a man with strong bisexual forces pushing him in opposite directions. Was he masculine or feminine, boy or man, black or white? Another well-known personality who portrays both archetypes, but in harmony rather than in conflict, is former governor Sarah Palin, vice-presidential candidate and spokesperson for the Republican Party. Feminine and stunningly attractive, Palin is also ambitious and hard as nails, thereby portraying a powerful animus as well. In her own words, she noted that the only difference between a "hockey mom," which she saw herself as, and a pit bull was lipstick. It was a funny line, which propelled her to the national and international arena. From a Jungian perspective, Sarah Palin had hit an anima/animus grand slam.

THE SHADOW

The shadow subsumes the id. It is our animal instincts, our sex drive, and our aggression, but more than that, it is the predator in us, "our uncivilized and disowned raw urges"—our killer instinct—"our most powerful and dangerous archetype."[18] Jung asks, why do we kill to survive? How is it that the force that created the universe and life on Earth made us killers and will later kill us? This is a religious question and it calls into play all the essentials of the shadow. Yes, it is the dark side; yes, it is linked to evil, horror, the devil, and war. But that is only one aspect of the shadow. It is the mystery of life itself, and in that sense, it is the other side of God. Not only is he a life-giver, he is also a life-taker.

Jung is pointing out that man cannot comprehend the full nature of reality. There is no way we can truly understand why "God" constructed a world where one animal kills and eats another for survival. Seen from that light, the universe is incomprehensible. That is the shadow. It is what we *cannot know* about ourselves. It is the unconscious in the full meaning of the term. As Jung says with a laugh in a movie interview, "The unconscious really is unconscious." We do our best, for instance, through dream interpretation, to understand the depths of the unconscious, but we can never truly comprehend what the unconscious really is, because, by its nature, it is beyond our comprehension. Why? Because it *is* unconscious! Just as a person can never see the back of his own head, we can never truly understand the magnitude of the psyche. That is all part of the shadow.

Certainly Freud was aware of this aspect of the psyche, for the shadow is really none other than the id expressed in more elaborate form. And if the reader digs deep enough into Freud's massive book *The Interpretation of Dreams,* one finds in the subchapter on regression the essential basis of Jung's ideas on the collective unconscious.

REGRESSION

Freud writes:

> Dreaming is on the whole an act of regression to the earliest relationships of the dreamer, a resuscitation of his childhood, of the impulses, which were then dominant, and the modes of expression, which were then available. Behind this childhood of the individual we are then promised an insight into the phylogenetic childhood, into the evolution of the human race, of which the development of the individual is only an abridged repetition influenced by the fortuitous circumstances of life.

Stating that part of the source of this insight stems from Nietzsche, Freud concludes that

> we are encouraged to expect, from the analysis of dreams, a knowledge of the archaic inheritance of man, a knowledge of psychical things in him that are innate.
>
> It was now my desire to transfer my authority to a younger man who would, quite naturally, take my place on my death. I felt that this person could only be C. G. Jung.[19]

Fig. 19.2. Sigmund Freud, Stanley Hall, and Carl Jung,
Clark University, 1909

From Jung's point of view, although he had great respect for Freud and wanted to continue to be a part of Freud's psychoanalytical society, by 1913 their differences had become too great, and so Freud shunned him. From a psychological point of view, where Freud for many years, saw Jung as his successor and thus as a surrogate son, Jung saw Freud as a surrogate father. But just as Jung had rebelled against his own father, a pedantic preacher who young Carl was forced to listen to as he ruminated in church, Jung also rebelled against Sigmund Freud. And, as mentioned earlier, just as Jung felt closer to God sitting on a rock by a stream than sitting in his father's church, in a way Jung replays this motif as he rejects Freud's emphasis on psychosexuality, because this focus had limited too much the nature of the dream life, and thereby limited the sum and substance of the psyche.

As we can see from the above quote, Freud agreed with the idea of the collective unconscious and came upon it years before Jung did. Where Freud disagreed with Jung was in its emphasis. Let us return to that 1909 boat trip and Jung's dream about the house with the attic, ground floor, basement, and sub-basement. Jung speculates that the dream represented an expansion of Freud's conscious/preconscious/unconscious model.

"Who were those two skulls at the bottom of the sub-basement?" Freud wanted to know. "My wife and my mother-in-law," Jung lies.

In his autobiography, Jung tells us that this was indeed a lie, because he realized that if he told Freud the truth—namely, that he did not think that the dream was an Oedipal dream and that he did not have death wishes toward Freud but rather that he saw the dream as a possible extension of Freud's theories—such a statement would have at that time caused an immediate split in their relationship. No one knows. Jung's intuition may have been on target.

Be that as it may, one can't escape the ironic conclusion that this dream was a brilliant instance of condensation. In other words, both men may have been right! On the one hand, the dream certainly did foresee Jung's foray into expanding the unconscious to include what he called the collective unconscious. And this expansion was a worthy endeavor, which has had a profound impact on depth psychology, art, religion, and man's view of himself and his relationship to his creator. Yet on the other hand, Jung does, through his actions, generate a death of his relationship with Freud. One way or another, Jung's theories do, in a way, advance and in that sense surpass those of his mentor. But at the same time, following Freud's idea of the Freudian slip, one has to also ask oneself, why did Jung suggest that the two skulls were his wife and his mother-in-law? Did Jung harbor some resentment toward his wife and, in that sense, symbolically wish her death?

This analysis reminds me of the joke about a troubled man who goes to see a psychiatrist. The psychiatrist shows the man the Rorschach inkblot cards. "What do you see?" he asks. "Two naked women," says the man. The doctor holds up another inkblot. "That's two more naked women," says the man. "And this one?" asks the doctor. "That's a naked man and a naked woman making love." After going through five or six of these, the psychiatrist comments, "Sir, I think you really have a sex problem." "I have a sex problem?!" replies the man in astonishment, "You're the one showing all the dirty pictures!"

The reason why I'm suggesting that Jung would unconsciously wish the death of his wife is because he was, at this time, beginning to have an affair with the young psychoanalyst Anna Wolff. Keep in mind that Jung continued this affair, and at least one other, for decades. Further, as mentioned above, Jung saw Wolff at least once a week on a regular basis during all this time, and he often invited her to his home to Sunday dinner with his wife and children present. Here is a clear repudiation of religious values. Jung's father, we remember, was a preacher, so he grew up in a religious environment. Adultery is a sin. One way or another, the only way to sin is to deny God, or some aspect of God's teachings. How would Jung's mother-in-law feel about him if she knew about the affair? And if Jung could symbolically kill off God to enjoy his hedonistic lifestyle, he could certainly, while he is at it, symbolically slay his wife, her mother, and the moralist Sigmund Freud in the process.

Further, Jung lived in an area where there were castles, stone stairways, basements, and sub-basements. One could argue that this dream, and Jung's earlier dream about the ritual phallus, which also lay in an underground chapel, in part stemmed from his wanderings in his father's church or any other structure that was made of stone and fit the bill. In other words, it did not necessarily stem from some mystical collective unconscious but rather from his natural environment. So when Freud is sitting on the boat listening to Jung's house dream and he asks Jung about the two skulls, it is quite possible that Freud did indeed know that Jung was avoiding the obvious truth, namely that the skulls represented Freud and Jung. In other words, Freud most likely knew at that instant that Jung was indeed lying. Freud intimated later that he didn't trust Jung, but at the same time he had enormous respect for Jung's great intellect. "When one thinks of the disagreements between Jung's various private and public utterances," Freud writes, "one is obliged to ask to what extent this is due to his own lack of clearness and how much to a *lack of sincerity*."[20] [Emphasis added.]

"In 1909," Freud continues, "Jung and myself were invited . . . to Clark University [where we] found, to our great astonishment [that our respected colleagues] knew all the psychoanalytic writings and honored them in their lectures to their students." After lecturing in German, both Freud and Jung were awarded honorary degrees.[21] A year later,

Jung became president of the International Psychoanalytic Society, Freud's organization.

In Freud's thousand-page collected works compendium, which was put together by A. A. Brill in 1938, Freud informs the reader that anti-Semitism was the reason he was unable to obtain a full professorship at the University of Vienna. In fact, it was for this reason that Freud left Vienna to begin his work with the medical doctor and hypnotist Charcot. Later, in "History of the Psychoanalytic Movement," which Freud wrote in 1914, he informs the reader that he overlooked the anti-Semitic sentiments of Carl Jung and his Zurich group for a variety of reasons. These included Jung's "conspicuous talents," his contributions to the field, his independence, and "the impression of energy, which his personality always made. He also seemed prepared to enter into friendly relations with me, and to give up, for my sake, certain racial prejudices, which he had so far permitted himself to indulge."[22]

Freud felt that for the sake of the psychoanalysis, he had to expand and relocate its center from Vienna to Zurich. This decision would also serve to shift the psychoanalytic movement from a Jewish community in Austria to a Christian community in Switzerland. It was also the reason that Freud stepped down as president. He needed Christian backing to spread his views to the rest of the world. This created conflict and jealousies on the home front, so Freud compromised to agree that the center of the International Psychoanalytic Society would correspond with the residency of its president, and elections would be held every other year.

Another problem Freud was having was theoretical. For Freud, "the theory of repression is the pillar upon which the edifice of psychoanalysis rests."[23] Another pillar that caused the repression was "the autoerotic activities of the early years of childhood." This almost always lay at the heart of a person's neurosis. Thus the key to the cure was to uncover these socially dangerous repressed memories so that they could be released. Often in the process a transference took place, namely, the patient would project onto the analyst the feelings he or she had toward a key parent. Since Freud was male, many of his women patients would see him as a father figure, and the way they related to him would give him insights on how they, when they were children, related to their fathers. Transference also can cause a patient to fall in love with the analyst.

Jung was at first in agreement with the idea of the child having sexual instincts and even lectured on the topic at Clark University in 1909.[24] However, by 1913, Jung and the Zurich group changed the core of the theory by replacing the sexual libido with an abstract idea, namely by making the Oedipus complex symbolic rather than visceral. The mother became a symbol for the "unattainable which must be renounced in the interests of cultural development . . . [and] the father who is killed in the Oedipus myth [now] represents the 'inner' father, from whose influence we must free ourselves in order to become independent."[25]

Freud vehemently held fast that "the study of the individual man has shown and always will show that the sexual complexes are alive in him in their original sense. That is why the study of the individual was pushed back by Jung and replaced by conclusions drawn from the study of racial history."[26] Freud is suggesting that Jung took an interest in the collective unconscious as a way of avoiding confronting his own libidinal underpinnings.

Freud continues his astute criticism. "Jung," Freud states, "made it a rule to direct as little as possible of the therapy of the past and to place the greatest emphasis on the return of the current conflict" as a way to deflect the patient away from the seed cause of the neurosis, a psychosexual problem that stemmed from childhood.[27]

Several pages earlier, Freud discusses the "infantile wish . . . namely the child's desire to observe the sexual act between adults." In the case of the boy, he fantasizes, on the one hand, taking the place of the father in the fantasy, or on the other hand, "identifying himself with the suffering woman."[28] Here is a potential bombshell, because it may be that Freud has finally revealed the particular source of his own Oedipal complex, the possibility that he came upon his parents during the sexual act and fantasized himself replacing the father and maybe also the mother. The use of the phrase "suffering woman" is also most curious, because it may very well have been that the mother enjoyed the moment as much as the father. One way or another, Freud had deep-seated memories associated with the Oedipal complex, so much so that they caused him at times to faint. Thus they did indeed lie at the heart of his own neurosis. If he had come upon his parents as they engaged in sexual intercourse and thereupon identified with both parents, one could certainly begin to understand why Freud would have such difficulty reconciling these deep-seated libidinal memories.

What Freud saw happening was Jung's desire to take the most intimate act possible between a man and a women, sexual intercourse, and to take childhood psychosexuality, which can involve satiation while breastfeeding during infancy, anal satisfaction during the toilet-training stage, and autoerotic pleasure during the genital stage, and transform these id-related urges into a new "religio-ethical system."[29] In other words, Jung was taking the roll-in-the-mud blood and guts of the theory and intellectualizing it, perhaps the same way he rationalized his need to have adulterous affairs throughout his career while he maintained the facade of the spiritual mystic.

> In 1912, Jung boasted . . . to me . . . that his modifications of psychoanalysis had overcome the resistances to it in many persons who hitherto wanted to know nothing about it. I replied that this was nothing to boast about, that the more he sacrificed of the hard won truths of psychoanalysis, [e.g., "suppression of the sexual factor"], the less resistance he would encounter.[30]
>
> SIGMUND FREUD

Just to make things clear, I happen to have enormous respect for Carl Jung's contributions to the field of depth psychology. I am also well aware of the literally thousands of pages of writing he has done in the field, and I consider his autobiography, *Memories, Dreams, Reflections*, one of the most important books written in the field. I also think that his concepts of the archetypes and collective unconscious were superb expansions of Freud's theories. Further, I also agree that many people's problems can be more Jungian; that is, more spiritual. However, if one looks at the world, one finds that psychosexuality is alive and well. All too often, people are confounded and even toppled by their id. For instance, just look at the lives of our politicians, such presidential contenders as Gary Hart and John Edwards, New York governor Elliot Spitzer, or California governor Arnold Schwartzenegger. All of these leaders were toppled because of illicit affairs. And then we are bombarded by the soap-opera lives of rock and Hollywood stars like Madonna, Marilyn Monroe, Elizabeth Taylor, Paris Hilton, Lindsay Lohan, and Michael Jackson. True, after Madonna became a mother, she began to study the Kabbalah, or mystical teachings of the Old Testament, but she has made her living by being sexually outrageous, and through that means, both she and Michael Jackson, for decades, were the most famous celebrities in the world.

20

The Dynamics of Mind

The UCS is living and capable of development and maintains a number of other relations to the PCS, amongst them that of cooperation. . . . Consciousness regards the whole sum of mental processes as belonging to the realm of the PCS. A very great part of the PCS belongs to the UCS and has characteristic derivatives of the UCS and this is subject to a censorship before it can pass to consciousness. . . . It is not only what is repressed that remains alien to consciousness, but also some of the impulses which dominate our ego and which form the strongest functional antithesis to what is repressed.

SIGMUND FREUD

There is a difference between a "defense" mechanism and a "coping" mechanism, and that difference is self-knowledge. A person can repress a painful memory, or the person can suppress it. With repression, the situation is truly forgotten. With suppression, the person is aware that he or she is storing the unpleasantry. In either case, the event still has energy or cathexis. According to Freud, repressions are *always active*. That is the key to understanding the dynamics of the mind. Unpleasant buried experiences are forever seeking expression, forever charged with cathexis. Therefore the defense structure must constantly be on guard.

Energy from the censor must be diverted to maintain the repression. This energy is counter to repressed cathexis (and thus we use the term *countercathexis*).

CATHEXIS

A concentration or accumulation of mental and physical energy stored in some complex or memory. Cathexes can be withdrawn or neglected or they can be suppressed or "repudiated." If the complex is important enough to be charged with cathexis, the complex will be active, and therefore the energy will seek expression, either directly through the conscious apparatus or indirectly through dreams, prelogical or symbolic activity, or through some other avenue such as anxiety or physical stress.

COUNTERCATHEXIS

A suppression or repression of energy. Any mental energy that is prevented expression either consciously or unconsciously is blocked or countercathected. The mechanism for this procedure, which stems from the censor, involves defense and/or coping mechanisms that oppose repressions, as well as opposing the id's natural desire to express itself. Humans countercathect all the time to simply keep at bay the amoral id. Some people rigidly defend against unconscious amoral longings. They therefore construct a "countercathectic barrier," one that automatically represses the vast majority of desires. These people can be characterized as having a "stiff upper lip." All the defense mechanisms are forms of countercathexes.

Note the term *amoral,* which is different from *immoral.* The id is beyond human understanding. It is our primitive self. If a person has a dream involving pornography or murder, this is neither good nor bad. It just is. One cannot control one's unconscious, because it is unconscious. This is a part of the primitive self that has its own conscious component. In the same sense, if a hawk swoops down and steals a pet rabbit, rips it apart, and feeds it to its young, this of course is not immoral. It is amoral. The universe is constructed on certain principles that, for humans, are harsh. Eat and be eaten. Jung called this aspect the shadow, which essentially was another word for the id. Our predator instinct is neither good nor bad, but it does seek expression in aggressive and pornographic imagery. If a human acts on these impulses, that is often immoral. Throughout the centuries, this distinction has been misunderstood. Many people are plagued by their unconscious, when in fact it is another realm operating with its own set of laws not easily translatable to the outside world.

HYPERCATHEXIS

Any expression, realization, or release of energy. This type of energy distribution occurs when a wish impulse receives an extra amount of cathexis, through the process of thought, volitional behavior, or through unconscious expression. The very process of thinking involves hypercathexis because attention becomes bound to unconscious or preconscious complexes.

In Freud's book *Wit and Its Relation to the Unconscious,* he tells us that "under certain conditions, a train of thought with a purposive cathexis (e.g., a repressed or suppressed memory left with its own excitations) is capable of attracting attention of consciousness to itself, and in that event, through the agency of consciousness, it receives hypercathexis."[1] If awareness is not attached, a Freudian slip may occur. The goal of psychoanalysis is to make the person become aware of the complex. Insight would thus be achieved through self-awareness.

SUBLIMATION

Freud's solution for dealing with painful complexes, unacceptable infantile wishes, or instinctual urges is to *transform* them into activities that are compatible with society. "Where id energy was, ego shall be." There are many forms of sublimation: artistic expression, attending a movie or concert, competitive sports, exercise. As you can see, some types are much more active than other types. One could look at Jane Fonda's career, which shifted from acting in the sex spoof *Barbarella* and playing a prostitute in *Klute,* to making the more family-oriented film *On Golden Pond.* As she aged, Jane's sexual energy naturally upgraded, and at the same time, she was able to work out some long-held emotionally charged issues with her famous father, Henry Fonda, who, of course, was also in the film, playing the father of the character her character played.

As we know, however, the sex drive is not that easy to tame. As she got older and won an Academy Award, Jane Fonda was not going to continue to make such overtly sexual movies. She transformed some of this drive into her exercise tapes. In this fashion, she could continue to express her erotic nature, neatly transformed through the persona of an exercise guru. In this fashion she could still dress in an evocative fashion with headband and leotards, and at the same time help the masses keep themselves fit. Exercise is one of the best ways to sublimate, that is, to burn off excess stress. These tapes helped Jane earn tens of millions of dollars and at the same time transformed her into a business executive. In this new role she was able to attract Ted Turner, one of the so-called masters of the universe, the creator of CNN (the first worldwide news organization), owner of the Atlanta Braves, and an America's Cup sailing champion. Their power marriage lasted about a decade.

As Carl Jung has suggested, the whole idea in alchemy of changing base metals into gold is a metaphor for sublimation, that is to say, changing one's raw nature into a spiritual one. According to Gurdjieff's philosophy, self-transformation or self-evolution is the goal of human existence.

"Do you believe," Adler remarked, "that it is such a great pleasure for me to stand in your shadow my whole life?"[2]

SIGMUND FREUD

Freud began his view of sublimation as mostly a corrective way for dealing with repressed material. It was only after he interacted with more ego-oriented colleagues, such as Alfred Adler, that he began to modify his view. For Freud, the id remained the almighty powerhouse of the personality. Nevertheless, he saw as a goal that the ego should increase its say in the destiny of the person.

Adler, of course, talked a good game. Like Freud, his work transcended his personal *mishegas*. Because of Freud's philosophical difficulty with Jung, he looked to Adler to take over the Vienna Psychoanalytic Society, and Adler became president around 1909. Although an ego psychologist, Adler himself had a disagreeable nature and suffered from feelings of inferiority. He therefore assumed that man's greatest drive was the drive for superiority. This essentially was Freud's aggressive drive. Adler, however, took this two steps further by "underestimating the importance of unconscious material,"[3] and by suggesting that the sex drive was actually a form of the aggressive drive. That was why, Adler speculated, the man wanted to be on top of the woman during sexual intercourse. Adler had essentially removed key cornerstones of Freud's theory, associated with the primacy of the unconscious and psychosexuality, and replaced them with emphasis on ego functions and a form of machismo, which was characterized as a drive from inferiority to superiority. The bumping up in importance of ego functions Freud could live with, and in fact he was indebted to Adler for this expansion of his theory. But replacing the sex drive with aggression was too much for Freud, and so he booted Adler out of the Vienna Psychoanalytic Society in 1911 and recaptured the presidency. Jung would leave Freud's sphere two years later.

CONFLICT-FREE EGO SPHERE

Peaceful internal development or expression. Freud's model tends to pit the ego against the superego and id in a never-ending battle. It thus appears that the normal person is always in conflict. Heinz Hartmann, on the other hand, realized that the ego often involved itself in functions that had nothing to do with working out unexpressed desires from the id or guilt from the superego.[4] For example, the wish to read a novel, attend a class, work on a puzzle, or watch a nature show on TV stems from a pure ego instinct associated with the concept of curiosity. "Perception, intention, object comprehension, thinking, language, recall-phenomena, productivity, to well-known phases of motor development, grasping, crawling, walking, and to the maturation and learning implicitly in all these and many others [are areas that] . . . develop outside of conflict. . . . Adaption obviously involves both processes connected with conflict situations and processes which pertain to the conflict-free sphere."

Freud created a dynamic model that involved the expression and transformation of energies. Physical or libidinal energies could be expressed mentally (e.g., a boy is aroused by a girl in a short skirt and wants to sleep with her), or a mental energy could be expressed physically (e.g., a woman decides to exercise and calls up a friend to go jogging). Otto Fenichel and other writers have described the lack of energy in the neurotic. In all such cases, as the unconscious is the true psychic reality, complexes from the unconscious (whether repressed or suppressed) are opposed by the censor. Looking at just the case of repression, we can set up the first stage of the model as follows:

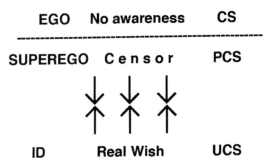

Fig. 20.1. When there is repression, the real wish is blocked by the censor so that the ego is not even aware of the conflict.

Note that in figure 20.1 that the unconscious real wish, situated in the id, is blocked by inhibiting energies from the preconscious activity of the censor, essentially located in the superego. Said in another way, the hypercathexis from the id (the wish that wants to be released) is countered:

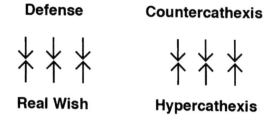

Defense **Countercathexis**

Real Wish **Hypercathexis**

Fig. 20.2. According to Freud, the real wish is always seeking expression or hypercathexis. However, if repression exists, countercathexis blocks the wish from being expressed.

The real wish is thwarted because it is blocked by the censor. This real wish may be (1) a painful repression or immoral thought, or (2) a valued desire stemming from the true self, for example, an aspiration. Note that both types of repressions, one based on conflict and the other simply a hidden positive wish, are frustrated in essentially the same way. They both are trapped in the unconscious, and they both will seek expression in various ways, such as in prelogical behavior or through the mechanism of the dream.

THE DREAM

The political writer who has unpleasant truths to tell to those in power finds himself in a like position. If he tells everything without reserve, the Government will suppress them. . . . The writer stands in fear of the censorship; he therefore moderates and disguises the expression of his opinions. He finds himself compelled . . . either to refrain altogether from certain forms of attack, or to express himself in allusions . . . or he must conceal his objectionable statement in an apparently innocent disguise. . . . The stricter the domination of the censorship, the more thorough . . . the disguise, and, often enough, the more ingenious the means employed to put the reader on the track of the actual meaning.

SIGMUND FREUD

Freud saw every dream, as well as every psychoneurotic complex, as a wish fulfillment residing in the UCS. Both seek expression through the mechanism of the PCS, and in both cases, the complex must confront the censor. There are two levels to a dream:

Manifest content: The actual dream
Latent content: The hidden meaning

Between the two lies the censor:

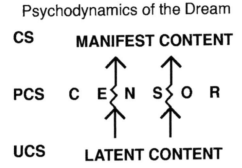

Fig. 20.3. The censor, weakened by sleep, is still strong enough to distort the hidden meaning of the dream so that the manifest content is different from the latent content.

If self-awareness is involved then the CS co,mes into play: the person remembers the dream. The goal of dream interpretation is to figure out how the censor distorted the dream to allow it to escape to the body through the CS apparatus. An analogy would be a pressure cooker with the jiggle (censor) on top. The steam (latent content) must pass through the jiggle in order to escape (manifest content). The jiggle is necessary because the steam would be too powerful if left to its own devices. In the same way, the dream—dealing with highly charged issues (repressed memories)—needs to be diffused through the censor and thereby be released/hypercathected from the body.

Notice that the dream could go through the conscious apparatus *without* arousing awareness. In fact, most dreams pass this way. When a dream is remembered, however, the person has brought attention to it. Nevertheless, the real meaning most often remains obscured. In these instances, the repressed material stays repressed and no insight is imparted, thus no pain is felt. "It is my unshakeable conviction," Freud wrote, "that the most complicated and the most accurate operations of thought . . . may take place without arousing consciousness."[5]

Cloris may have a dream of pulling on the arms of three slot machines and winning tons of money on all three and have no idea of the real meaning of the dream, that is, her wish to have an affair with the three men in her office (e.g., pulling their penises). Since this idea is abhorrent to her conscious self, the energy can neatly be released through the mechanism of the dream, and what's more, she can tell the dream to the three men and thereby hypercathect even more of the energy attached to this dominant complex.

A person often makes use of the conscious apparatus without arousing awareness. According to Freud, this type of activity is preconscious activity, in that the PCS is using the CS apparatus. Numerous examples of this procedure while awake are discussed below.

AUTOMATISMS

Any repetitive psychomotor pattern that becomes a habit. Examples of automatisms would include the very act of walking, going down a staircase, driving, touch typing, handwriting, talking, playing a musical instrument, and numerous personal habits such as nail biting, mustache stroking, cigarette smoking, tapping, certain facial gestures, hand movements, and so on. These are preconscious activities that can become conscious.

For instance, a good typist just allows his or her fingers to fly across the keys. This procedure can be slowed down if more CS attention is attached to the procedure. Losing your keys when you enter your apartment would be an example of doing something preconsciously, without awareness. Driving past your exit on a highway is another example. Why would a person drive past his or her exit? Because the person's attention is not on the road; the person is lost in thought. The mind has actually split as the CS is involved in the thought while the PCS is driving the car. If someone steps on the brakes up ahead, the driver sees the red taillights and automatically hits his or her own brake. Automatisms or habits allow the mind to advance to more important tasks while the PCS takes over the rote procedures.

As Heinz Hartmann and Otto Fenichel tell us, some automatisms have symbolic significance. For instance, suppose a person is a three-pack-a-day chain smoker. Obviously, this habit is self-destructive. A psychoanalyst cannot ignore the link between the habit and the wish, on some level, to self-destruct. The lighting up of the cigarette allows certain psychoneurotic complexes to be expressed in the guise of cigarette smoking. Cloris, discussed above, who wears spiked heels and tight-fitting short skirts at work and spends many of her weekends at the gambling casino, is expressing a lustful UCS in numerous symbolic/prelogical ways. We can map this out as follows:

1. Censor Blocking Access to Motility

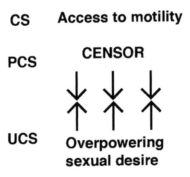

CS   **Access to motility**

PCS   **CENSOR**

UCS   **Overpowering sexual desire**

Fig. 20.4. In a repressed situation, the overpowering sexual desire is thwarted by a powerful censor that prevents the impulse from obtaining consciousness, that is, access to motility, i.e., self-expression.

We see here that the UCS wish is blocked by the censor and therefore cannot get access to the CS apparatus. In other words, the energy cannot escape. It is trapped in the mind and in the body or brain.

2. The Rigid Personality. If the censor or superego is extremely rigid, a countercathectic barrier will be set up between the UCS and the PCS. This is a wall that cannot be crossed. The energy is trapped. See below:

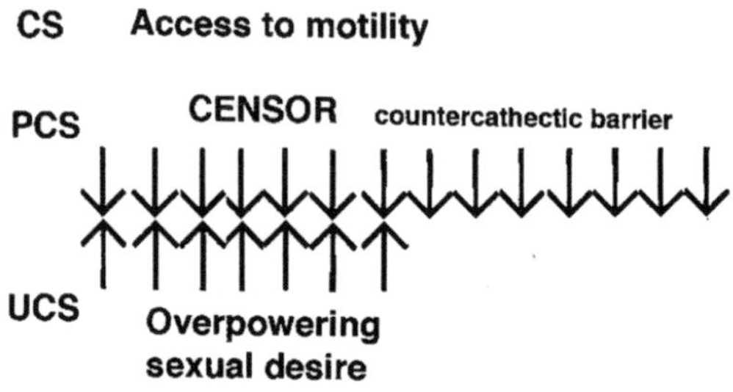

CS   **Access to motility**

PCS   **CENSOR**   countercathectic barrier

UCS   **Overpowering
sexual desire**

Fig. 20.5. In the case of the countercathectic barrier,
the impulse simply hits a brick wall in the rigid personality and
so real desire is never expressed. At the same time, because of
its unswerving nature, energy is saved because the fight
is over before it really starts.

Every time the unconscious desire attempts to express itself, it runs into a roadblock. This schema is indicative of a person with a rigid censor. Rapaport suggests that because the block is so fixed, energy is saved, unlike in the case of the neurotic whereby some energy is hypercathected, that is, released, and some thwarted.

3. A Psychoanalytic Model for Psychosomatic Illness. Repressed energy that is not allowed to be expressed through the conscious apparatus can be redirected to attack different body parts. Figures 20.4 and 20.5 display an impasse, whereas figure 20.6 explains potential ramifications. Remember, the energy, which Freud calls libido, seen as arrows in the diagrams has to go somewhere. Keep in mind that these complexes are *always* active. Thus they will still seek expression in some other way. One possibility (fig. 20.6) would be for the energy to turn back into the body, thereby causing any of a variety of psychosomatic illnesses. Any repressed desire or anger—it doesn't have to be sexual—can be diagrammed this way.

In all cases of repression, the initiating energy is thwarted from being

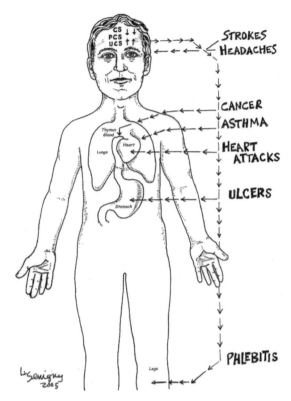

Fig. 20.6. The psychoanalytic model shows how stress can cause physical illnesses. Drawing by Lynn Sevigny.

released by a powerful censor located in the preconscious. Simplistically, we could say that because the person is stressed, some part of his or her body becomes affected.

This simple diagram explains why most people die. Stress in the system causes something to give. Usually it is the heart or the brain, that is, heart attacks or strokes, that do the most damage. However, if the thwarted or stressed-out energy attacks the immune system (e.g., via the thymus gland), the T-cells and the B-cells will be weakened and the person may become susceptible to cancer. This does not mean that every person who is diagnosed with cancer got it because of this type of psychodynamics. What it does mean is that in some instances this may be the case. In effect, the mechanism for psychosomatically induced cancer would be similar to how AIDS works. In both cases the very cells needed to attack incoming viruses are weakened. Other examples would be ulcers or asthma whereby the stress becomes localized in the stomach or lungs.

4. **Dreams.** Referring to figure 20.3, during dreams some of this energy can be released, but it gets *distorted* by the censor. This, for the sake of discussion, would be a fourth way for the energy to be released. According to this theory, the manifest content, the actual dream, contains a hidden message as to the real source of the tension. The reason the energy can be released through the conscious apparatus in this manner is because the censor is weakened by sleep.

5. **Circumventing the Censor.** The last way energy can be expressed is outlined by Otto Fenichel in his masterwork *The Psychoanalytic Theory of Neurosis.*[6] It is by *circumventing the censor* through prelogical or symbolic behavior. Jake is angry at his father so he picks fights with his coworkers for little or no reason. This would be a form of displaced aggression. The diagram would look as follows:

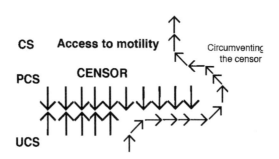

Fig. 20.7. One way for the real wish to escape is to circumvent the censor. Direct confrontation with the defense structure is avoided and the impulse is expressed, but in a distorted, prelogical, or symbolic fashion, e.g., a schoolteacher is overtly harsh to the girl students because when he was in high school he could never get a date.

Here we see the energy is blocked, so it travels along the barrier and skirts around it. Thus the complex can now be expressed through the conscious apparatus, but in such a way that the censor does not know that the repression is being released. Jake thinks that he is picking fights because of the stupidity of his coworkers. In actuality, he fights all the time for no real reason at all. His coworkers get angry and this causes bickering. What is really happening is that Jake is hypercathecting, that is, releasing trapped angry energy stemming from the constant criticism he received from his father when he was growing up. No matter what he did, he could never measure up to his father's expectations. Much of this anger is deeply ingrained or repressed. It has to be released some way. Part of this energy may affect Jake's heart. He may have high blood pressure, and part of it is released prelogically, through the symbolic act of the numerous arguments that he constantly manufactures.

To recap, we have described five different ways repressed material attempts to escape the system: (1) the energy is simply blocked, and the repression is in some form of stasis; (2) the energy is blocked by a powerful countercathectic barrier; (3) the energy turns inward and attacks the body, causing psychosomatic illnesses; (4) the energy is expressed through a distorted means, like the mechanism of the dream; and (5) the energy skirts around the censor and is expressed in prelogical ways through some odd behavior or quirk. In all cases, we are talking about ways for the repressed energy, which is countercathected, to be released or hypercathected. Additional ways are discussed below:

6. **Overpowering the Censor.** Sometimes the pain can only be endured for so long, and the person explodes in a fit of anger or rage. In this instance, the countercathexis is simply overpowered. Jim came into the apartment one night exceedingly drunk and smashed the furniture to bits. The alcohol allowed the censor to be weakened and the deep-seated anger that he felt could be contained no longer, so destruction ensued. Steam was let off in a moderately violent way.

7. **The Last Straw.** When this occurs, that is, when the dam breaks, a number of other repressed complexes may see their chance for expression and so they pile out the opening as well in a tremendously charged

emotional outburst. This can lead to great destruction. Sometime it could be only one small straw that breaks the camel's back. The person cannot understand why so much rage was expressed for so small an incident. This is the reason: one additional crack in the censor weakens an already fragile structure. All of the hurts from numerous other complexes find their chance to escape the system as well. An analogous situation was seen politically in 1989 with the sudden expiration of the Soviet Union. The system had been weakened for numerous reasons over many years, and then suddenly the structure, which had been seen as such a bulwark, collapsed, and one great country was split, virtually overnight, into a dozen or more smaller ones.

8. **A Cartharsis.** A total release of emotional energy, a purging of the system. Billy's cat died, and once he started to cry, he couldn't stop. Alone in his apartment, he cried so long that his sides ached. Clearly he was not just crying for the loss of the cat. He certainly loved his pet, but what has happened is that numerous other trapped emotions that he had held in for so long—for being a man, for not allowing himself to cry—finally have an avenue out and so they hop on board. When someone begins to cry, oftentimes a concerned associate pats them on the back and says, "Don't cry." I pat them on the back and say, "Cry. This is your big chance."

This emotional outpouring can lead to what Arthur Janov calls *The Primal Scream.*[7] It is a total liberation of cathexis, and usually it is a positive experience because the crying allows the body to release so many trapped emotions and corresponding destructive toxins. Once someone experiences a primal, he may run out of tears and may not cry again for years. Every once in a while, a good cry is quite beneficial for the system. Janov went so far as to say that the physical body was enhanced because of the primal scream.

In primal therapy, Janov asked patients to spend an entire night alone before the session. They were not allowed to make phone calls or watch TV. If they usually smoked or drank, they were not allowed to indulge; they were to spend some quiet time just with themselves.

The next day, with the help of a trained therapist, the person would lie on the ground spread-eagled and began to free associate. As the body was disarmed, the censor also was weakened. Oftentimes because of this, deep-seated hurts and pains began to surface, and the person began to cry. Once the crying began, the faucet could not be shut off, and for the reasons explained above, he or she would experience the primal. According to Janov, in some cases men grew an inch taller after therapy, and some women's breasts purportedly got larger.

9. **Body Armor.** Here we see the ideas of Wilhelm Reich come into play. As expressed in his book *Character Analysis,* Reich suggested that if libido is repressed, it can get dammed in the physiology of the system and body armor results.[8] Various areas of the body become repressed, for example, Richard Nixon's upper lip, John Wayne's skewed walk, Jimmy Swaggart's head cock, Dick Cheney's sneer, Bill Buckley's bizarre facial expression and uptight demeanor. These are all signs of body armor. Libido has converted itself into physical blockages.

A person could become sexually blocked as well. Reich's idea was to combine psychoanalysis with massage, whereby the therapist worked out repressed areas of the body. In theory, the idea is sound, as mental stress can root itself in the body (see fig. 20.6 on pg. 197). In practice, as so many of his patients' problems were linked to their sexuality, it was often difficult for the doctor to separate sexual massage from normal deep tissue therapy. Reich had sexual relations with a number of his patients, and there is little doubt that he masturbated some of them or allowed them to masturbate in front of him.

Freud recognized that hysteria, for instance, in some of his women patients was the result of sexual stasis. Thus, the "cure" in those instances might be for the patient to have sexual intercourse (and an orgasm) with their husbands, or as Freud discussed concerning some of his neurotic female patients, "The only prescription for such troubles is the well-known one to us, but which we cannot prescribe. It is: *Penis normalis dosim Repetatur!*"[9]

In Reich's case, he saw the orgasm as a panacea, as the discharge of primal energies and the way to fine-tune the body. From the Kundalini chart (see page 135), it can be seen that sexual orgasm is only one level of libido release, and it is certainly not the cure for deep-seated neuroses. This is because the core problems may have had nothing to do with sex. Deep-seated pain stemming from childhood—say, by the abandonment of the child by one of the parents through divorce—is not going to be cured by having an orgasm, yet this is what Reich is implying. Creating a work of art, hiking a mountain trail, contributing to society, seeing a great play, having a revelation, standing in the presence of a true leader—these could all be seen as "orgasms" of a different order.

Nevertheless, as hinted by Freud, Reich was certainly right that the correct release of sexual tension through the orgasm is a healthy way to release bodily tension. Reich had upped the ante considerably for Freud, as Freud had spent his career studying the libido and stating that libido had both a mental and physical side. As a single energy, it could be converted from the mind, that is, through thoughts, into body or into physical action. This is what sublimation is: the conversion of raw id energy into some type of ego production. When id energy is poorly transformed, mentally this is seen as neurotic behavior; physically it can cause psychosomatic illness.

Freud was wrestling with the seduction problem at this time. At a meeting of Freud's inner circle in 1929, Reich confronted Freud with the method of his therapy.

> Freud's remark was, *"Die Kulture geht vor"* (culture takes precedence). I say he was irrational. I am sorry. . . . I said to him, "If your own theory says that the libido stasis . . . is at the core of the . . . neurotic process, and if the orgastic potency, which you don't deny (he never denied that), is a key to overcome that stasis . . . then my theory of the prevention of the neurosis is correct." But he didn't want it.[10]

A number of Freud's female patients felt that they had been molested by either their fathers or older male figures. At first Freud thought that these women had truly been violated, and then he came to consider the possibility that these ladies simply *thought* that they had been molested. Ultimately, it made no difference from a psychoanalytic point of view if the woman acted as though she had been molested. But some theoreticians saw Freud's modification of his seduction theory as his wish to bend to the dictates of society. It was distasteful to think that girls had been seduced by their fathers, even though this had occurred on numerous occasions.

If this were true, then Freud was guilty of what he accused Jung of, namely watering down his theory. It was more acceptable to suggest that the molestation was a fantasy rather than a practice more common than we would like to believe.

Unfortunately, there is an incest cult within this culture, small though it is, of a sub-group of men who get married with the hope that they will have female children so that later they can seduce them. In one instance, a father had sexual relations with two of his three daughters, and he was put in jail. The family relented, and withdrew the charges. The third daughter, then about thirteen years old, felt left out and wanted to be "inducted" into the family practice. Fortunately the oldest daughter was able to plead with her sister not to make this mistake, and the father, again, was removed from the household.

Reich, when he studied with Freud in the late 1920s and early 30s, had put Freud in a bind because Reich had taken Freud's theory to its ultimate conclusion. In his book *The Function of the Orgasm,* Reich states that orgasms are not needed for reproduction. This is certainly true in the case of the female, and even sperm can be released without ejaculation by the male. For Reich, orgasms were required to maintain some type of harmony within the system. Sexual frustration and the misuse of this energy was the cause of much that was wrong in society. Certainly one could make a case that the dysfunctional sexual nature of such zealots as Adolf Hitler, Manuel Noriega, Idi Amin, Saddam Hussein, and others resulted not only in their own bizarre, and often sadistic, sexual practices but also in their warped and repressive regimes. Misuse of sexual energy has also caused devastating scandals in politics, Hollywood, and within the Catholic Church. Priests are asked to be celibate, and according to Reichian theory, this simply is not possible. A person must have orgasms. From the yogic perspective, Kundalini energy must be released.

Reich expounded on different aspects of this theory in his important book *The Mass Psychology of Fascism.*[11] However, he stepped beyond the bounds of morality when he got sexually involved with his patients. Nevertheless, his theories on body armor and the need to express oneself in a healthy sexual way are certainly important keys to mental health. Due to Reich's highly controversial nature, he made it easy for Freud to sanction his dismissal from the psychoanalytic society. Reich was forced to flee one country after the next, accused of being a pornographer. He eventually immigrated to the United States in the 1940s and set up an experimental laboratory in Rangeley, Maine.

Reich, however, was dealing with many demons. As a child, he had witnessed his mother having an affair with his piano teacher. He made the mistake of telling his father and his mother committed suicide. Shortly thereafter, his father also allowed himself to die, essentially committing suicide by catching pneumonia while fishing. Clearly, sexuality played a key role in the destruction of his family. Although one of Freud's most brilliant acolytes, Reich was also mentally troubled and paranoid. Once in America, he began to experiment with something he called an orgone box, which was a telephone booth–size container made from layers of organic material, like wood, wool, and metal. This multilayering supposedly trapped orgone energy, which was some type of primal energy present in the universe.

It was Reich's contention that it was beneficial for humans to sit in such boxes. Of course, they had to be naked. Reich felt that these orgone boxes could be beneficial in alleviating the symptoms of cancer, and so, in the early 1950s, he began to sell orgone boxes around the country. At the same time, Reich was also experimenting with radioactive material, which he placed in smaller prototypes during animal experiments.

Unbeknownst to Reich, the placement of radium in such a box tended to generate deadly orgone energy, which Reich called DOR.

Fig. 20.8. Wilhelm Reich and his cloudbuster in Maine, 1956

Mice were killed in these experiments and people near these containers complained of headaches. At the same time, this experiment caused a tear in the very fabric of space-time. This, as some of you may have guessed, sent a signal to the extraterrestrials who came to Rangeley, Maine, to see what the humans were up to.

In order to protect himself, Reich designed a machine that he called a cloudbuster, which could create rain and also shoot down UFOs. Resembling a multibarrelled machine gun, the contraption was supplied with orgone energy from long hoses that were connected to a water source attached to metal pipes, which were aimed at the sky. UFOs could be dissipated because their energy was taken from them.

Reich was eventually arrested for transporting orgone boxes across state lines. Thinking that President Eisenhower would get him out of jail, Reich refused to recognize the court system. He said that only a body of scientists could analyze his work. Because of this defense, he was convicted of contempt of court, and so he stayed in jail, and that is where he died of a heart attack in 1957, at the age of fifty-nine.

One of my professors, Bruno Bettelheim, who knew Reich when they both attended Freud's lectures in the 1930s, met Reich in New York in the mid-1940s after Bettelheim was released from a concentration camp. Bettelheim, who during his heyday was considered by many to be the world's leading psychoanalyst, stated that Reich was "brilliant" when he talked about his theories on psychoanalysis outlined above, but when he discussed UFOs, he was irrational. In 1973, while in his class in psychoanalysis, I asked him about this meeting. In this one area, Bettelheim said, Reich had an "encapsulated psychosis." After Wilhelm Reich died, the U.S. government made a barn fire and burned his books. Part of this story can be seen in Dusan Makavejev's controversial movie *WR—Mysteries of the Orgasm*. Fortunately, copies of Reich's works survived, and they can be purchased at any number of sources online.

10. **Insight.** The very act of realizing, or gaining insight into, the painful repression through psychotherapy and/or dream analysis allows the complex to discharge. This is one of the best ways to release pent up energy, and it is the goal of psychoanalysis. Interestingly enough, the process of insight is a receptive state. In that sense, it is an essentially opposite way of hypercathecting (releasing energy). Creative expression is an active way to positively discharge energy; having an open mind is a passive way. Creative Expression can only be achieved through having an open mind, and thus, an open system.

11. **Sublimation.** Transforming the repressed or suppressed energy to a higher realm. People can sublimate in a variety of ways, such as through artistic expression, careers, hobbies, charity work, or more vigorously through physical exercise and sports activity. Building up a good sweat and pushing oneself into a second wind are two excel-

lent ways to discharge pent up libido while at the same time improving body functioning.

12. **Learning.** Influenced by David Rapaport's 1956 article "Activity and Passivity of the Ego in Regard to the Reality," I realized that a person could hypercathect in an active fashion, as in spontaneous expression, or in a passive fashion through insight or through learning. Energy is released in both instances, through active or passive means. The key here is that the censor must essentially be a two-way street. Energy can be *actively* released from the unconscious through the censor by:

- the various ways mentioned above (e.g., prelogical behavior or sublimation)
- creative expression
- action based on revelation

Information also can be entered into the unconscious in a *passive* way by being impressed into the unconscious through:

- the formation of memories based upon experience
- some open-minded process whereby the censor allows the conscious access to the unconscious material, for instance through psychoanalysis or dream interpretation
- contemplation and learning

One must be receptive for learning to take place, and energy is gained during this process. The Sufis have a term for this energy, *baraka,* which means "effectual grace."[12] Baraka can be transmitted from a teacher and received by a student.

If we go back to Freud's model of the ego, we see that it is often in conflict with the superego and the id: Elmer Fudd caught between the devil (sex and aggression) and the angel (conscience). The ego can also be trapped deciding between the demands of society or the demands of the self. In other words, there are two kinds of ego conflicts: Freudian psychosexual conflicts and humanistic-existential ones.

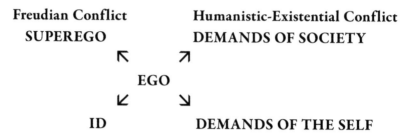

Fig. 20.9. The ego can be torn between the demands of the id vs. superego (the conflict portrayed on the left side of the ego) or between the demands of society vs. the self (conflict portrayed on the right side of the ego).

If the individual chooses the demands of society over the demands of the self, that person is a *conformist*. This is Whyte's "organization man."[13] He has followed the dictates of society to the detriment of self.

If, on the other hand, the person only follows the demands of the self, he or she may be a nonconformist, but the person may also be extremely unsuccessful, as in the *struggling artist* who, rejected by society, becomes an outcast.

A third way is that of the *neurotic*. This person is trapped, unable to decide between (1) the Freudian conflict, superego versus id (should Sally sleep with the cute milkman or should she be true to her husband?); or (2) the humanistic-existential conflict, in which the person is unable to choose between the demands of society versus the demands of the self (should Kate borrow the funds to go back and finish her college degree, which is something she has always wanted to do, or should she just continue on in her bank teller job and keep paying the rent?).

The key is to follow the demands of the real self and also figure out a way to make it in society. For want of a better term, I call this person the *creative artist*. This type of person expresses his or her real self but also, one way or another, he or she has learned how to survive, or better yet succeed, in society. A good way would be to earn a living at what one truly wants to do in life. Abraham Maslow called this person *self-actualized*. Such a person is happy in his or her life path.

That really is the key. Such people are goal oriented and have a sense of fulfillment as they go through life because, simply, they are enjoying what they are doing. Maslow differed from Freud in one key way: he based his model of mind on highly creative and productive people, whereas Freud, for the most part, based his model on neurotic and troubled individuals. Maslow found that self-actualized persons tended to be nonconformist, independent in thought, and when they were in the midst of their "work" they felt a oneness with the universe. All was right with the world. This, for Maslow, was called the *peak experience*. During these moments, there is no sense of time, hours fly by like minutes, and a sense of *awe* oftentimes dominates. There are some fortunate people who are in this "zone" when they are in their work—they may be artists, carpenters, car mechanics, or childcare workers—and there are other people who get there when they spend time close to nature. The easiest way to have a peak experience is to spend time in a natural setting such as a friendly forest, by the seashore, up in the mountains, by a brook or a lake, or in a pine forest.

Tony Robbins teaches in his "PowerTalk" tapes that to be happy, one should rethink his or her priorities. Karl says he will be happy just as soon as he earns his first $100,000. Tom feels he will be happy as soon as he is finished painting the house. Kate knows she will be happy the day she and Kip are married. What Robbins points out is that happiness can simply be claimed at any time. Instead of setting up a rule whereby a person cannot be happy *until* such and so occurs, this infomercial guru wisely suggests to simply reverse the rule: be happy in pursuit of the goal. That is the key. Decide that happiness is the first priority; the achievement of the goal is the second one. Although a simple idea, it is also quite a profound concept.

On another of Tony Robbins' tapes he explains why he is 6'7" tall. As it turns out, he had a tumor on his pituitary gland, and this caused an accelerated growth spurt during his teens. This author can't help but see that the tumor may have also triggered Robbins' third eye chakra of wisdom and knowledge of higher states. Having read literally hundreds of metaphysical books and having attended and given numerous seminars in the power of positive thinking and neurolinguistic programming at an early age, Robbins showed an uncanny ability to cull through all of this material to come up with key concepts that truly can cause a person to transform into a more optimum, functioning individual. Both Robbins and Maslow would agree that an essential key is learning to live in the moment. This idea reminds me of a greeting card that my father used to keep on his desk. It was a picture of a cow with the saying, "Don't forget to eat the roses."

If we return to the psychoanalytic model, some interesting things emerge. The neurotic wants to express her real self, but she is thwarted by the censor who blocks her from acting. Many people have dreams and desires of what they would really like to do, but they prevent themselves from acting because their censor tells them they should just stay put. This inner voice, which could be symbolized by a fist and a shaking first finger, may be the voice of a parent or spouse thwarting them, it may be peer pressure, or it may just be their own fear. These people are in conflict with themselves. Their real desire gets partially expressed, partially transformed into symbolic activity, and mostly repressed.

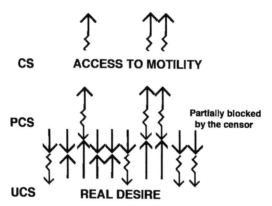

Fig. 20.10. Diagram of the neurotically blocked individual.
In the neurotic situation, the censor expresses itself in an uneven fashion, partially blocking trapped feelings and partially giving them access to the conscious apparatus.

Some energy is released, but soon after the censor reforms and sends most of the energy back into the unconscious.

Tex wants to be an artist. He goes to college, switches his major to art, and graduates with an art degree. After two years of struggling unsuccessfully to get his paintings shown, he buries his paintings in his basement, returns to school, and gets an MBA. After trying a few jobs, Tex ends up working as a real estate agent. He makes a lot of money, he sells a lot of houses. He also raises a family, but spends a good percentage of his time bitching and moaning about politics, particularly Hillary Clinton and what a horrible person she is. Unbeknownst to Tex, he harbors great resentment against a female gallery owner who, many years ago, when he was just out of college, promised to show his work and then reneged on the promise. Tex never picks up a paintbrush again, and lives the rest of his life in some form of denial.

Fig. 20.11. Rendition of Robin Williams, actor/comedian, on the cover of a magazine, à la the surrealistic artist Magritte. Drawing by Lynn Sevigny.

Every time the neurotic tries to express the real self, the censor countercathects and punishes. Numerous subclasses of this type include repressed, conflicted, and conforming individuals. Notice that the return arrows come from themselves, from their own censor. In conflict, they are in a fight with themselves, Neurotics are stressed out and thus more susceptible to disease and psychosomatic illness, as some of these return arrows can convert to physical energy and attack various organs.

PURE HYPERCATHEXIS

I first formulated these ideas in 1972–73 after taking a few courses on Freud's theories and psychoanalysis with Dr. Bettelheim. At that time, I encountered a revelation, because I asked myself, where is the return arrow? In the diagram below, the person is spontaneously expressing his or her real self. There is no blockage. The censor has simply allowed the individual to let loose. An example of a person who exemplifies pure hypercathexis would be Robin Williams. Anything goes. Whatever he wants to say or do, he does. His censor does not block him.

This is different from Monique, an exotic dancer who overtly appears to be uninhibited by stripping every night but actually is dominated by deep-seated repressions stemming from a dysfunctional child-

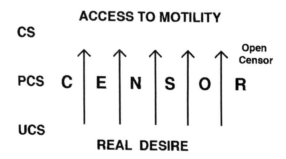

Fig. 20.12. Diagram of expression from the real self.
With an open censor, a person is easily able to express
real wishes and desires from the unconscious.

hood. Some exhibitionists have been seduced or molested by older men when they were children. So what looks like uninhibited self-expression is actually a neurotic reenactment of the dysfunctional psychosexual childhood event. A good measure of this would be the use of breast implants in such dancers. They are secretly very concerned with their appearance (active censor), and in a bizarre kind of way, they are also intellectualizing powerful sexual and antisocial forces.

Great artists, such as Picasso (1881–1973), Dali (1904–1989), and Marc Chagall (1887–1985), typify the idea of pure self-expression. Ernst Kris, in his book *Psychoanalytic Explorations of Art,* introduced the concept *regression in service of the ego* to explain this process. In essence, the ego or self delves back into the unconscious to dwell there in order to get in touch with the wellspring. Picasso's abstract and often erotic drawings and paintings vividly portray this ability of the ego to make use of unconscious forces. Drawing one's dreams would be another example. Note that many great artists, psychologists, and composers lived to ripe old ages. Both Freud and Jung were in their mid-80s when they died. Dali was well into his 80s, Picasso into his 90s, and Chagall was nearly 100.

This is what I realized: If people expresses their real self, they are not in conflict with themselves. They are not exchanging energy with the self. Rather, they are exchanging energy with the environment. The return arrow comes from the environment.

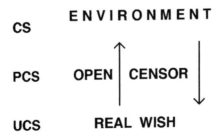

Fig. 20.13. In an open system, the individual is not blocked by the censor and thus is in a dynamic relationship with the outside world. Instead of exchanging energy with the self, the open person exchanges energy with the environment.

During hypercathexis, there is a free release of mental energy. Since the mind is an *open* system, new energy can now be put into the unconscious and mental growth can take place. Something is freed up and enlarged through true and creative self-expression.

A similar process takes place during the act of perceiving or learning. Input from the environment enters the mind through the open censor and the person is enhanced because of this. In the case of self-expression, we have *active* hypercathexis, and in the case of learning, we have *passive* hypercathexis. The term "an open mind" intuitively explains precisely this process. Someone who is a good listener is growing as a person because he or she is allowing new energy to be put into the system. In one of his more esoteric lectures, Gurdjieff discusses the process of *baraka,* a transfer of energy, which takes place from teacher to student during a situation of learning. In these instances, the censor is flexible and the person's real needs and wishes can be expressed naturally and spontaneously. When someone learns something, energy is gained from the environment. The same is true during creative expression.

According to the model, the main cause of death is the way a people handle stress. If they do not handle stress correctly, the energy attacks some organ of the body. Strokes and heart attacks are still the highest killers in society. There is abundant evidence to show that certain character types, in particular the type-A personality (overly ambitious), are much more susceptible to high blood pressure and heart attacks. Stress tends to cause the arteries to constrict, and liv-

Active Hypercathexis →→→ Expressive →→→→→→

SELF   ENVIRONMENT

Passive Hypercathexis ←←← Receptive ←←←←←←

Fig. 20.14. People in a dynamic relationship with the environment. They not only express what is inside of them, but they also continue to grow by taking in new input from the environment. This theory suggests that some actual form of energy is taken into the system if people have an open mind.

ing this way for thirty or forty years can bring on the attack.

If humans can learn to express who they really are, if they tune in to their unconscious desires, their real self, their soul consciousness as it were, according to the model, they will live longer. Furthermore, they will continue to grow throughout their lives.

Bruno Bettelheim pointed out the opposite occurrence in the life of the autistic child. According to his psychoanalytic model, due to a variety of factors—in particular the lack of love and affection from the mother (or primary caregiver) and perhaps a predisposition of the child to be cool or distant—instead of the ego being encouraged to grow, the ego of the newborn is thwarted, and thus it constricts and withers. A cold or uncaring mother causes the ego of the child to literally shut down, and the rage that it feels is turned onto the self. A similar process occurs in depression. The person attacks his or her own self-image, but all of this is done unconsciously. All children need to be nurtured, but in these instances, and for whatever reason, the child turns away from the mother, and the situation snowballs. Since we are talking about a newborn, certain neurochemical factors do not unfold correctly during this critical period, the brain may become malformed, and the ego becomes autistic.

Autistic children are self-abusive, they avoid affection, have a delay in language development, become preoccupied with restricted patterns of behavior, tend to show intense interest in parts of objects, and do not use the personal pronoun I. Bettelheim asked the simple question, "Why would a child bang his head against a wall?" And the simple answer was because the child did not like himself. How many normal people hit their head when they do something stupid? The cure for Bettelheim was to reverse the process. The goal would be to get the child to express

$$\search \qquad \swarrow$$

EGO

$$\nearrow \qquad \nwarrow$$

Fig. 20.15. The autistic ego is being attacked due to self-hate.
In this instance, the ego builds a wall around itself and shrinks.

himself in some way, any way, and then gain the trust of the child and give the child encouragement, love, and physical affection.

There is much controversy as to whether or not autism is caused before or after birth. Certainly the disorder can be caused by a variety of factors. Many cases of autism have nothing whatever to do with parenting styles, but rather are due to a malfunctioning brain, for instance, an impaired cerebellum or left frontal/temporal lobe. Clearly genetic factors play a role in many cases of autism. However, as shown on the television show *20/20*, pollutants in the air also are a factor. Thus it is clear that Bettelheim's theory was flat-out wrong for many cases of autism because parenting styles, in these instances, had nothing to do with the onset of autism.

Years ago there was a Foster Grant plastics industrial plant in a town in Massachusetts. Many of the youngsters who lived a few blocks away eventually gave birth to autistic children. Somehow the toxins from the surrounding air imbedded themselves into the psychophysiology of the male and female children playing near the plant. Twenty or so years after the fact, when these children themselves had children, a large number of them were autistic.

What we call "autism" is most likely a variety of diseases that have similar symptoms. The mistake that many critics of Bettelheim make is to assume that there is only one cause. The movie *Rain Man* portrays a psychoanalytic model for its cause, and this is the case in some instances. Due to problems with the mother, one child (Dustin Hoffman's character) became autistic and the other child (Tom Cruise's character) became angry, hostile, and isolated. Just as the cure in the film was for the brothers to bond and love each other, the cure for psychoanalytically curing autism is for the abuse to be replaced by nurturing.

Bettelheim did have success treating autistic children by encouraging them and by having his specially trained attendants give the children *love, affection,* and *encouragement.* These are the keys to help any child grow.

Interestingly, I had a student in the year 2000 who had an autistic son. Since her husband worked at a fertilizer plant, she suspected that toxins in his system may have negatively impacted the embryo or the growing fetus. This student was committed to helping her child. For her class report, she showed movies of the child from the age of two until his present age of five. At first the child showed the typical signs of autism: there was self-destructive behavior, avoidance of seeking affection, and ritualized activities. After intense daily therapy involving long hours, which included the key factors of love, affection, hugs, and encouragement and another important ingredient, *maintaining eye contact* with the therapist, the child developed remarkably well, and now functions at an almost normal capacity in grade school. My thinking was that through the hugs, special attention, and the maintaining of eye contact, the child's brain was forced to adapt in a more positive way so that it had a greater chance of developing normally. In more difficult cases, advances have been made in teaching the ability to be affectionate by bringing in young animals such as puppies and kittens. Bonding often does occur between the autistic child and the pet. How can anyone resist a kitten?

There is a great secret to be learned by studying all the varieties of autism. Some autistic children are "savants" in particular areas. They may display a photographic memory, have exceptional musical or artistic abilities at the level of genius, or have uncanny mathematical skills. A number of autistic savants can describe the day of the week for any day in history or multiply strings of numbers in their heads. What is so amazing is that the ability is not taught. It just comes naturally. The prevailing theory to explain these fantastic abilities is based on the idea of the brain compensating for loss in one area (e.g., higher cognitive/social functions) by enhancement of abilities in another primal area (right hemisphere) usually associated with memory and mathematical abilities.

Note that no matter what the ultimate "cause" of the autistic disorder, the key to mental health is for the subject to hypercathect, that is, to express the inner self. The ego grows through love, encouragement, and spontaneous expression. People with open minds continue to grow through life, and thus, rather than dissipate energy in self-destructive ways, the energy is utilized to help the person continue to expand and develop.

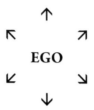

Fig. 20.16. A healthy ego, which receives support, encouragement, and love, will grow and expand through spontaneous self-expression.

21

Collective Construct Realities

Fig. 21.1. The organization man. Drawing by Lynn Sevigny.

It is obvious to fight tyranny; it is not easy to fight benevolence, and few things are more calculated to rob the individual of his defenses than the idea that his interests and those of society can be wholly compatible. . . . One who lets the Organization be the judge ultimately sacrifices himself.

WILLIAM H. WHYTE JR.

Whyte states that as beneficial as the large corporations can be, they are also static, delusory, and self-destructive. During the inevitable conflict between the individual and society, the organization man is caught in a bind because the company provides a livelihood but at the expense of the worker's individuality. This Whyte calls a "mutual deception."[1]

Adorno, one of a group of critical theorists, sought to combine Marxist theory (which analyzed society from an economic viewpoint) with that of psychoanalysis (which factored in the role of the unconscious of the individual), as combined shapers of human history. Adorno noted that during the process of identification with and the wish to be accepted into the group, there is a transfer of libido from the self to the leader (in the above case, the corporate image) and also ensuing self-repression. Paradoxically, although in some sense the ego weakens, primary narcissism is involved as the "other" becomes psychologically merged with the self. This is the essence of the psychodynamics of the conformist.[2]

An example of this occurred in rather dramatic fashion in my presence in March of 2003, during the very week President Bush took this country to war against Iraq. This was a controversial war, and many countries opposed the invasion, including China, Russia, Germany, and France. In retaliation to the French, the administration suggested that the term "french fries" should be replaced with the term "freedom fries."

I happened to be in transit at an airport at this time and found myself standing on line at a concession stand attempting to get lunch. The man in front of me ordered a hamburger with "freedom fries." The poor fellow behind the counter, who happened to speak with a foreign accent, had no idea what the man ordered, so he said, "Excuse me?" in a polite voice. And every time the man asked for "freedom fries," this was answered by "Excuse me?" again, in a polite voice. Since they were not on the menu, and because of the absolute absurdity of the situation, the man finally acquiesced and ordered french fries. Here was a classic example of over-identification and transfer of libido to the leader at the expense of the self.

The inherent standardization of the marketing of products, production, and consumption, the mechanization of labor, and the development of mass transportation, communication, and urbanization also worked to strip the individual of his uniqueness[3] and therefore, perhaps, cause the worker to resent individuals who were not consumed by corporations. The corporate view, which the critical theorists associated with the term "instrumental reason," became the very embodiment of rationality itself, thereby structuring, restructuring, and in that sense controlling consciousness.

An example of *instrumental reason* shaping our view of reality can be seen in the decision by cell phone companies to produce only one wireless phone per line. They could just as easily have created multiple phones for individual cell numbers just as they do with landlines. The outrageously high price of greeting cards seen in every drugstore is another example. Instrumental reasoning is self-validating. Because corporations do things the way they do, then that must be the way it should be done—that is the thinking. The point is, corporate or government logic, although it controls our thinking, may in fact be irrational.

An excellent example of such an organization man can be seen in the Jack Nicholson character Schmidt, in the 2003 movie *About Schmidt*. Forced into retirement, Schmidt finds out that his life had been the corporation. Now, with nothing to do, he has absolutely no idea who he is, and he faces the sad fact that his contributions to his family and the world have been ultimately meaningless.

Another example from real life, from Wall Street, which occurred in the 1990s, concerns how stock options were handled. Against every rule of accounting, the Congress, corporations, and even Securities and Exchange Commissioner Arthur Levitt agreed not to count stock options as future debt. Essentially what this meant was that corporations, as a rule, overestimated profits by as much as 20 percent because they collectively agreed to hide this clear future debt. In a TV interview for *Frontline,* Levitt admitted that he caved under pressure from such senators as Christopher Dodd and Joe Lieberman. This was one of the reasons why the market crashed at the turn of the present century, because the bottom line of the entire market was overinflated by precisely this factor.

GROUP FANTASY

The term "group fantasy" generally refers to a worldview that may or may not be substantiated. It could be based upon fact, conjecture, or faith. It is a broad term closely associated with the idea of a collective or shared aspiration, assumption, avowal, belief, bias, canon, construct reality, conviction, credo, delusion, desire, doctrine, dogma, dream (as a conscious aspiration), faith, hallucination, hypothesis, illusion, indoctrination, interpretation, motif, paradigm, prejudice, premise, presumption, tenet, theory, wish, worldview, or *Weltanschauung*. Accepted natural laws could be seen as group fantasies. They are constructed realities formulated by human observation or experimentation to explain natural phenomena. They are not actually laws so much as lawful interpretations, which would be subject to change as more data is accumulated. For instance, there is a law of gravitational attraction, but no one truly knows exactly what gravity is.

Another example of accepted natural laws are black holes in space, which are reported on as if they are actual phenomena, when in fact they are construct realities made up by physicists.

Group fantasies tend to revolve around generally accepted interpretations of historical events. DeMause writes that group fantasies can "produce group dynamics, which can lead to a breakdown of group fantasy, a period of paranoid collapse, and an attempted restitution through the formation of group delusion. . . . [This] result[s] in a group-trance, which may require discharge in violent historical action."[4]

> We will achieve peace in the Middle East when the Arabs learn to love their children more than they hate the Jews.
> GOLDA MEIR, FORMER PRIME MINISTER OF ISRAEL

The rash of suicide bombers in the Middle East during the dawn of the present century is a case in point. Not only have bombers been promised martyrdom, they have also been promised scores of virgins waiting for them in heaven after they murder the infidel. This psychosexual delusion, which serves to cathect powerful polymorphous perverse id desires through the guise of the superego, is couched as a religious belief. It is preached in places of worship throughout the Middle East, so that tens of thousands, if not millions, of young people are indoctrinated into this way of thinking. It is not an understatement to say that the entire fate of present-day civilization rests, to some extent, on this outlandish construct reality.

The inner psychological mechanism for a group fantasy, for deMause, is a "massive displacement onto the public stage of feelings connected with the individual's search for love."[5] Through this collective imaginary worldview, people are able to express "important unconscious tasks[6] . . . [and] act out and defend against repressed desires, rages, and prohibitions, which have their origins in childhoods common to the group."[7] In pursuit of maintaining the group fantasies, deMause states that people will use ordinary defense mechanisms like repression, reaction formation, and rationalization.

An example of this can be seen with the National Rifle Association. Because the second amendment gives Americans the right to bear arms, any attempt to restrict any kind of gun from being marketed is portrayed as an attack against one's civil liberty. Many a politician has gone down in flames for trying to modify any aspect of this powerful second amendment group fantasy, even when deranged individuals use certain kinds of assault rifles to kill unarmed civilians.

THE HERDING INSTINCT

We are all pawns from the chessboard, and we're playing our parts in a drama that is neither fiction nor unimportant.

PART OF BOB LIVINGSTON'S RESIGNATION SPEECH AS
SPEAKER OF THE HOUSE, AS HE CALLED FOR PRESIDENT
CLINTON'S IMPEACHMENT FOR LYING ABOUT A SEXUAL
LIAISON WHILE HE HIMSELF WAS LYING TO HIS WIFE
ABOUT HIS OWN AFFAIR, DECEMBER 19, 1998

A major problem to consider in analyzing group fantasies is to understand the psychology of group dynamics. The group itself can have many levels (or subgroups) to it. For instance, there is the family unit, cohorts or friends, the local community, professional colleagues, the local culture, or the historical period. Just as the group attempts to cause the individual to conform, so too the individual tries to transform the group.

Take the case of body piercing. Sometime in the mid-1990s, a few bold adolescents began to get their noses and eyebrows pierced. In about 1997, this morphed into the piercing of the belly button, septum, lips, nipples, cheeks, and tongue.

Between the years 1995–1998, I noticed a total of three students (out of approximately five hundred) with their tongues pierced, two females and one male. It was quite uncommon to have a college student with his tongue pierced at that time. The male, who also had his lip pierced, was making a living piercing others. Within the next three years, by 2001—in conjunction, by coincidence, with the rise of the sale of cell phones and the ubiquitous increase in e-mail addresses—the number of students with their tongues pierced increased to about five per semester. In other words, it became quite common. This would correspond roughly to a tenfold increase within five years. There is little doubt that hundreds of thousands, if not millions, of young people have had their tongues pierced between the years 1999–2008.

Clearly the need to belong to the tongue-piercing group easily outstrips any fear associated with the pain and continuing discomfort that this procedure entails. For the female student, tattoos at the base of the spine have followed a similar trend.

Where the youth of today easily subsume these new fads, the older generations would see, particularly in the case of body piercing, the activity as being bizarre and incomprehensible. In 2002, I asked my Abnormal Psychology class what they would think if everyone began chopping off the top half of one pinky. The class overwhelmingly agreed that there was nothing wrong with this behavior. I felt like I had stepped into the story of the *Emperor's New Clothes*, and I was the only child. A fad that supposedly enhances oral sexual practices, tongue piercing has become a bizarre norm, one which, no doubt, will disappear in a few years just as telephone booth stuffing and goldfish swallowing did in years past. What about clitorectomies, I asked the class. The female students became outraged. It was okay to pierce a tongue or chop off half a pinky, but they drew the line at removing the female pleasure center, a common practice in many African nations.

PERSONAL MYTHS

Feinstein[8] and Krippner[9] have supported this term, which can be applied to both the individual and the group. Defined as "cognitive structures that underlie consciousness,"[10] in and of themselves personal myths reflect an agreed-upon mental reality, which may or may not reflect the actual state of things or events. Krippner notes, "Any version of reality is at its core a mythological construction."[11] He emphasizes the importance for an "observing ego" to reflect on the substance, meaning, and ability to verify the personal myth.

Myths are not "falsehoods," says Krippner, but rather they are cognitive mechanisms that are either "functional or dysfunctional."[12] On a group level they "provide the understanding and guidance that determine the success [or failure] of the culture."[13] Note how the myth of the "great American" played a key role in the invasion of Iraq in 2003. The goal of ousting the horrible leader Saddam Hussein was admirable, but the myth will be sorely tested as the problem of helping transform this fragmented and highly complex culture plays out.

The word *guidance* is important for both Feinstein and Krippner, because one's personal myth tends to direct the course of one's life. Highly complex structures, personal myths involve, on the exterior, "conscious attitudes and beliefs," and on the interior "the basis of our [Freudian] unconscious . . . pattern[ing]."[14] Genetic factors associated with the Jungian collective unconscious, which Jung called the archetypes (shared racial memories or instincts), should also be reflected in one's personal mythology.

Why does a person join the Peace Corps, become a doctor, or run for president? Personal myths play a major role as shapers of our life path.

Archetypes, as building blocks of the collective unconscious, for Jung[15] are, by definition, the formative patterns, psychic structures, and organizing principles that make up the basic template from which the personal unconscious arises. Dreams, as shapers and also reflectors of personal striving, from this perspective can also reflect mythological motifs found in modern cultural patterns as well as in primitive religious beliefs.

In animals, archetypes appear as preprogrammed behavior patterns, such as the stalking reflex seen in kittens and various courting rituals in different species of birds. For Jung, "nest-building" is also an expression of an archetype. In humans, these mentally related, culturally linked survival instincts are more difficult to discern. Could the new interest in body piercing be a reemergence of an ancient courting instinct? Road rage may also be a manifestation of the Darwinian instinct to survive.

22

Dreams and
the Collective Psyche

Jung points out that human events occur through an interaction of conscious and unconscious processes. Jung has proposed a profound insight here, as he is suggesting that the unconscious, as an autonomous force or entity, plays a direct role in shaping people's actions and world events. Further, the unconscious is creative. We like to think that our future is determined predominantly by conscious decisions. But Jung is suggesting quite a different view. Unlike Freud, who is emphasizing unconscious libidinal factors in shaping behavior, Jung is recognizing another aspect of the unconscious, a sagacious side aligned with a biblical view, which is separate from the conscious self but which still has influence over this outer husk. Of divine origin from this point of view, the unconscious is a source of "higher" consciousness. Proof for this hypothesis lies in the simple fact that dreams often give the dreamer advice.

Clearly the unconscious "knows" or "perceives" things that the conscious does not. Although it lives and/or operates in its own domain, it can interact and motivate the conscious.

As Jung stated in a filmed interview, "The unconscious really is unconscious!" And then he laughs, because it's funny. If it is *unconscious,* then it's unconscious, that is, it remains unknowable or unrealizable to the so-called conscious mind—that is, to *us.* In other words, there is a very active dimension of mind with its own rules and modus operandi that is separate and distinct from the waking state and world we humans know and, in that sense, inhabit.

> My contacts with astral beings did not make my childhood particularly easy. . . . I was very young when I realized that though the visitations I experienced seemed perfectly normal and not in the least frightening to me, other people did not react the same way. Attitudes varied from simple disbelief to a barely concealed conviction that I was a bit mad.[1]
>
> ROSEMARY BROWN

This treatise is in some measure an exploration of the numerous aspects of this realm. Where does it begin, and where does it end? If a person has a vivid dream about a dead relative, is it not possible that some form of communication with the departed has taken place? I can tell you from my own personal experience, having had a number of key dreams with my father—who passed away in 1996—they felt like real experiences, close encounters, so to speak, with the dead.

I've had a few dreams and visions with the dead. The first major one occurred the very day my father died. On the drive down to his funeral, I felt compelled to pull over and get out of the car. At that moment, I had an overwhelming feeling of the presence of my grandparents and my uncle hovering above me in the clouds. My grandparents died a half-century earlier, when I was a boy, and my uncle, my father's brother, died shortly thereafter. In 2005, my first cousin, Hilary Gold, died. A few days later, much like the Albert Brooks movie *Defending Your Life,* I had a dream of seeing Hilary on a line to get into heaven. She waved to me from beyond a fence as she moved with the crowd. And the most recent event occurred just last week as I write this, in July of 2011, the day after my twelve-year-old nephew Bentley Seifer died in a swimming accident. On the drive up to Burlington, Vermont, where he lived, I saw quite clearly a vision of Bentley lying on a table or bed being cared for by my Aunt Lucille, who had passed away at the age of eighty-six just three months earlier. Sitting in the background behind her was my mother, Thelma Seifer, who passed away at the age of eighty-eight, two years earlier. I am not a person who has many visions. These were very unusual events for me. I am not suggesting that I definitely had contact with the other side, but what I am suggesting is that this is a possibility. The subjective experience has validity. It just can't be "measured" or neatly catalogued in the outer world.

Once one begins to study the topic of life after death, one finds much evidence. A number of interesting scientific studies were done with the medium Mrs. Piper by psychologists Richard Hodgson and William James at the turn of the twentieth century.[2] Much like the modern-day TV medium John Edward, fraud was never detected, and Mrs. Piper was able to impart compelling evidence that she was in touch with the other side.

A more recent and perhaps even more astounding example is the story of Rosemary Brown, who has written upward of four hundred symphonies in the style of many dead composers such as Beethoven, Chopin, Bach, and Rachmaninov. In her mind-boggling autobiography *Unfinished Symphonies: Voices from the Beyond,* and in an interview she did for *60 Minutes,* Rosemary Brown states overtly that the ghosts of these composers, headed usually by Franz Liszt, appear in her room and simply tell her which notes to write down. When one considers that great composers such as these may compose ten or twenty symphonies in their entire lifetime, her accomplishment is that much more astounding, given also that the compositions are written in such varied styles. In an interview, hospice pioneer Elisabeth Kübler-Ross also claimed that during her later practice the spirits of some of her dead patients often came back to visit her.[3]

Along a similar line, if I have a dream with a famous person—for instance, I have had dreams with Bill Clinton when he was president, or more recently with the actor Michael Douglas—who is to say that in some sense our psyches did not communicate on this other unconscious level?

An analogous way of looking at this wider view of the psyche can be seen if we link the idea of "consciousness" to daytime and nighttime.

During the day, the sun is out, we are awake, and we can see and operate in our world. At night, the sun goes down, and the moon comes out, as do all the stars. If a person had never seen nighttime, that is, if he had never been awake or conscious during the night, would he ever imagine that there were hundreds of billions of other stars beyond our sun? Clearly, the answer is no.

At night, the waking self slumbers and this larger self that expands into the infinite firmament awakens. Just as our reality is limited to the sphere of the earth during daylight hours and extends into the infinite nighttime sky at night, so, too, does our consciousness stay limited when one is awake and extend into vast realms when the moon comes out.

When a person awakens, he may or may not remember his dreams. It does not mean that he has not dreamed if his conscious self does not remember anything. We have all had the experience of having a dream disappear, or in a sense withdraw back into the unconscious before our very eyes. We know we had a vivid dream, had been, in a sense, in another full and rich world, and we have an inkling of what it is all about, but as we awaken and search it out, the vision simply vanishes before our eyes. Freud would call this repression, the tendency for the psychic event to recede back into the unconscious.

Freud also suggested that there were infinite layers of primary and secondary processes in the psyche. The primary process refers to the realm of the unconscious. This realm is always active and always thinking. The secondary process, or censor, overlays and inhibits the primary process. If we did not screen out our unconscious when we awaken, we could not operate in the outer world. Psychedelic drugs have the ability to, in a sense, withdraw the veil, that is, remove the secondary process, so that the subject has more direct experience with the primary process. In common terms this is what "tripping" is. Schizophrenics also tend to live in the unconscious dimension as they have little ability to screen it out. Like drug trippers, they are, in a sense, dreaming even while awake.

If there are infinite unconscious layers, overlayed with infinite censors to screen out these layers, we could, for the sake of discussion, number them. For instance, one of my students constantly dreamt about elevators. Let's say for arguments sake that the elevator dreams refer to layer fifty-seven in her unconscious. If she also dreams about beach houses on a regular basis, these dreams could operate in the realm of layer seventy-nine. Perhaps she has forgotten, or she does not even know, that she constantly dreams about beach houses. She only knows she dreams about elevators. But one night she dreams about a beach house and she has the distinct feeling during the dream that she has been to this same beach house in a previous dream. This is a déjà vu experience within the realm of the dream. Depending on her level of awareness, she may or may not ever know that her mind enters and reenters layer seventy-nine in her unconscious on a regular basis. This is the point: people may have an entire unconscious world that they live in, but they might not even know this world exists. Why? Because it is unconscious! It is my contention that all humans function much like my student. Every night each of us enters realms our conscious selves do not even know exist. Only through tuning our attention to dreams can we ever discover the truth of this statement.

If one keeps a dream diary, one finds that the mechanism of repression still operates. This is to say, even though the subject has written down the dream, the experience most often still recedes back into the unconscious, so that months or years later, when the dream is reviewed, there is not necessarily a strong conscious memory of the psychic event. But there it is, because you wrote it down.

Do psyches intermingle at these deeper levels? I suggest that they might. I believe that our minds are open-ended systems. Most dreams are restricted to the realm of the personal unconscious. They deal with day-to-day activities, emotions, conflicts, and problems from the past that still influence our behavior. But some dreams may pass beyond this realm, either to the land of the dead or to a collective realm where the deeper parts of other souls can be found. At the deepest strata of mind, all minds are one.

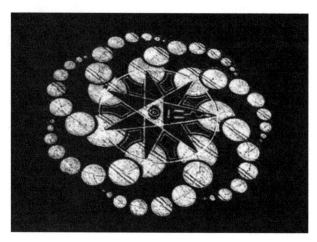

Fig. 22.1. Crop circle, England ca. 1990

In designing this section, I wanted to include a picture of a mandala, which was one of Jung's favorite symbols. The search for an image led me to crop circles, many of which are fantastic mandalas. Although crop circles may indeed be created by humans (as opposed to extraterrestrials), they do represent in a symbolic sense the point of this book, namely that the more we learn about the mind, the more we corkscrew inward. These spiraling images resonate with me as pictoral depictions of the search for the source of one's soul, oversoul, or unconscious self.

JUNG, THE MANDALA, AND THE SEARCH FOR GOD

Think of the world as a bicycle wheel, with a metal core at the center and spokes leading out to the tire, which runs around the perimeter. At the surface of the tire, we are individuals. Each spoke would correspond to each separate human. The depth of the rubber of the tire would correspond to the conscious, preconscious, and unconscious of each individual. And most of us are barely aware of the real depth of the tire, let alone the entire wheel. However, as the person moves toward the center, the individual unconscious is transcended. The next layer would be what Bruce Taub-Bynum calls the "family unconscious," which would be the shared psyche of a family. People more closely attuned to each other would have the capability of intermingling more in this second tier.

According to the early twentieth-century occultist Richard Ingalese, there are entities called "dwellers of the threshold" who prevent humans from getting past their own unconscious, past the tire, so to speak. These dwellers are really our fears. It is a fear barrier that keeps humans from delving very far into this unconscious realm.

At deeper levels, according to F. W. H. Myer's idea of the universal mind or Jung's idea of the collective unconscious, we are all interconnected. Jung says that the mind of man as a collective realm is structured with archetypes, primordial symbols, or primeval instincts, from which the collective psyche is constructed.

Essentially taking a biblical view, Rudolf Steiner suggests that these archetypes are autonomous and have their own consciousness. Considered messengers or angels, these formative patterns deep in the psyche are, in some sense, higher conscious entities closer to the source. Farther up the hierarchy toward the center would be the archangels. And at the apex sits God in the center with Michael on one shoulder and Lucifer on the other. The deeper we go into our own psyche, the closer we can get to the Supreme One. This essence is present in all humans and, in fact, is in all things. This relates to Leibniz's idea of the monad. Each psyche is a microcosm that contains within it all the principles of the macrocosm and reflects the macrocosm. This idea would also bear a link to the process of holography, three-dimensional photography, whereby each section of the hologram codes for the whole. A mirror operates on the same principle. If a person looks at himself in a large mirror he sees the one entity. If, however, the mirror is broken into a thousand pieces, each little mirror also reflects this one whole entity. The principle of cloning also shows this monad theory operating. Every cell contains the information to construct a new entire being. At the periphery, we are individuals; at the center, we are One.

23

Tarot and the Tetragrammaton

And I looked, and, behold, a stormy wind came out of the north, a great cloud, with a fire flashing up, so that a brightness was round about it; and out of the midst thereof . . . came the likeness of four living creatures. And this was their appearance. . . . They had the face of a man; and the four had the face of a lion on the right side; and the four had the face of an ox on the left side; the four had also the face of an eagle. Thus were their faces. . . . And the living creatures ran and returned as the appearance of a flash of lightning.

EZEKIEL 1: 4–13

Looked at from a biophysical perspective, the brain and body are formed from DNA, our genetic source. If we analyze the composition of DNA we find that all of life is made up from four molecules or DNA bases: thymine, adenine, cytosine, and guanine. Thymine can only pair with adenine (TA or AT) and cytosine can only pair with guanine (CG or GC). The specific arrangement of these base pairs in the zygote, the fertilized egg or seed, accounts for all of life. This sequencing could be seen as a complex binary system, with AT or TA corresponding to 0 or −0 and

CG or GC corresponding to 1 or –1. Just as all computer programs can be broken down to a series of 0s and 1s, so can DNA, except some form of directionality for the 0 and 1 has to be taken into account. The only difference between a virus, a pine tree, a tyrannosaurus rex, a kangaroo, a fly, or a human is the sequencing of these four bases. Arrange them one way and you get a fly; arrange them another way, you get Jeff Goldblum.

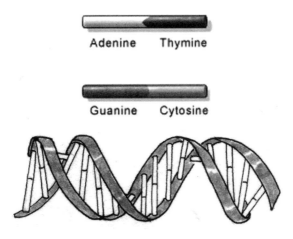

Fig. 23.1. DNA

DNA in the fertilized egg directs the growth and production of the embryo into the baby. Within this DNA code is not only the blueprint for the entire body but also a blueprint for the mind. The mental apparatus has some structure at birth. This, for Jung, would be the collective unconscious. On top of this primal foundation of mind, which is present at birth, the experiences of the individual will develop. This new part, which occurs after birth, would include the personal unconscious, habits, memories, and the rest of the psyche developed through experience.

Returning to the biophysical aspect, if we break down the four bases of adenine, thymine, guanine, and cytosine into their components, we find that they, in turn, are made from five elements, carbon, nitrogen, hydrogen, and oxygen for the construction of the base, and these four plus phosphorous in the spiral backbone. If we think of the DNA double helix as a twisted ladder, the rungs could correspond to the AT/TA and CG/GC combinations and the rail, which holds the rungs, corresponds to the so-named backbone.

So now we are down to the level of particular atoms, as these five elements can, in turn, be broken down further to electrons, protons, and neutrons. The only difference between oxygen, nitrogen, hydrogen, phosphorous, and carbon, from this perspective, is the number of protons and neutrons in the nucleus and the number of electrons circling this center. However, we can even take this one step further, for a neutron is really the combination of a proton and an electron. Thus, the entire periodic table of elements can be seen as simply the special arrangement of electrons and protons, yin and yang, plus and minus, 0 and 1.

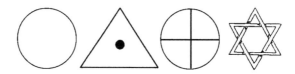

Fig. 23.2. Circle, triangle with dot in center,
circle with cross in center, Star of David

Turning to NUMEROLOGY: its mystical correspondences provide a key as to how the One split itself into the many. We start with 0 and 1, the All, the single entity before the big bang. The zero is a circle and therefore can symbolize oneness or nothing. So we see in the zero the idea of both 1 and 2, duality. This primary circle and its self-reflection is 2, yin and yang, male and female. The number 3 corresponds to the tension between the opposites, the yin/yang symbol as one entity, and also the trinity: Father, Son, Holy Ghost. Three is also a triangle. And this triangle as a single unit, with a dot in the center, corresponds to 4. The trinity as a gestalt is the fourth element. Place the divine cross in a circle and you get four quadrants. This is how 3 becomes 4, how 3 is 4.

$$3 + 1 = 4$$

Note that in this instance, the 1 is really a different form of 3, it is the 3 as a single unit, the triad as a gestalt, 3 = 1 where "three" is seen as one thing. 3 + 1 does not only equal 4, it also equals 6 because it is, seen in this light, 3 + 3. This is also how the trinity relates to the Jewish star, how Christianity and Judaism are interlinked: ✡ is two interpenetrating trinities. Seen as arrows, one trinity, with its base on the ground and its apex in the sky, points above ↑, and the other arrow/trinity points below ↓. As above, so below. The laws that exist in the higher world exist in the lower world. This is another way of saying the microcosm reflects the macrocosm.

Four is also the tetragrammaton, or fourfold nature of God: fire, earth, air, and water. These four elements, according to the ancients, account for all existence. Curiously, not only are there four dimensions, four cardinal points (north, south, east, west), and four bases in DNA accounting for all of life, there are also four laws to the universe, according to classical physics:

Strong nuclear force: the binding force within the nucleus
Weak nuclear force: the binding force within the neutron
Electromagnetism: the binding force between molecules
Gravity: the binding force between large bodies like planets and
stars

Fig. 23.3. Derived from Phoenician script, the Hebrew word for God,
read from right to left as YHVH (Yod Heh Vav Heh).

The tetragrammaton is also, in Hebrew, the name for God, YHVH, which in English translates into Yahweh or Jehovah. Note that there is a repeating element in this sacred name. So again, we note a complex binary arrangement, YH and VH, reminiscent of the female and male chromosomes in genetics, XX and XY. These four components also relate to the four animals of lion, bear, eagle, and man. And if we combine all four animals, 4 + 1, we get 5 or the Sphinx.

Five also relates to the hand ✋, with 4 fingers + 1 thumb, whereby the thumb, in a sense, equals the four fingers, 4 = 1. It is also the fifth

Fig. 23.4. Sphinx. Drawing by Lynn Sevigny.

element, Akasha or prana, or in DNA, phospherous, the element not found in the bases but found in the backbone.

Six, as stated above, is the Jewish star and the credo "As above, so below." Seven is the sacred octave, the rainbow and also the seven stages the initiate takes to enlightenment symbolized by the seven chakras. Eight can be seen as two intertwined tetragrammatons, two interpenetrating squares. It is also 7 + 1, or the first stage of the second octave, $8 = 2^3$, whereas nine is the reverse, 3^2. Nine is the last single digit. It relates to the spiral, to gyroscopic properties, and to the ends of old laws and the beginning of new ones. Nine also correspond to the nine stages of enlightenment (actually 7 + 2 hidden chakras) as espoused in Kundalini Yoga. Nine can be seen as three trinities, which, when set up correctly, creates a spiral:

H
Y V
H
Y V
H
Y V

Fig. 23.5. Spiral

The trinity, YHV as a totality, is the next H. The first level once achieved becomes the first step for the second stage. This is most clearly seen in the Major Arcana of the tarot, which are the twenty-two steps, or mythological motifs, that the soul takes on its journey through life. Extrapolating from P. D. Ouspensky and also Mouni Sadhu's masterwork on the tarot, we come up with the following:

Fig. 23.7. The twenty-two steps of the Major Arcana.
Drawing by Lynn Sevigny.

THE TAROT

This Clavicle . . . lost for centuries . . . [is] a hieroglyphic and numerical alphabet, expressing by characters and numbers a series of universal absolute ideas.

ELIPHAS LEVI, CA. 1860

While researching the tarot during Easter one year, I happened to watch a movie on Jesus of Nazareth. It struck me as synchronistically peculiar that Jesus's Last Supper was on the last day of the seven days of Passover (the Jewish holiday celebrating Moses's escape with his people from Egypt) and that his body rose seven days later. This total span of fourteen days had a midpoint and transitional seventh day (Palm Sunday), which marked the passage and remembrance of the old religion (Judaism) with the dawning of a new one (Christianity). Could this be symbolized by the card of Death and Rebirth (card #13) of the tarot?

As the movie progressed, I began to see some other visual comparisons between the pictures of the tarot and various scenes. During the trials of Jesus and Barabbas, the Roman governor presides. He is flanked by two men, one standing for good, the other for evil. The seventh card of the tarot depicts a similar symbolic triad. In the center is a soldier with a white sphinx to his left and black sphinx to his right. According to the movie, the Roman governor Pontius Pilate (played by Rod Steiger) lets the people decide who is to be saved. Out of fear or ignorance, Barabbas is freed, leaving Jesus to be executed.

A few scenes later, Jesus is nailed to the cross. He has two criminals on either side of him, and at Christ's feet are the two Marys, one a reformed prostitute, Mary Magdalene, and the other, the Virgin Mother. In looking at one version of the Death card, there are two women at Death's feet. These women symbolize transmigration of the soul, for the female is the life bearer, carrying the fertilized seed from one dimension to another. The Death card is also a card of rebirth. Jesus, at the end of the film, tells the viewer that his message to man is that life does not end with the destruction of the body. One's spirit travels on.

Shortly thereafter, I came upon a passage in the Old Testament that completely describes the tenth card: the Wheel of Fortune. (See the opening quote about the four animals: lion, eagle, man, and ox and the wheel within a wheel from the book of Ezekiel.)

In the New Testament, Corinthians 40–42 describes a direct correspondence to the seventeenth, eighteenth, nineteenth, and twentith cards:

There are celestial bodies and bodies terrestrial; but the glory of the celestial is one, and the glory of the terrestrial is another. There is one glory of the sun, and another of the moon; and another of the stars; for one star differeth from another star in glory. So also is the resurrection of the dead.

It is well known that the Kabbalah, or mystical interpretation of the Old Testament, is intimately linked to the tarot. The above passages not only verify this observation but also suggest that the Jewish Kabbalah may be a mystical interpretation of the New Testament as well.

Kabbalism talks of a covenant with God. This is a contractual arrangement whereby man and God are in an interpenetrating partnership with each other. The Kingdom of God is within each of us. This is the secret of the tarot.

The word *tarot* is of Egyptian origin composed of the prefix "tar" (road) and the suffix "ro" (royal), thus "the royal road to wisdom." Interestingly, Freud used a similar term to describe dreams, which he called "the royal road to the unconscious." And like the dream, the tarot at first appears unintelligible, making use of pictorial images such as kings and priestesses, horses, trees, swords, and stars, the ever-changing juxtaposition of the cards reportedly revealing a seeker's identity and linking to his or her future. It is the occult Rorschach, psychokinetically allowing the initiate to subconsciously order the cards himself in revealing his latent destiny.

The tarot has been traced back to at least the thirteenth century to the alchemist Raymond Lully, but Eliphas Levi, the nineteenth-century

Kabbalist, and many others speculate its origin is pre-Egyptian, probably Chaldean or Babylonian times. Since the occult has always been plagued with persecution and death (e.g., the witch trials and burnings of the 1500s and 1600s), it has also been speculated that contained in the tarot is a hidden message concerning just who and what man is. Each picture contains a chapter's worth of information. Intriguing symbols also abound (see the cards above).

Together, all the cards contain metaphysical and secular concepts, most hidden deep within the graphic, yet puzzling, structure. The deck consists of seventy-eight cards, which, in turn, are made up of two distinct packs: the Major and Minor Arcana (Mysteries). These two decks probably evolved separately, as they serve separate functions, and later they were sandwiched together.

THE MINOR ARCANA

The Minor Arcana is essentially an exact replica of a regular deck of cards except for the inclusion of an extra picture card, a Page card or second Jack, so to speak, for each suit. The other difference is that instead of diamonds, hearts, spades, and clubs, we have pentacles, cups, swords, and wands.

The playing-card deck probably was developed from scribes as an ancient way to record the events of the year, and this evolved into the calendar, the 4 suits standing for the 4 seasons and the 13 cards in each suit standing for the number of weeks for each month: 52 cards in the deck, 52 weeks in the year. The Minor Arcana has an extra card for each suit/season. If we consider that the regular deck is a form of a calendar, the extra card for each suit would correspond to an overriding theme for the season in question. In the regular deck, there are 2 jokers, whereas the Minor Arcana has, in a sense, 4 jokers, only they are called Page cards.

In this theory, each card in a suit stands for a different week for a different season, 13 weeks in summer (hearts/cups), 13 weeks in fall (clubs/wands), 13 in winter (spades/swords), and 13 weeks in spring (diamonds/pentacles). Say there was a violent lightning storm during the third week of the summer. A lightning-storm card could be created to symbolize that week. Perhaps the king's brother died by drowning on the sixth week of the summer; a card could be created to symbolize this tragic event. And say, overall, it was a particularly hot summer. After each week of the summer, a different card would be placed down, and at the end of the 13 weeks an overarching theme for that summer would be symbolized by a Page or Joker card, which in this instance would be a card depicting great heat. If these summary cards were kept by the ancients, along with the other 52 cards for the 52 weeks, they would thereby have a fairly accurate record for every week and season throughout their recorded history (e.g., a rainy autumn, three years ago, a tornado the fourth week of the spring the year before that, and so on).

This theory allows for each card to signify a different manifestation of God's will, symbolized by the weekly and monthly changes either in weather or daily events. The Minor Arcana also appears to be linked to the game of chess, with the picture cards corresponding to the king, queen, bishops, knights, and castles and the cards 1–9 corresponding to the pawns.

THE MAJOR ARCANA

There is a secret doctrine concerning the tarot. Part of this doctrine involves Hermeticism, a form of alchemy, which is an ancient process of self-transformation achieved through initiation or direct experience of the Arcana, which are the great mysteries (or universal truths). Mouni Sadhu, whose book on the tarot is highly regarded, informs us that truth exists independently of man's knowledge or ignorance of it. The mysteries are inherent in the understanding and study of the name of God, the tetrad, or fourfold nature of God, and his many manifestations symbolized by the twenty-two cards of the Major Arcana.

Note how in spelling the word *tarot,* the motif of a letter beginning and ending the word is present: the T. This same motif is present in the tetragrammaton, whereby the H is the repeating element in YHVH.

T

A   O

R

TAROT: Major Arcana (counterclockwise)
ROTA: Wheel (counterclockwise starting at bottom)
TORA: Law (clockwise starting at top)

Each card stands for a different principle of metaphysics and mysticism. Each has a numerological as well as symbolic significance, which tarot writer Eden Gray says forms an "inner thought that ha[s] rightly been called [a] door[way] leading to hidden chambers of mind. The study of [the cards] can be a fascinating pursuit in itself, conducive to contemplation and meditation."

In plotting out the Major Arcana in relationship to the tetragrammaton, the fourth card, or Emperor, not only symbolizes the synthesis of the first three cards of Magician, High Priestess, and Empress, but also signifies the beginning stage for the second of seven tiers, which would be the fourth, fifth, sixth, and seventh cards. Likewise, the seventh card, or Chariot, not only signifies the end of the second phase but the beginning of the next phase. The other transition cards are: The Wheel of Fortune, Death, The Tower, and the Sun cards. When looked at in this light, one can see that the Major Arcana signifies the spiraling stages that one must go through in order to reach universal truths, symbolized by the last card, the World.

There are twenty-two cards and seven stages (see below), whereby the fourth card is the last of the first tier and the first of the next tier, and so on. From the numerological point of view, this can be seen as 3 + 1 = the Trinity plus the One = the tetragrammaton. Here is the link between 3 and 4, where three as a gestalt *is* four, symbolized by a triangle with a dot in the center. Note also that twenty-two cards divided by seven stages is another famous number, π, pi: the relationship of the diameter to the circumference of a circle. So the tarot can also be seen as an occult symbol for the wheel of life. Mathematically, this is also the sign of infinity, as there is no end to π.

I: 1. MAGICIAN

2. High Priestess   3. Empress

II: 4. EMPEROR

5. Hierophant   6. Lovers

III: 7. CHARIOT

8. Strength   9. Hermit

IV: 10. WHEEL of FORTUNE

11. Justice   12. Hanged Man

V: 13. DEATH

14. Temperance   15. Devil

VI: 16. TOWER

17. Star   18. Moon

VII: 19. SUN

20. Judgement   0. Fool

21. WORLD

By plugging in the twenty-two stages above in this manner we can now begin to understand the tarot's esoteric construction. The Fool card is really the Magician Card, traveling through every stage. That is why it appears right before the end of the series, right after position twenty. No matter where a person is in life—whether Tiger Woods, Rupert Murdoch, Bill Clinton, Senator John McCain, or Rosie O'Donnell—he or she is always the Fool. Look at the life journey of some of the greats like Frank Sinatra, who was often the Fool but who also owned the world, or Elvis Presley or Marilyn Monroe, who both died as the Fool.

A good example of this can be seen in the field of sports. Bill Parcells had been the head football coach of the New York Giants and as such took his team to the Superbowl twice and won both times (in 1987 and 1991). This was an extraordinary achievement involving such cards, or way stations, as the Magician, Wheel of Fortune, and Strength. Parcells then became head coach of the New England Patriots and, as Emperor, took them to the Superbowl in 1997. However, one day *before* the game was played, Parcells, greedily influenced by the Devil, announced that he was returning to New York to coach the Jets for a tidy salary. His timing was horrible. The Patriots played terribly in the Superbowl and lost handily—Death card. Parcells had reached the top, that is, the World, but he was still the Fool and paid the price by generating tremendous ill will. He should have used the Hermit card and Temperance and kept his plans quiet until after the big game.

In the political arena another example of the Fool card was evident in the 2008 election in which Senator John McCain battled Senator Barack Obama for the presidency. Where Obama, a Democrat, former professor of constitutional law from the University of Chicago, Harvard graduate, community organizer and bestselling author, had been a U.S. senator for only two years, McCain, a Republican, former Vietnam prisoner-of-war veteran and war hero, had been in the House of Representatives for two terms and then had been a senator for twenty years. McCain had wanted to choose as his running mate Senator Joe Lieberman, a conservative Democrat, longtime friend, and also the vice-presidential running mate for Al Gore when Gore, a Democrat, ran for the presidency in 2000. In terms of the tarot, McCain was striving for such cards as the Chariot (combining opposites), Temperance, and Judgement. However, the Republican Party had demonized all Democrats. Thus, had McCain kept Lieberman on the ticket, he risked both the Devil card and the Tower, in other words, the wrath of many members of his party who could not abide with the radical decision to choose a running mate from the opposing party.

Unable to choose whom he wanted, McCain became the Hanged Man. He was forced to sacrifice some key element of his core self to continue to obtain party backing. He therefore spun the Wheel of Fortune and chose Sarah Palin, a Republican governor from Alaska with only two years experience whom he had met once for about an hour. How could Senator McCain, with all of his know-how, choose a neophyte as a running mate, someone he really didn't know, when his age was such a factor in the race? The most important decision he had to make was done in a cavalier manner, and that decision alone cost him the race. I personally knew at least five individuals who switched their vote because of this decision. With the World card within his grasp, McCain instead played the Fool.

The first stage for all humans is that of initiation. In the case of a young man, he (the Magician) meets the girl who is, for him, the High Priestess. They marry, and she becomes the mother (the Empress) of his children, and he becomes the father (or Emperor). So, the Magician is the Emperor after a period of time, 1 becomes 4, and he has now attained the first of the seven stages. The first three cards of each stage become the fourth card, which encompasses the precepts of the previous three, to end that stage and begin the next one. The Magician graduates to become the Emperor, who graduates to become the Chariot, Wheel of Fortune, Death, Tower, Sun, and World. The Fool signifies the journeyman who travels to each position along the way.

Once the Magician has reached the stage where he has a wife and family, he, as Emperor, encounters the next stage, which is the realm of duality: two acolytes before a deacon, the struggle of the love with his mate, the yin and yang of his existence, the Chariot driver. Can a person reconcile the opposites within himself? Can he harness the two opposing horses? Perhaps the singer Michael Jackson could be seen as a man struggling with his chariot, two opposites pulling at him. Is he a black man or a white man, male or female? One person who successfully rode the Chariot was Hillary Clinton, who dealt with the darkness of her husband's infidelity by emerging bathed in light.

One way to reconcile the opposites, to achieve what Jung calls *individuation,* is to use Strength. How does one open the mouth of the lion? Only if the lion allows the person to open the mouth. This is the feminine principle to Strength, using the other person's force or momentum to achieve one's own end. The fighting strategy known as judo is based on this principle. Gandhi and Martin Luther King were two people who symbolized the card of Strength, the eighth major card. If the Dalai Lama wants to gain independence for Tibet, he knows the best way is that of the eighth card: place China in a situation whereby it wants to grant some form of autonomy to Tibet. In a war, obviously, the Tibetans could never oust the oppressor.

One way or another, if the journeyman can reconcile the opposites, he or she can graduate to the next level, which is the Wheel of Fortune. One could look at the presidential election of the year 2000 as corresponding to this card. It was a coin toss who would be president—Gore or Bush? It boiled down to a virtual tie in the state of Florida. Gore won the popular vote throughout the country, but Bush squeaked out the majority of the electoral votes when calculated state by state. After the vigorously contested Supreme Court ruling, Gore decided to concede through sacrifice, and two years later he sacrificed yet again by deciding not to run for the presidency in 2004. Gore is the Hanged Man. Bush is the Emperor, and sits on the other side of the Wheel as the ruler of Justice. Both men, however, also face the Death card, the death of an old self and the birth of a new self.

In the case of George W. Bush: after becoming president, he faced a heavy triumvirate of the Tower, Death, and Devil cards in the form of Osama bin Laden, the Middle Eastern zealot who choreographed the 9/11 attacks, which killed over three thousand Americans and caused the destruction of the Twin Towers in New York and partial destruction of the Pentagon in Washington, DC.

The Tower card is oftentimes the heaviest of all the cards. It is a card of total destruction. For instance, the stock market crash in 2001, after the 9/11 attack, and the burst of the dot.com bubble were massive examples of the Tower card, as in both instances millions of Americans lost vast percentages of their long-held capital. If we go back a few years to President Clinton's impeachment, he was tempted by the Devil, in the form of a twenty-one-year-old intern, Monica Lewinsky, with whom he had an affair, and he faced the wrath of the Tower—potential total destruction. No doubt, this was a hell on earth for the sitting president, but he survived and thereby was able to enjoy the Moon, the Star, and the Sun, in part through the success of his wife, Hillary, the first lady who became a New York senator and later secretary of state. Hillary's card would be that of the Empress.

If we were to map the rise of Barack Obama from senator to president, we could say he started in life burdened or blessed with the Chariot card: his mother is white and his father black, his mother American and his father African. Obama learned in his later youth to reconcile his opposites.

In college Barry Obama reclaimed his birth name Barack, which, similar to the Hebrew word *baruch*, means "blessed." At Harvard Law School, Barack became editor in chief of the *Law Review*. This position would entail the cards of Emperor and Justice. His mother died when he was a young man; he thus experiences early on the power and complex energy of the Death card. He married well. His wife, Michelle, herself a graduate of Harvard Law School, began as the High Priestess and then, through motherhood, attained the role of Empress. Michelle's mother, who moved into the White House, might represent the cards of the Hermit and Strength. She stands in the background and gives her family support.

Obama turned to religion, the Heirophant, through the Reverend Wright, who, through his bombastic rhetoric, becomes the Fool. Obama must confront the Death card once again as he is forced to shed this relationship.

Even before the 2008 election, Obama is perceived throughout the globe as a rising star, symbolized by the Star, the Sun, and the World cards. As president, he aspires to remain the Emperor as he constantly confronts, once again, the card of polar opposites, the Chariot, through the divisive battle between the Republicans and Democrats. His master cards at the time of writing, July 2011, seems to be Temperance, the Magician, and Judgement.

After the Magician takes his entire journey through life, he is still the Fool. The great ship, the Titanic, would correspond to the hubris of the Fool. It thought it was invincible, but much like Icarus who did not listen to his father and flew too close to the sun, the unsinkable Titanic sank and thus faced the Death card and Judgment day.

If a person has led a good life, he will be judged well and enter the holy kingdom, which is the World card. In life, people can also achieve this stage, but it is very difficult. Such greats as Walt Disney and Jacques Cousteau have achieved this status while alive. In this day and age, Barbara Bush, the wife of the senior President George Bush and mother of another president, has certainly attained the World card. However, and most importantly, so has *anyone* else who has raised or been a part of a happy family and lived a good and fulfilling life.

24

The Dream Diary

I'm in a dark alley with a door that gets progressively smaller, and I need to get out. I see the light at the end of the last door but get stuck in it because it is too small.

A DREAM OF A STUDENT

As part of the process of self-transformation, the initiate must learn more about himself. This can be done in a number of ways. One is by self-remembering, that is, by being conscious of the self at all times, or at least as often as possible. Notice that when you sit and consider yourself, there are three aspects to the process: the actions of yourself, your ability to observe these actions, and the link between these two aspects. One can become more aware of the self during the day, but one can also become more aware of the self at night even while one is asleep. The best way to remember your dreams is to simply *command* your unconscious before you go to sleep and say to yourself: I WILL REMEMBER MY DREAMS!

Remember, this will not work unless you put the exclamation point at the end of the sentence. Purchase a blank notebook, which will become your dream diary, and write down and date every dream you have upon awakening. If you do nothing else, you will at least log a good percentage of your unconscious.

HOW TO ANALYZE A DREAM

It is condensation that is mainly responsible for the strange impression produced by dreams, for we know nothing analogous to it in the normal psychic life that is accessible to consciousness. We get here, too, ideas which are of great psychic significance as nodal points or as end-results of whole chains of thought. . . . In the process . . . the whole set of psychic connections becomes transformed into the intensity of the idea-content (i.e., the symbol in the dream).

SIGMUND FREUD, *WIT AND ITS
RELATION TO THE UNCONSCIOUS*

When you are going to sleep and have a dream, who is the author of your dream? Freud called this entity the unconscious. In many ways I prefer Lobsang Rampa's term *oversoul,* as it implies that there is an intelligence inside each of us that is communicating and giving us guidance. Keep in mind that this dreaming self is a thinking entity, which, from a phylogenetic point of view, is hundreds of thousands, if not millions, of years old. It is the primal psyche from which our modern minds emerged.

There are seven steps to analyzing a dream. The following were derived from a lecture given by Stanley Krippner, circa 1980.

1. Write down the dream.
2. Put down the feeling tone. In the above dream about the shrinking door, we could say frustration.
3. Pick out three or more key symbols. In this instance:
   a. Diminishing door
   b. Dark alley
   c. Light
4. Now let your mind go and form five to ten quick associations with each symbol. Do not edit during this process. Any crazy thought is acceptable!
   a. Feeling of getting trapped, being closed in, squeezed, Alice through the Looking Glass, the Doors rock group

b. Mugged, city at night, cobblestones, London, secret passway, short cut, tall cold buildings, dumpster

c. Solution, the way out, warmth, savior, happiness, bright, moth to a flame

5. Now go through your associations, editing the list, and see where the analysis takes you. Keep in mind that the following mechanisms of dream-work have been compiled to a great extent by the master himself, Sigmund Freud:

a. **Displacement:** Does one symbol really stand for another? Sometimes you dream about Sally, but you know she really stands for Roselyn.

b. **Condensation:** Oftentimes two symbols get sandwiched into one. Dreams are efficient and often make their point in as simple a way as possible. Sally and Roselyn might combine into some unknown person who sits beside you in a car. This person, most often, is another side of yourself with the attributes you have that are in common with the two individuals who have been sandwiched together.

c. **Reversals:** Sometimes in order to understand the dream the person should take the very opposite of the overt message. A person may dream about attacking someone else, when in fact it is the person himself who is the target.

d. **Magnification:** Oftentimes dreams magnify situations to make a point. A lady dreams that her child is kidnapped. This is a common theme in dreams, and it does not mean that the child is in danger. Rather, the dream is asking the dreamer to reconsider how much time she is devoting to her child. The dream prompts the dreamer to become a more vigilant and accessible mother. As a teacher, I often dream that I come to the final and leave the tests at home. This dream simply warns me to make sure I leave the house fully prepared!

e. **The manifest and the latent content:** The manifest content is the actual dream. The latent content is the hidden meaning. Between the two is the censor whose role it is to keep unwanted or unpleasant thoughts/truths hidden from the conscious mind. It is the task of the dreamer to delve into and beyond the censor to uncover the real meaning of the dream. These steps help in this task. The censor in dreams often shows up as a policeman or as a series of gates. The censor works to distort the hidden message. In the dream above, the censor is the diminishing door. If the dreamer can pierce through his own blocks or fears, enlightenment may ensue.

    f. **Potential sources:** Dreams often go over the day's events. They may also be prompted by ongoing problems or conflicts, themes stemming from childhood, somatic situations such as a stomachache, and spiritual strivings.

    g. **Wish fulfillment:** Freud felt that most dreams contained a hidden wish.

6. After going through your major symbols and their associations and editing the list, keep following the trail. Sometimes an insignificant or vague part of the dream is the key, because this is the part that is most defended against. Use an open mind to allow the dream to unfold before your eyes. Then write out your analysis, and if you are lucky, you get to participate in "the Aha! experience."

7. **The Aha! experience.** This does not happen all the time, but sometimes you know that you have nailed the dream. By following this process you may be surprised, because when you have uncovered the hidden meaning, you will know that you have solved the dream. Keep in mind, however, that dreams are paradoxical, contradictory, allegorical, and most importantly, *multidimensional.* There is oftentimes not just one single meaning to a dream, but like any symbol, for instance, the American flag, there can be many meanings to the single event. Dreams dwell in a world with different laws, rules, and regulations from the so-called conscious world. What I am saying is that many times, even after completing this process, the dream is not completely revealed. Nevertheless, if you gain any

insight, and you will if you go through these steps, you have succeeded.

Another aspect to this process is something called **lucid dreaming**. This is when you know you are dreaming while you are dreaming. The goal is to bring the conscious mind into the unconscious realm. One trick sometimes used is to come to the dreaming process prepared. Say you always wear your watch. See if you are wearing this watch while are in a dream. This act may serve to allow you to become aware while you are dreaming.

When you are lucid dreaming, you can sometimes gain the ability to change a dream so that you are no longer the victim. Tribes from Micronesia tell us that if you can stand up to a bad guy in a dream, that entity may become your ally. If the dream is seen as an out-of-body experience as it were, a journey of the soul, much like Wendy being led by Peter Pan, you may have the ability to fly to other realms and dimensions. This would be the ultimate trip, to prove the theories outlined above and meet the higher beings that dwell in this realm of the unconscious. If you achieve this by transcending the personal unconscious, please let me know. See my e-mail address at the end of the book.

Some lucid dreamers however, are really fooling themselves because they think that they have obtained the ability to control all their dreams. If they are in fact controlling *all* their dreams, then they are not really dreaming, because the nature of the dream presupposes that this other self, the unconscious, oversoul, or guru within, has taken over to give us a message. It is the one in control, not your outer self. If the conscious entity has always taken control, this is simply a clever defense against confronting the true unconscious. The lucid dreamer is certainly on the master journey, and he should be able to control some dreams or some aspects of the dreams, but it is a tricky course. The idea or goal is to break through the fear barrier, so that the journeyman can enter the next strata where he will be the initiate once again, but on this deeper plane. See Carl Jung's autobiography *Memories, Dreams, Reflections* for an accounting of such an explorer.

25

The Cultural Myth

Comparative anthropology lends support to Jung's view that all humans share some basic psycho-neurological (and thus instinctual) framework, which guides so many human events (e.g., child rearing, loyalty to the community, marriage ceremonies, need for a leader, religious beliefs, rites of passage, sense of humor, sense of justice). Clearly, the rise of patriotism, shown by a significant increase in the purchasing and display of the American flag after the 9/11 attack in New York City in 2001, was a manifestation of an archetypal instinct being triggered.

In my own case, after the event I simply had the urge to go out and purchase an American flag, which I did. I later found out that hundreds of thousands of other Americans purchased a flag that same day. This surge of patriotism would be caused by the trigger of a tribal archetype.

ICONS

Cultural myths find expression in such forms as media, rituals, fables . . . [and] history books. . . . Personal myths are expressed directly through the individual's verbalizations . . . images . . . affects and behaviors . . . [They] shape . . . experience by determining how and what we perceive. These mythological templates give structure to reality in a manner analogous to the shaping of dough by a cookie cutter. They are the colored glasses through which we see the world.

DAVID FEINSTEIN

Take, for example, Superbowl Sunday. Essentially an entire nation gathers together to watch the culminating professional football game of the season. This event, one way or another, not only shapes the way we view and experience contemporary America; the game also serves to unify the country and even plays a role in defining the country's place in the world arena.

The myth of the cultural icon is a powerful vehicle for cathecting the archetypal need to manifest a God that can be seen and felt. At the same time, the perpetuation of such myths helps sell products. Elvis Presley, James Dean, Marilyn Monroe, John Lennon, and John Wayne are cases in point. These were highly flawed individuals who, in truth, only had an appeal to restricted segments of society when they were alive. However now, much like Lenin and Stalin in the defunct Soviet Union, these idols have been resurrected, anointed as it were, to unprecedented levels of adoration. They are safe symbols, in part because they are dead. The need for society to keep them alive also reflects another archetypal wish for our own everlasting life.

EXTRATERRESTRIALS

The group fantasy that Earth has been contacted by extraterrestrials is a common motif that derives from an ancient wish to make sense out of the universe. From a deMausian perspective, it is a search for love; from a Jungian view, it is a search for meaning and for God. Major adherents have traditionally been society's stargazers. In ancient times they were astrologers: today they are generally astronomers. Stemming from the 1700s and 1800s, these scientists have included such people as William Hershel, discoverer of the planet Uranus in 1781, French astronomer Camille Flammarion, who in the late 1800s often discussed the concept of the plurality of worlds and his belief that Mars was inhabited, and Percival Lowell, brother of the president of Harvard University, who, during the height of the Gilded Age in the 1890s, photographed the famous canals of Mars with his large telescope located in Flagstaff, Arizona. Because of the prestige of his name and great telescope, Lowell often gained the front page of the major newspapers with his staunch belief that Mars was inhabited.

Jumping ahead three generations, we come to two well-known late-twentieth-century university-educated professors, astronomer Carl Sagan from Cornell University and physicist Allen J. Hynek from Ohio State. Both wrote popular books on their own theories that intelligent life existed elsewhere in the cosmos. Where Sagan doubted that *our* solar system had yet been penetrated, Hynek, as head of a leading UFO organization, stated on numerous occasions that we had indeed been visited by UFOs.

As witnessed by the extreme popularity of nineteenth-century science fiction writers from Jules Verne and George du Maurier, Orson Welles's famous *War of the Worlds* radio play in the late 1930s, which was an updated rendition of H. G. Wells's famous book of the same title, and present-day movies, such as *ET, Star Trek, Star Wars, Close Encounters of the Third Kind, X-Men, X Files, Galaxy Quest,* and *Men in Black,* there is a powerful need for humans to believe "we are not alone."

GROUPTHINK

Cultural myths and group fantasies are closely tied together. Structured hierarchically within civilized settings, these myths greatly determine the course society takes. Their vehicles of indoctrination can range from intimidation to persuasion, disinformation, promises, platitudes, and propaganda. Everything from religious ceremonies to corporate marketing techniques, community projects, governmental elections, media topics of the day, and war are ruled by construct realities. Without them society could collapse. Cultural crises are closely associated with the destruction of generally accepted views. Stock market crashes, social unrest, and postcombat trauma are all linked in this way.

The loss of a cherished belief that has become an integral part of a group fantasy can cause panic, terror, moral decay, or fear of catastrophic consequences.[1] A good example of this was the incredible bailouts of the banks by both President George W. Bush as he left office in

2008 and President Barack Obama shortly after he took office. The fear was that if the banks were not saved, the entire economy of the world could collapse. Due to this fear, our capitalist country used a socialist mechanism of partnering with the banks by lending them nearly a trillion dollars, which resulted in plunging the country into greater debt. In the interim, many of these loans have been repaid. Ironically, much of the success that the banks achieved after this crisis was not due to any intrinsic change in the way America conducts business; the bailout did not result in a dramatic resurgence in the production of goods or the creation of real wealth, but rather to the simple fact that the stock market rebounded—and so the banks made money on the uptick! The point is, these banks were really perceived as "too big to fail." Based on this premise, the country had no choice but to save them, and so both a conservative Republican president whose philosophy railed against such action and a more liberal Democratic president who also believed in fiscal responsibility were forced into the unprecedented action of lending enormous sums of money to companies that, in a truly capitalistic society, should have gone belly up.

Even to include this analysis in this text risks the very trepidation being discussed in this chapter, namely the pressure to stay "politically correct" and to avoid, in a psychology book, these kinds of discussions. That's how powerful group fantasies are. They dictate how we are to think. If the system is bucked, the messenger is most often the one that pays the price.

A clear example of this occurred in 1991, when filmmaker Oliver Stone released *JFK,* a realistic movie about the Kennedy assassination. Much of the story was based upon Louisiana Attorney General Jim Garrison's hypothesis that Kennedy was not murdered by a lone gunman, but rather by a renegade faction of the CIA (see his book *On the Trail of the Assassins*). The viciousness of the assault against Stone in the press was staggering. And a weaker man than Oliver Stone would have been devastated.

Another example occurred right after the 9/11 attack in New York City in 2001. Satirist Bill Maher suggested that the act of the suicide terrorists was not cowardly at all, particularly as compared to the launching of bombs at a distance, which is what the United States did in Afghanistan to retaliate against al-Qaeda, the organization that planned the treacherous venture. Maher's popular television show *Politically Incorrect* was pulled almost immediately, and it has been off the air ever since. The punishment of Maher, whether his comments were right or wrong or misunderstood, was a clear signal to all other media talking heads to be wary. From a psychoanalytic standpoint, it would have been better to let Maher continue with his show, even if his statement was obtuse or disrespectful to the many who died that day, because ultimately we all suffer if people like him are silenced by this kind of censorship. Maher came in conflict with the edginess of the situation. These terrorists struck America at the core of its belief structure, and anything that seemed unpatriotic, even if it was misunderstood, was deemed a threat to the prevailing order.

Fortunately for Bill Maher, he resurrected his career several years later when a racier rendition of his show was picked up by HBO. The same, however, could not be said about newsman Dan Rather. Even though Rather had been one of the most important, if not *the* most important, newsmen on TV for a generation, he was fired from his position when he released suspect documents that supported the premise that sitting president George W. Bush had let his National Guard pilot's license lapse during the Vietnam War. What was so astonishing about the event was that the facts of the case were not in dispute. Bush's pilot's license did lapse at that time. Rather was let go ostensibly because he presented documents about the case that may or may not have been forgeries. Since President Bush was sending the military into combat in Iraq at the time, his past was newsworthy, but the network bowed under pressure and killed the messenger instead.

Other powerful group fantasies that appear sacrosanct are the suggestions that Ronald Reagan and JFK were the greatest modern presidents since FDR: Dwight D. Eisenhower, the five-star general who led the D-Day invasion, or George H. Bush, a president with over fifty combat missions as a pilot during World War II, former head of the CIA who rescued Kuwait from Saddam Hussein notwithstanding. (Reagan never served in the military.)

> Mr. Gorbachev, tear down this wall!
> PRESIDENT RONALD REAGAN SPEAKING IN WEST BERLIN,
> JUNE 12, 1987. THE WALL CAME DOWN TWO YEARS LATER.

In the case of Ronald Reagan, in 2003 a miniseries called "The Reagans" was scheduled to be released on CBS. The part of the president was played by longtime actor James Brolin. Due to the critical nature of the show, it was pulled and ended up playing on HBO, which has an audience base millions smaller. Since the movie does not portray Reagan as a demigod but rather as a flawed human being, no critic has had the gumption to review the movie, and thus the myth of the Reagan presidency has been maintained!

> And so, my fellow Americans, ask not what your country can do for you, ask what you can do for your country.
> PRESIDENT JOHN F. KENNEDY'S INAUGURAL ADDRESS,
> JANUARY 20, 1961

With respect to JFK and the Cuban Missile Crisis stand-off against Russia, Kennedy has achieved demigod status because of the way he handled the affair. To briefly recap: In 1962, the Russians began placing nuclear warheads onto Cuban soil, an island just ninety miles off the coast of Florida. With the real possibility that a nuclear war would ensue, instead of retaliating militarily either in Cuba or directly against Russia, standing against many of his military advisors, Kennedy chose a less bellicose path. Instead, he placed a naval blockade around Cuba thereby preventing the Russians easy access. This gave the American president time to negotiate through a back channel with his counterpart, Soviet premier Nikita Krushchev. The crisis was passed when Krushchev agreed to withdraw the warheads in exchange for similar concessions with the U.S. removing comparable warheads from Italy and Turkey.

True, Kennedy showed great muster and negotiating skills at that moment. His actions were directly related to getting the world to avoid a nuclear war. However, when Kennedy became president, just two years earlier, he had inherited a war plan against Cuba. Known as the Bay of Pigs invasion, Kennedy pulled back support while the operation was underway. This resulted in the deaths of some of the forces, and the arrest of about a thousand Cuban rebel forces and a number of covert CIA operatives. Had Kennedy not balked during this invasion, had he given the troops the air support they had expected, the Cuban Missile Crisis never would have happened, and Castro may even have been toppled. The world would have never faced the possibility of a nuclear war in 1962 had Kennedy supported the coup against Castro the year earlier. I personally met one navy pilot in the mid-1980s who displayed great disdain for Kennedy because he was sitting on the tarmac in Florida with a bevy of other navy pilots waiting for the expected go ahead that never came.

The very fact that America was halfheartedly behind the invasion gave Castro the moxy to allow Russia to place nuclear warheads on his soil to begin with! Thus, where most historians see Kennedy in a very positive light, other historians and Kennedy adversaries see him not only as weak but also as the ultimate cause of a situation that almost led to a nuclear war. Although there remains a small segment that generally spurns Kennedy, in general the overarching cultural myth of his greatness prevails. And to be fair to Kennedy and his vision, man's landing on the Moon is a direct result of his initiative, as is the civil rights act. Do these epochal achievements fully offset JFK's previous decision, which almost led the world to Armageddon? To ensure the myths of the greatness of these two presidents, the airport in Washington, DC, was renamed after Ronald Reagan, the airport on Long Island, New York, was renamed after Kennedy, and the image of John Kennedy was placed on the 50¢ piece.

People stripped of important group fantasies, even when their private fantasy systems remain intact, nevertheless feel they are going crazy.

The most dramatic examples, perhaps, are those found in anthropologists' accounts of groups who are suddenly "decultured," who lose their rituals and beliefs through traumatic contact with Western or other cultures.[2]

If conditions are right, chaos, mob action, or group hysteria can ensue. Over time, with the threat of such a loss, all of the ego defenses come into play. In these instances, it seems, the truth does not set us free!

CLIQUES AND CLANS

In the case of subgroups of a culture such as fraternities, policy makers, or scientists, extreme forms of peer pressure can produce a "group norm [which] bolster[s] morale at the expense of critical thinking."[3] Guiding factors associated with maintaining agreement, conformity, continuity, homogeneity, sameness, stability, and unity tend to predominate.

"Shared illusions" can be created in a variety of ways such as when the group blindly follows a misguided leader, or "when a dissident begins to voice his objections to a group consensus."[4] In the latter case a homeostatic mechanism begins to operate. "Typically, a cohesive group . . . develops a set of norms requiring loyal support of past decisions. Each member is under strong pressure to maintain his commitment to the group's decision and to support unquestionably the arguments and justifications they have worked out together to explain away obvious errors in their judgment."[5]

I cover an iconic watershed example of this in my previous book *Transcending the Speed of Light.*[6] In George Gamow's text *Thirty Years That Shook Physics,* Gamow, a founding father of quantum physics, mentions that in the 1920s Goudsmit and Uhlenbeck measured electron spin as greatly exceeding the speed of light.[7] Since this measurement violated Einstein's sacrosanct theory of relativity, which stipulates that nothing can travel faster than the speed of light, the finding had to be suppressed. Following in the footsteps of Hermann Minkowski, the young physicist Paul Adrian Dirac decided to call electron spin the square root of negative one, which is an imaginary number. (There is, by definition, no square root of a negative number, because a negative times a negative is always positive.) By doing so, Dirac was able to combine quantum physics with relativity. In the process, not only did he receive the Nobel Prize, the neat violation was swept under the rug.[8]

Janis continues by noting that the "shared commitment" to the ongoing belief keeps the pressure to maintain the illusory status quo. Doubts are inhibited "to insiders as well as outsiders . . . [as each group member] comes to rely upon the group to provide . . . emotional support for coping with the stress of the decision-making."[9] If the decision of the group was clearly immoral or unethical, individual members may suffer from feelings of "shame, guilt, depression, and related emotional reaction associated with lowering of self-esteem."[10]

Concerning deviants, Janis noted that at first (in general) the group rallies to convert the renegade, but if the group repeatedly fails, communication diminishes and eventually the dissident is excluded. In the George Orwellian sense, "Groupthink . . . tend[s] to override critical thinking."[11]

26
Thought Transference

Dreams create favorable conditions for telepathy.
SIGMUND FREUD

We find groupthink occurring in our own field of psychology with regards to the subfield of parapsychology. Over fifty years ago J. B. Rhine established in rigorous experiments that thought transference can occur in card-reading tests, yet mainstream science and psychology have maligned him and/or dismissed his results. What is so interesting about this continual prejudice is not only that the evidence from a statistical standpoint is overwhelming but also that the experiments can easily be duplicated. All one needs is a deck of cards and a willing subject.

If the subject can guess the suit held up, that is, spades, hearts, diamonds, or clubs, to a degree that is statistically significant, this is ample proof that thought transference has occurred. For instance, in a run of 52 cards, blind chance demands that a subject would guess right roughly a quarter of the time, which translates into 13 hits. If the subject can *consistently* obtain a correct score of, say, 18 or more hits, this has significance from a simple statistical standpoint. Anecdotal evidence for telepathy in card reading can be seen just about every week on TV during the poker tournaments. Certainly intuition and card counting play a role, but I have seen quite a number of instances where one of the players guesses exactly the hand of an opponent. In my own case, way back when I was in high school, my bridge partner Ken and I were playing poker one night and he began betting wildly with a 7, 9, 10, and Jack. Sure enough he pulled the card that gave him the inside straight. Walking home, I said, "Ken, how could you bet so crazily with that hand?" and Ken replied, "I could hear the 8 of clubs calling me from the top of the deck."

Rhine's easy-to-do experiments, which began in the late 1920s, utilized a special deck of 25 cards designed by Karl Zenar, which contained five symbols,

(Star ★, Cross ✚, Square ❏, Squiggly lines ≈, Circle ○)

and five of each to make up the deck. Any score above 5 in a simple run of 25 would be a score above chance. Similar experiments had also been successfully performed by various British scientists such as Sir Oliver Lodge and Sir William Crookes in the late 1800s.

From these experiments, Rhine and others noticed a number of findings. For instance, if a person did not look at the cards, but simply shuffled the deck and then had someone guess, if a score was statistically significant, this would suggest that the information was derived directly from the cards themselves and not from another mind, since another mind did not know the answer. This would be *clairvoyance* or a *mind-to-matter link*. In fact, *telepathy* or a *mind-to-mind link* could be seen as a form of clairvoyance because the brain is made up of matter. Displacement effects were often discovered. In this instance, a person's guesses would match the pattern of the deck but be off usually by one card. This would suggest that the person's mind could somehow tune in to the layout of the deck, but the timing was off. Intuition apparently plays a role in these instances, as does the structure of the unconscious.

Another of Rhine's more intriguing results became known as negative ESP or negative psi. This is to say, a person does so poorly on the test, say none or only one correct, that this terrible result is also statistically significant! Chance demands that a person obtain a score of about 5 correct in a run of 25 because the odds are one in five that the person will be right. If a person consistently gets a score below this mean of 5, this too has significance. In general, Rhine discovered that *attitude* played a role. If people believed in ESP they tended to obtain a score *above* the mean and if they doubted the existence of ESP they tended to obtain scores *below* the mean. Believers are called sheep and non-believers are called goats.

In my own studies with Zenar cards in class, I try to create a "psi-condusive" environment, that is, I first discuss the topic of ESP in a positive light. Also, when I stare at the cards, I try to look beyond the cards so as to create a double image of the card in my brain. Essentially what I am doing is causing each eye to process the cards independently. Through the years I have had many individuals do exceedingly well. In one instance in 1983, *PM Magazine,* a national television show of the day, brought cameras into the class. During that run, I had one student get 11 cards correct and another student get 12 cards correct. This is an astonishing result in a class of twenty. We were definitely in a psi-conducive state that day.

In another class one student only guessed on 13 of the 25 cards. I told him, as I always do, to leave no blanks, but he refused to fill in the other cards. He didn't know the term, but he had guessed on what are called "confidence calls," that is, those times when he was somewhat sure of the answer. He got 6 cards right. Many students through the years have had 8 or more right. In another instance, a student got 11 correct out of 25. The following semester a student in the back of the class got 10 correct, which is also a very high score. I commented how well he did and he said, "Don't you remember last semester, I got 11 right?" I remembered the instance but not the student, because he was a very quiet person who was barely noticeable in the class.

An eye-opening, fascinating, sometimes frightening and occasionally hard-to-believe book.

. . . The Russians are actually investigating ESP and its use. The authors are utterly serious, so are the Russians.[1]

In 1975, I was teaching night courses at two separate colleges: the University of Rhode Island Extension Division and Providence College School of Continuing Education. A student from the URI class told me she had a dream of me talking to two priests. She did not know that I was teaching at Providence College, which is a Catholic school, and in fact, I had spoken to two priests the day before. Speaking to two priests in the same day was an extremely rare event for me. When we did a run of the ESP cards, she got 12 correct including 5 in a row correct. The odds of this in a single run are thousands to one that this is chance. The following year another student came to class claiming to be a witch. She often dressed in black or in leather. She, too, got 12 correct during our experiment including 5 correct in a row. In 2008, I had another student get 12 right including the last 10 right in a row!

Since there is a one in five chance of getting any one card correct, getting 5 correct in a row would be $1/5 \times 1/5 \times 1/5 \times 1/5 \times 1/5 = 1/3,725$ (i.e., 0.0037 level) where one out of twenty (0.5 level) or one out of a hundred (0.01 level) would be the standard measures for statistical significance. The calculation for getting 12 correct in a run of 25 is more complicated, but as you can see, 12 correct would be 7 correct above the mean, which is highly significant. One must also take into account that isolating one person from a class complicates and reduces the odds. The main point, however, is that the validity of telepathy in card reading experiments is easy to scientifically verify, yet the establishment continues to ignore this elephant in the room.

The full equation for calculating the entire run is as follows:

$$z = (x - pn)/\sqrt{(npq)}$$
$$z = (12 - 5)/\text{square root of } (25 \times 1/5 \times 4/5)$$
$$z = 7/\sqrt{4} = 7/2 = 3.5$$

where:

x = number correct

n = total number of cards

p = probability of getting one card right by chance

q = probability of getting one card wrong by
   chance
z = the z-score refers to placement on the bell-
   shaped curve away from the mean, which has
   a z-score of 0

Looking up the figure 3.5 on a z-score chart puts the odds of getting 12 right by chance in a run of 25 ESP cards at 0.0002 or 1 out of 5,000, when an extreme test for significance is at the 0.01 level, that is, 1 out of 100. The .05 level of significance is 1 out of 20.

The point of these stories is twofold:

1. Don't accept these figures at face value. Rather, I am suggesting that you, the reader, conduct these experiments yourself. They are simple to do, but they should be done with a positive attitude. Goats, please don't attempt this!

   The literature from the skeptics is staggering, accusing Rhine of using see-through cards, and so on. What is so exasperating about all of this is that these critics never conduct the tests themselves. This is not like climbing Mount Everest.

2. What is more important than continuing the tunnel vision tactic of doubting the thousands of positive studies done over the last century is to *turn our attention to the underlying neurological mechanisms involved.* Consider how much we can learn not only about the structure of brains, how they are physically constructed and interact, but also what we may learn about the structure of space-time and matter itself. Other countries such as Russia and China have been studying these phenomena for decades, and it is about time that the West caught up and took this field of study seriously.

Concerning dream telepathy experiments, in the 1970s Ullman, Krippner, and Vaughan established credible evidence in their classic book *Dream Telepathy.* Using EEG equipment to ascertain when their subjects were dreaming, these researchers would wake up their subjects during telepathy tests after they had completed a REM dream cycle. The images from the dreams of the receivers often corresponded in remarkable ways to the target "transmitted" by the sender. For example, during one night, the target was a picture of a Fabergé crystal Easter egg with paintings of two houses on it. The receiver dreamt of a house in one dream and two huge bald heads, which she described as "eggish" in another dream.[2]

In my own case, I have had numerous hits during dream telepathy experiments in my classes. My procedure is simple. A particular night is chosen, and on that night I stare at a randomly selected picture and think about each student in the class. The students, at the same time as they go to sleep, *command* their unconscious to "dream of what Professor Seifer is staring at." One night I stared at a picture of two rams colliding in a large computer ad promoting their increased "ram" capacity. One of my students, a nurse, dreamt that goats were running through the operating room. In another example I stared at a picture of a flower in a test-tube. A student dreamt about searching for flowers in a pharmacy. In a third instance, I stared at a picture of a bridge and a particular student dreamed that night of a bridge. The following semester, I stared at a picture of a boat, and that same student dreamt of a boat.

I have also experienced instances of spontaneous telepathy linked to dreams. For instance, on August 22, 2002, I had a vivid dream about bidding $200 for a piano that a person said had been used in a play. "I thought about where I could put it in the house. . . . I could fix it up, but really, there was no room, so it didn't seem worth it." A few hours later I was driving to a store just a few blocks away, and there on the road was a ramshackle piano, which was being offered for free to anyone who wanted to take it.

Another vivid instance occurred February 12, 2000. I had a dream about many starlets wanting to be with me. These included Sharon Stone, Winona Ryder, Michelle Pfeiffer, and Susan Sarandon. This was an unusual (and pleasant!) dream for me. When I awoke, I noticed in the newspaper that Roger Vadim had died. Vadim, the French film

Fig. 26.1. Roger Vadim and Brigitte Bardot

director, had been married to or had affairs with Brigitte Bardot, Catherine Deneuve, Jane Fonda, Jeanne Moreau, and Susan Sarandon. I will say, that as an adolescent, I was somewhat enamored with Brigitte Bardot. Her delightful movies used to play on television. This would be in the early 1960s. Perhaps this old cathexis created a bond with Vadim.

One way or another, these types of activities have gone on in my life for many years. The secret is to keep a dream diary. One of the most astonishing examples of thought transference occurred to me in February of 1976. On February 15, I had a dream about a roll of Mercury-head dimes all dated 1927. (These were the dimes that were minted before the Roosevelt dimes, ca. 1916–1945, and I do have a collection of these dimes. However, to my knowledge, I had never dreamed about Mercury dimes before that night.) During my next night class, I lectured about the significance of the dream from a psychoanalytic point of view. After class, a student approached to tell me that he "wasn't going to say anything, but" he had sold a roll of Mercury-head dimes that very weekend! This fellow kept a log of incoming calls, writing down the exact times. At 2:17 on February 13, he received a call from a man interested in the coins. And on the following day, Saturday, at 9:27

the fellow called back agreeing to the purchase price. Note the extreme precision of the event with the subject, the Mercury-head dimes, and the numbers, specifically 1, 9, 2, 7, all matching.

The subject of telepathy, and specifically the work of J. B. Rhine and Ullman, Krippner, and Vaughan, has been all but ignored by the scientific community because of the strong antagonism mainstream scientists have toward serious consideration for studying *any* form of ESP.

This is unfortunate for a variety of reasons, foremost being that if telepathy is discounted at the outset, how could the neurological basis for the phenomena ever be uncovered? That is the point. Everything else is a smokescreen. Andrija Puharich speculated in his masterwork *Beyond Telepathy* that one could start with a simple resonance model of DBP (direct brain perception). This would explain the numerous instances of telepathy seen between twins including twins reared apart. If the process of thought involves some type of vibration, which of course it does, then the resonance model is an excellent starting point, as it is in accord with the fundamental basis of simple physics. An example of this would be identical tuning forks placed in a room of different-size tuning forks. If one of these is rapped and caused to vibrate, the other one shaped just like it will vibrate in synchrony.

One of the more stunning analogous examples of the power of the resonance effect can be seen in the old classic Memorex audiotape machine commercial whereby singer Ella Fitzgerald hits a particular note and thereby shatters a wineglass. The question the advertisement raises, "Is it Ella Fitzgerald or Memorex?" became one of the most well-known commercial slogans of all time.

It is simply indisputable that "thought is vibration," and if that is so, then by definition resonance effects between brain/minds can take place. This simple law of physics provides a fundamental mechanism for beginning to understand this complex phenomenon. With our new technologies for looking into the brain (e.g., the MRI), it is imperative for the scientific community to step up to the plate and begin once again to study this exciting and fertile field of research.

One of the most compelling examples supporting this model con-

Fig. 26.2. The Jim twins. Note similar tree stools.

cerns the Jim twins. These two identical twins, who by coincidence had the same first name, were separated at birth and raised by non-biological parents. The two Jims did not know that they were twins. Both Jims married a Linda and divorced these Lindas to marry women named Betty. They named their sons James Allen and James Alan. Both had dogs named Toy and both drove Chevrolets, smoked Salem cigarettes, and vacationed on the same Florida beach. They also suffered headaches at about the same time in their life, made doll furniture in their basements, and put circular benches around the trees in their backyard. To me, the most obvious explanation is some form of telepathy. One twin falls in love with a Linda and this emotion, through a form of resonance, becomes implanted into the brain and psyche of the other twin. He therefore seeks out a Linda to fulfill the feeling. One names his dog Toy, and this name is implanted into the brain of the other twin, and so on. Both twins also died on the same day.

Keep in mind that there are numerous other instances of amazing coincidence between twins. On more than one occasion, when the twins separated at birth finally meet, they find they are wearing the same outfits. In one case, both female twins had seven rings on their fingers. In another instance of identical female twins, one twin experienced the pregnancy cramps occurring in the other twin. Again, a simple resonance model seems the most likely mechanism for information transfer. In my instance, since I owned a set of Mercury-head dimes, I would be the one more likely to pick up the sale of such dimes by one of my students because my brain is already prewired to receive this kind of information. Telepathy occurs most frequently to people closely attuned to each other, either by blood, love, or similar interests.

Puharich continued his speculation by studying the molecular arrangement of the neurotransmitters active during various psi-conducive states, for the senders, adrenaline, and receivers, noradrenaline. Since telepathy often occurs during the REM cycle when the subject is sleeping and dreaming, one could begin the study there with EEGs and MRIs of the brainwave states of senders and receivers during the process of dreaming.

The term "telepathy" for "shared feelings" was coined by F. W. H. Myers in the 1880s. Ullman, Krippner, and Vaughan note that telepathy often occurs when the targets chosen contain emotionally charged data. It is well known that telepathy often occurs during crises. For instance, the mother of one of my friends, when a child, was ironing one day when she suddenly knew that something had happened to her father, and this was so; he had been in a car accident.

> Human learning presupposes a specific social nature and a [neurological] process by which children grow into the intellectual life of those around them.
>
> LEV VYGOTSKY

Freud had suggested that telepathy might occur when information from the primary process of the unconscious was transferred to the secondary process, which is more closely linked to the awareness function. What is important to realize is that human brains and psyches are open systems.

27
Occult Schools, Avatars, and Seed Men

Ouspensky, an ardent Gurdjieffian, discusses the role of the occult, which he calls the esoteric, as a repository of secret knowledge. In his text *New Model of the Universe,* he writes,

> In order to understand the possibility of the existence of the inner circle and the part played by the esoteric schools in the life of humanity, it is necessary to be in possession of such knowledge concerning the essential nature of man and his destiny in the world as is not possessed by modern science. . . . According to the idea of esotericism, as applied to history . . . no civilization ever begins of itself. There exists no evolution, which begins accidentally and proceeds mechanically. Only degeneration and decay can proceed mechanically. . . .
>
> Esoteric schools are hidden from the eyes of ordinary humanity; but the influence of schools persists uninterruptedly in history. . . . Esoteric knowledge can be given only to those who seek, only to those who have been seeking it with a certain amount of consciousness.[1]

Ouspensky states further that esoteric knowledge does not have to be found in secret societies. It does, however, involve the transmission of knowledge to an inner circle of humanity who believes that (1) things have an inner meaning and (2) things are connected but only appear to be separated.

275

Knowledge is present to all, but they people endowed with the ability to see behind the veil can appreciate esoteric knowledge. "The biblical story of the Golden Calf is an illustration . . . of how the people of the outer circle behave at the very time when the people of the inner circle are striving to help them."[2]

Astrologer Dane Rudhyar suggests that esoteric schools, which he calls "occult brotherhoods,"[3] inevitably tie into other dimensions and therefore incorporate the idea of extraterrestrials. Rudhyar suggests that certain individuals on Earth, who are often referred to as avatars one way or another, have within their beings knowledge that can lead a culture to transcendence.

> What we are witnessing in our twentieth century and to a lesser extent this occurred also towards the close of the last century is the coming of human beings who incorporate within themselves the seed harvest of the culture of the race or nation in which they have been born, and in some creative manner who release this harvest to those who, by dharmic connection, will become attracted to, or fascinated by it. They are seed men.[4]

I would suggest that individuals like J. B. Rhine, Ullman, Krippner, and Vaughan, Lobsang Rampa, Gurdjieff, P. D. Ouspensky, Uri Geller, Sigmund Freud, Carl Jung, Rudolf Steiner, and the Dalai Lama fall into this category.

CULTS

Whether Hale-Bopp has a "companion" or not is irrelevant from our perspective. However, its arrival is joyously very significant to us at "Heaven's Gate." The joy is that our Older Member in the Evolutionary Level Above Human (the "Kingdom of Heaven") has made it clear to us that Hale-Bopp's approach is the "marker" we've been waiting for—the time for the arrival of the spacecraft from the Level Above Human to take us home to "Their World"—in the literal Heavens.

MARSHALL APPLEGATE, HEAVEN'S GATE LEADER, SAID SHORTLY
BEFORE HE AND THIRTY-EIGHT OTHER MEMBERS COMMITTED
SUICIDE AS THE COMET HALE-BOPP PASSED BY EARTH, MARCH 1997

In Evans's text *Cults of Unreason,* he sees cults as "stop-gaps"[5] for people in society, ways for them to deal with life's mysteries and also the unsettling feeling associated with the rapid pace of our times. "These gaps, we will have to agree, need plugging. And if science and present-day philosophy . . . are unprepared to offer help, while the great world religions offer only outdated, time-worn and implausible concepts, then the field is ripe as never before for . . . pseudoscientific philosophies, quasi-technological cults and new messiahs to emerge. They are in fact already here."[6]

Evans lists as cult figures: L. Ron Hubbard, the founder of Scientology; Tuesday Lobsang Rampa, a reputed Tibetan lama and prolific author purportedly residing in the body of a British fellow; ufologist George Adamski, whose "encounter in the Mojave desert with a long-haired Venusian wearing dark glasses and ski pants with whom he engaged in telepathic contact . . . reads like a desperate travesty of the most simple-minded science fiction";[7] Wilhelm Reich, renegade psychoanalyst who claimed to have discovered the secret force of the universe (i.e., orgone energy); and Gurdjieff, "a fiercely moustached Russian Greek [who supposedly] . . . offered some important slice of Wisdom of the East to Western man."[8]

Evans wrote that many cult figures have an association with higher states of consciousness, flying saucers, and a "preoccupation with gadgetry of arguable practical value."[9] The Scientologists, for instance, promulgated an "E-meter" to obtain through biofeedback special states of consciousness; Reich had both an "orgone accumulator—for obtaining and generating the secret universal life force, and also a cloudbuster—for producing rain and shooting down or dematerializing UFOs."[10]

The Evans text predominantly looks at these individuals in a negative way. The cult figures are described as false messiahs, although they "do their level best to fill a serious vacuum caused by the rejection of religion and the attempt by modern science to deny the realm of the unknown."[11] In fact, if one were to study the lives and positive effects these people have had on the world, as I have done in a number of treatises on Lobsang Rampa, Wilhelm Reich, and Gurdjieff, one could discern many positive contributions. Scientology, for instance, has helped actor Tom Cruise, a staunch supporter, and also helped train Ingo Swann,[12] a man who has been repeatedly tested with positive results for remote viewing by the American Society for Psychical Research, the CIA, and Stanford Research Institute. Wilhelm Reich has written one of the most important textbooks in psychoanalysis, *Character Analysis,* which attempts to explain how neuroses can root themselves in repressed areas of the body. Lobsang Rampa has penned over a dozen treatises on higher states of consciousness, which are not only entertaining but also contain much key wisdom not easily found elsewhere in the literature. And the Gurdjieff teachings on the nature of the mind have helped to spawn numerous beneficial treatises in the field, including an approach to psychotherapy known as psychosynthesis developed by the Italian psychoanalyst Roberto Assagioli. Gurdjieff's theory places the will at the center of the personality instead of the Freudian unconscious. For some reason, the will as an important component of the psyche is almost never discussed in texts on psychology. Evans hypothesizes that cults exist in order to discover the Holy Grail, the supposed secret behind the universe. It is for the reader to discover which so-called cult figures are essentially bogus philosophers and which have something important to say.

Fig. 27.1. Gurdjieff in Washington, ca. 1935

28
Gurdjieff (1874?–1949)

Man has real individuality inherent in him; it is his own birthright, his birthright, which he has sold for the mess of pottage of false personality.

C. S. NOTT,
TEACHINGS OF GURDJIEFF: A PUPIL'S JOURNAL

Sometime in the 1870s, midway between the Black and Caspian Seas, 250 miles from the cradle of civilization, Georgi Ivanovitch Gurdjieff was born. This was in Alexandropol, a nineteenth-century city in Armenia, melting pot for Persians, Russians, Assyrians, Christians, Sufis, Jews, Muslims, and other peoples. Gurdjieff himself was descended from the Russians on his mother's side and from Cappadocian Greeks on his father's. The latter were a race of people who could trace their lineage back over eight thousand years. The young Georgi knew his father as a carpenter, but Mr. Gurdjieff had been a wealthy shepherd until a famine destroyed his entire flock. He told his son stories of Atlantis and legends of higher knowledge, and he recommended that in life one should provide for a happy old age. In volume I of *Beelzebub's Tales to His Grandson*, Gurdjieff describes his first great teaching, which came from his grandmother.

When my grandmother—may she attain the kingdom of heaven—
was dying, my mother took me to her bedside. . . . [She] placed her

dying left hand on my head and in a whisper, yet very distinctly, said: "Eldest of my grandsons! Listen and always remember my strict injunction. In life, never do as others do. . . ." And just from this it began that in my entirety a "something" arose which I should now call an "irresistible urge" to do things not as others do them.[1]

Gurdjieff is a complex subject, not easily categorized. Thus it helps to keep in mind that as powerful a thinker as he was, he was also a flawed individual, at times a rogue with large libidinal appetites, a spectacular sense of humor, and the ability, much like Thomas Edison, to put people on. Coming from a man of great personal magnetism and a philosopher of serious purpose, Gurdjieff's teachings remain as an important compilation of ancient sacred knowledge combined with his own inventive philosophy. His second "great teaching" can be found in this same allegorical, satirical, and sometimes imponderable three-volume treatise, of which the first draft was completed about 1928. It was obtained from the mysterious "Mr. Alan Kardec" during an "absolutely secret séance" whereby the great Kardec came in touch with one of the "chief life principles of the Great Universe." The weighty dictum, which should be memorized, was as follows, "When you go on a spree, go the whole hog, including the postage."[2]

Gurdjieff's second book, *Meetings with Remarkable Men,*[3] is much more readable and remindful of, perhaps, a novel by Mark Twain. Made into a motion picture directed by Peter Brook, unfortunately the film in no way captures the significance of the text. In *Meetings,* Gurdjieff discusses his wanderings in Egypt, Tibet, and Mongolia in search for the highest states of consciousness. Along the way, the reader becomes enmeshed in many of his fantastic exploits.

A rug merchant and also sly businessman, Gurdjieff describes how he made his first fortune, having set up "The American Traveling Workshop" in northern Persia, in Ashkhabad. This city is now the capital of Turkmenistan, located about two hundred miles from the Caspian Sea. In his shop, he promised to fix and repair any appliance, no matter what. And this became a highly successful endeavor.

The styles of the day were changing, and in one instance, the long-line corset was being replaced by just the bra. When some of the local ladies would stop by to have the whalebones removed to update their undergarments, this gave Gurdjieff an idea. "Hurrying off to all the shops in the city," he purchased hundreds of the long-line corsets at highly reduced prices, because the shopowners were glad to get rid of the obsolete inventory. "However, I did not stop at this," he said. And so Gurdjieff sent out buyers to "all the towns along the Central Asiatic Railway" and obtained the entire outmoded inventory, over six thousand corsets, from such places as Bukhara, Chardzhou, Kizil-Arvat, Krasnovodsk, Merv, Samarkand, and Tashkent. Then seamstresses were hired to cut the lower part off and resew the bottom of the bra with fancy lace. Now he had the "latest fashion from Paris," which he resold to the same merchants for a hefty profit.[4]

Traveling with a group of truth seekers, Gurdjieff describes numerous escapades, including the riding of camels in Egypt and the purchasing of stilts to travel through sandstorms in the Gobi Desert. Finally, after years of searching, he came upon a secret school called the Sarmoung Brotherhood, a group allegedly founded 4,500 years ago in Babylon. J. G. Bennett writes in his classic biography *Gurdjieff: Making a New World* that this school was linked to the Masters of Wisdom, a branch of the Sufis called Khwajagan. These were the builders of society, realistic people who believed in one supreme spiritual force and also in individualized access to this force. Influenced by Zoroastrian tradition and Mithraic and Chaldean teachings, these were the first monotheists, establishing their own culture thousands of years before the Hebrews. Their teachings are a basis for both the Judeo-Christian religions as well as Islamic and Buddhist traditions. Bennett summarizes the essence of their teachings:[5]

1. Be present at every breath. Remember yourself always in all situations.
2. Keep your intention before you at every step you take.
3. Your journey is toward your homeland. Remember that you are

traveling from the world of appearances to the world of reality.

4. Solitude in a crowd. Learn not to identify yourself with anything whatsoever.
5. Remember your friend God. Let the prayer of your tongue be the prayer of your heart.
6. Struggle with all alien thoughts.
7. Be constantly aware of the divine presence.

THE WORK

There are two kinds of doing—mechanical, automatic doing, and doing according to your real wish. Take some small thing, which you are not able to do, but what you wish to do. Make that your God. Let nothing interfere. Only strive to fulfill your wish. If you succeed in that small thing, I will give you a bigger task.

GURDJIEFF

After twenty years of searching, Gurdjieff returned to the West, reestablishing himself in Moscow in 1912 in order to teach the secret wisdom he had acquired. Three years later, the writer and mathematician P. D. Ouspensky, himself a world traveler and seeker of higher knowledge, became one of his students. Ouspensky describes his first meetings with the elusive Gurdjieff in the definitive work *In Search of the Miraculous:*

We arrived at a small café in a noisy though not central street. I saw a man of oriental type, no longer young, with a black moustache and piercing eyes, who astonished me first of all because he seemed to be disguised and completely out of keeping with the place and atmosphere. I was still full of impressions of the East. And this man with the face of an Indian raja . . . in a black overcoat, velvet collar and black bowler hat produced the strange unexpected, and almost alarming impression of a man poorly disguised, the sight of whom embarrasses you because you see he is not what he pretends to be and yet you have to speak and behave as though you did not see it.[6]

In one of their early meetings, Gurdjieff summarizes the scope and intent of his entire teaching:

> "Have you ever thought about the fact that all peoples themselves are machines?" G. asked. . . . "Men are machines and nothing but mechanical actions can be expected of machines."
>
> "Very well," I said. "But are there no people who are not machines?"
>
> "It may be that there are," said G. "Only not those people you see. And you do not know them. That is what I want you to understand. . . . But there is a possibility of ceasing to be a machine. It is this we must think of and not about the different kinds of machines that exist."[7]

29

The Behaviorists

The problem is not whether machines think, but whether men do.

B. F. Skinner

In one sweeping statement, Gurdjieff both accepts and repudiates the field of behaviorism, which suggests, really demands, that men are machines, that they operate essentially automatically in response to rewards and punishments. The seeds of behaviorism go all the way back to Aristotle's idea of the tabula rasa and then to the works of John Locke and Thomas Hobbes (see chapter 2). All ideas stem from outside impressions and reflections of such impressions. Radical behaviorists John Watson and B. F. Skinner who followed went one bold step further to suggest that the mind itself was unimportant to the field of psychology, because all human action could be explained by simply studying what a scientist could see, that is, overt behavior. The father of behaviorism, Ivan Pavlov, however, was not that obsessed with outlawing the works of the psychoanalysts and other mind psychologists. In fact, Pavlov felt that higher cognitive functions stemmed from a hierarchical arrangement of reflexive neuronal action.

Pavlov's famous work on classical conditioning with his salivating dogs suggests that all learning stems from simple reflex action: a stimulus generates a response (S-R). What we call thinking evolved from this S-R procedure.

If we liken this idea to the modern computer, it is possible that Pavlov may indeed have been right. Either a neuron fires or it doesn't. It is either on or off. In the same sense, all complex activities of the computer—its ability to read e-mail, generate graphics, beam out music, perform complex mathematical processes, create animated figures, change recorded voice to typed copy, animate robots that can destroy other robots or mow the lawn, fly airplanes, send a rocket ship to the moon, and so forth—are based on two simple decisions: either a circuit is on or it is off. The only thing a computer chip listens to, ultimately, is a binary code, 1 or 0, on or off.

Take, for instance, this sentence. It can be converted to numbers.

A = 1	H = 8	O = 15	V = 22
B = 2	I = 9	P = 16	W = 23
C = 3	J = 10	Q = 17	X = 24
D = 4	K = 11	R = 18	Y = 25
E = 5	L = 12	S = 19	Z = 26
F = 6	M = 13	T = 20	
G = 7	N = 14	U = 21	

So the word TAKE becomes 20-1-11-5, FOR becomes 6-15-18, and so forth. Now, to go to the next step, the numbers that we use in our base ten system, 1, 2, 3, 4, 5, 6, 7, 8, 9, 10 can also be transcribed into a binary code, so that the entire alphabet could be transformed to just zeros and ones. Thus TAKE becomes 10100-1-1100-101, FOR becomes 110-1111-10010, and so on.

Base 10	Binary Code
0	0
1	1
2	10
3	11
4	100
5	101
6	110
7	111
8	1000
9	1001
10	1010

An easy way to understand this is to see that a base 10 system goes up by the square of 10 to 100, 1000, 10,000, 100,000, and so on. The same is true for a base 2 system: from 2 to 4, to 8 to 16, 32, 64, and so on. So, where 10^2 is 100 in base 10, 2^2 is 100 in base 2. Where 10^3 is 1,000 in base 10, 2^3 is 1,000 in base 2, and all the in-between numbers are slotted in, in a similar way.

$$10^1 = 10 \qquad 2^1 = 10$$
$$10^2 = 100 \qquad 2^2 = 100$$
$$10^3 = 1000 \qquad 2^3 = 1000$$
$$10^4 = 10,000 \qquad 2^4 = 10,000$$

In this way, the alphabet of twenty-six letters can be converted to just 1s and 0s, and all larger numbers can also be transcribed as such. The bar codes on books, food store items, and so forth are all based on this binary system. Essentially what this means is that if we look at the brain as simply a complex arrangement of neurons, then indeed, Pavlov's idea bears merit. All higher cognitive functions can be broken down into a hierarchical arrangement of neuronal S-R events. Either a neuron fires or it doesn't, just like a computer chip. This concept of mental complexity was completely ignored by Watson and Skinner, and worse, their idea of eliminating the mind from the field of psychology altogether actually became a leading motif in a major, if not the dominating, branch of American psychology throughout most of the twentieth century.

Pavlov had trained a dog to salivate to the sound of a bell in three steps.

1. An Unconditioned Stimulus ⇒ an Unconditioned Response

MEAT   SALIVATING

(automatic)   (automatic)

The aroma of the meat causes the dog to automatically salivate.

2. An Unconditioned Stimulus + a Conditioned Stimulus ⇒ an Unconditioned Response

MEAT   BELL   SALIVATING

The meat with a bell ringing causes the dog to salivate.

3. The Conditioned Stimulus ⇒ a Conditioned Response

BELL   SALIVATING

(learned)   (learned)

Now the bell causes the dog to salivate.

Watson liked to think he had uncovered the science of human behavior. Therefore he could shorten the terms of these steps to make them look like a mathematical certainty:

$$1.\ US \Rightarrow UR$$
$$2.\ US + CS \Rightarrow UR$$
$$3.\ CS \Rightarrow CR$$

Simply stated, by ringing the bell every time the dog was fed, the dog became conditioned to salivate to the sound of the bell, because this sound had been associated with his desire to eat. Pavlov argues that the dog *learned* to salivate to the sound of the bell, and further, that all forms of learning operate in the same fashion, as an extension of the reflex action and the use of association. The important thing to remember is that the bell is neutral, that is, Pavlov could have gotten the dog to salivate to anything, the sound of a can opener, the sound of a refrigerator opening, the flash of a yellow light, the waving of the Russian flag. Anything. That is the point. And based on this simple process, all animals, including humans, can be conditioned to learn and operate much like machines. This became known as classical conditioning or respondant conditioning.

Based on the work of Edward Thorndike, Skinner reversed this process to achieve astonishing results in training animals, and this was called operant conditioning. Where Pavlov fed the dog and then it salivated, Skinner waited for the animal to do a desired response *first,* and then the animal was rewarded. For instance, if you feed the dog first, it will not jump through the hoop. It must jump through the hoop, and then you feed it. And in the same sense, if the boss pays his salesman *before* he sells his cars, the salesman will not be motivated to sell very many cars. The trick is to reward the worker *after* he performs a required task. This idea was expanded to what became called schedules of reinforcement, where rewards, punishment, and negative reinforcement techniques could be implemented. Reward: time-and-a-half for overtime. Negative reinforcement (and punishment): docking pay when someone is late; and so on. Like Pavlov's dogs (technically like Skinner's pigeons) we all jump through the hoop so that we can get paid later.

So it seems that Skinner's idea of reversing the process to respond first and then reward later was the better plan. However, this was not the entire story. John Watson, who had taught at the University of Chicago and Johns Hopkins (ca. 1910–20), was also editor of *Psychology Review,* and because of that, he gained great control over the future direction of the field of American psychology. Since he was at odds with such diverse psychologists as William James and Sigmund Freud, a great bifurcation occurred in the field. For instance, when I was a graduate student at the University of Chicago in the early 1970s, the antipathy on campus between Freudian psychoanalyst Bruno Bettelheim and Skinnerian Israel Goldiamond was legendary. Where Goldiamond wanted to treat stutterers by shocking their tongue when they stuttered, that is by using aversive therapy as Watson might do, Bettelheim was revolted by this procedure because it ensured that such people could never be cured of the root cause of their problem. Yes, maybe the stuttering might be better controlled, but Bettelheim understood that if the stuttering was ultimately caused by some psychoanalytic action, say a repressed hatred toward one of the parents, the energy involved with the symptom would simply shift to some other area of behavior.

Although John Watson made a career out of arrogantly dismissing such things as Freudian psychology, this did not stop the married professor from having a well-publicized affair. The irony of course was that Freud's theories could much better explain Watson's libidinal activity than any behavioral model. Watson was fired from the university. Fortunately for him he made his way to New York City where he enjoyed a new career in the field of advertising.

What Watson did essentially was to replace Pavlov's meat with attractive women and replace Pavlov's bell with a name brand. By using this simple procedure, that is, by pairing sex with a product, Watson made a fortune for himself and revolutionized the field of advertising. Note that a powerful stimulus—usually sex, but also animals, humor, patriotism, and so forth—can be used to sell any product. That is the key. The American flag can sell Toyota cars, cowboys on horses can sell Marlboro cigarettes, Britney Spears can sell Pepsi-Cola, talking frogs can sell Budweiser beer. Hundreds of billions of dollars are invested every year in the simple three-step program set up by Pavlov outlined on page 287.

1. Unconditioned Stimulus   ⇒   Unconditioned Response
      (automatic)   (automatic)
  SEX, PATRIOTISM, HUMOR ⇒ GETS ATTENTION OF VIEWER
          US   ⇒   UR

A powerful stimulus will gain the attention of the viewer.

2. Unconditioned Stimulus + Conditioned Stimulus ⇒ Unconditioned Response
     SEX + PRODUCT   ⇒   GAINS ATTENTION OF VIEWER
   HUMOR + PRODUCT   ⇒   GAINS ATTENTION OF VIEWER
      US + CS   ⇒   UR

Pairing a powerful stimulus (US) with the product (CS) occurs in the second stage. This still creates an unconditioned response (UR).

3. Conditioned Stimulus   ⇒   Conditioned Response
    (learned stimulus)   (learned response)
  PRODUCT GAINS ATTENTION OF VIEWER

In the final stage, the viewer tends to purchase the product that has been paired with the powerful stimulus.

The Mighty Duck: Aflac is boosting sales and name recognition with its ubiquitous duck, and now the marketing icon is also reaching audiences in Japan.

GOLIATH.ECNEXT.COM

LIFE/HEALTH: MARKETING

For example:

1. DUCK $\Rightarrow$ GAINS ATTENTION OF VIEWER
2. DUCK + AFLAC INSURANCE $\Rightarrow$ GAINS ATTENTION OF VIEWER
3. AFLAC INSURANCE $\Rightarrow$ GAINS ATTENTION OF VIEWER

Aflac Insurance uses funny duck commercials to gain the attention of the viewer. Geiko Insurance uses a gecko who speaks with a British accent. In both cases, once these humorous commercials were created, the sales of insurance in these companies increased dramatically.

For cigarettes, there is the Marlboro man. Marlboro ads use a variety of powerful unconditioned stimuli. Besides the handsome cowboy, there is usually a horse or group of horses in their ads, as well as mountains, a stream, cowboy boots, and a cowboy hat. Marlboro is using such symbols as the perfect man, sex, the archetypal cowboy, horses, and nostalgia for the Old West, when men were men, when life was less complicated, to sell their product.

Many beer commercials use pretty girls. Foreign car companies often take highly American symbols to sell their product. Toyota often has either an American flag or a banner with red, white, and blue. Toyota also uses parades and, in the past, famous baseball players to sell their cars. Subaru tended to use the American farm as a backdrop. Ace Hardware used Suzanne Somers, an attractive blonde woman, as their symbol.

It needs to be remembered that in this view, the individual mind is unimportant to controlling behavior. It makes no difference what a person thinks. In advertising, which uses classical conditioning, simple powerful stimuli are used. The stimulus, green gecko with a British accent, yields a response, laughter and attention of the viewer. To be more specific, name recognition. Gecko/Geiko, Duck/Aflac. In the case of Skinner's operant conditioning, which is essentially the reverse of classical conditioning, the subject must perform a task first before he gets a reward; if the worker doesn't perform his job, he doesn't get paid. Ergo, he performs his job.

There were many theoreticians who were appalled by this simplification of human activity. In fact, the humanistic psychologists uncovered a flaw to the idea of removing the mind from the equation, because one *needed* a mind not only to come up with Skinner's theory but also to create the goals necessary for the animal to achieve in order to get rewarded. Said another way, Skinner had used his mind to come up with a theory that stated that the mind was unimportant in explaining human behavior. It was an inherent contradiction.

Another problem the behaviorists ran into was that not all people respond the same way to reward systems. Take, for instance, the starving artist. He gets punished for his activity because he cannot sell his product, yet on he goes writing his books, painting his paintings. It seems some people are motivated by intrinsic rewards, not extrinsic ones. The realm of dreams of course, also, could not be explained by the behavioral paradigm, nor could complex mental activity. Finally, after nearly a century of Skinnerian dominance, a new field called cognitive behaviorism has come into being. Many of the rules outlined by Pavlov, Watson, and Skinner remain sacrosanct, but mental attitudes are now included.

30

Tony Robbins on the Cause and Cure of Depression

Whether you are happy or not is not a question of whether the happiness is there. It's there inside of you at levels of intensity and depths you have never dreamed of, but you've got to open the spout. You've got to let what's in you, out. You've got to realize that you are at one with the source. You've got to remember that there is nothing outside of you that is going to create it for you. . . . The only way to really have this ongoing happiness is to change your focus, to change some of your core beliefs, to realize you do not have to do anything to be happy. You do not have to be responsible to something to be happy. You don't have to achieve to be happy. You can happily achieve. You don't have to choose between the two.

TONY ROBBINS, 1993

A core problem with the Watsonian/Skinnerian behavioral model was that the observant scientist can readily see that most animals do not blindly respond to stimuli. Anyone who has ever owned a cat knows that if she is not interested in a particular kind of food, she won't eat it—even if she is hungry. In fact, I have a theory about humans, cats, and dogs. My belief is that humans train dogs and cats train humans. Partly I'm teasing, but I think it is fair to say that our pets do not blindly eat and act like robots. They connive, and, depending on their level of intelligence, do things in such a way to get what they want. Their wheels are turning. As much as we try to train them, they try to train us.

As an exercise in my advanced psychology classes, I will ask the students the following question: "How many of you would move to North Dakota for one full year under the following conditions: You can do whatever you want, you can work, whatever, as long as you do not leave the state for that year, and if you do that for one full year, I will give you a check for $100,000 after taxes."

Many of the students will agree to this, but some will not. The point of the question is that the same stimulus will not always yield the same response. If, for instance, a person is earning $180,000/year, they would be taking a cut in pay to do this deal. Obviously, they would most likely decide not to take the deal. Other people will not go because they do not want to leave their family, their house, and so on.

What a number of psychologists began to understand was that in between stimulus and response there is a mental activity taking place.

$$\text{Stimulus} \Rightarrow \text{Cognitive Appraisal} \Rightarrow \text{Response}$$

When you read the North Dakota offer, it was something you considered. No matter how fast the reaction, some thought had to take place. Then the deal was either accepted or rejected. Likewise, in feeding your pet, his or her response—even just to gobble down the food—might be more rapid, but it is not a blind response. Other examples that contradicted the prevailing behavioral paradigm were things like latent or vicarious learning, that is, learning by watching others, delayed responses, and behaviors that go on even when a person is being punished.

Why is it that some people get upset in bumper-to-bumper traffic and other people do not? Obviously, attitude plays a big role. Compare, for instance, how different Robert De Niro and Woody Allen might respond in a traffic dispute. Their reactions will differ because their personalities are different.

Some people's baseline belief structures may be irrational. What type of lens does a particular person see the world through? An extreme example of this point is 9/11. Al-Qaeda was able to recruit eighteen men willing to go on a suicide mission, in part because they were under the belief that they would become martyrs on the earth, and go to a heaven where there would be seventy-two virgins waiting for them after death if they died while killing the infidel.

For more everyday examples, think about people who complain or criticize all the time, misers who must split a restaurant bill down to the penny, or people who seem to be chronically unhappy.

Two psychologists who have emphasized the importance of the cognitive aspect in influencing behavior are Albert Ellis and Aaron Beck.[1] Ellis suggests that people's irrational assumptions are often the cause of behavioral problems, but the situation is compounded because oftentimes these assumptions go unnoticed. Ellis has listed a number of "musts" that people set up for themselves, which is often the cause of their problem. "I must be loved by everyone who knows me," "I must get an A on every test or I am not a good person," and so on.

Beck expands on this premise by suggesting that people set themselves up for failure by using automatic nonrational thoughts such as "I never do anything right." Beck points out that common statements such as these are obviously incorrect, as all people do *some* things right, but these kinds of automatic thoughts go on all the time. The end result is that people essentially program themselves to fail or feel bad about themselves.

"This always happens to me" is another example. Magnifying the negative and minimizing the positive are additional maladaptive thinking styles Beck discusses. For example, let us say it is Marley's birthday. She receives sixteen birthday cards, but she does not get one from Uncle Errol, her favorite relative. She may become very upset because she has discounted the positive, the sixteen other people that were considerate enough to send her a card, and she magnified the negative, the one person who forgot.

Beck points out that people play entire scenarios in their head, and then they act on those scenarios, which may or may not reflect reality. Suppose old Uncle Errol actually went out and got Marley a birthday card and put the wrong zip code on the envelope. Marley had only looked at the situation in a negative way and became unhappy, when in fact, her assumption was completely faulty. The key is that people like Marley do this all the time as a habitual way of dysfunctional thinking.

Perfectionists also set themselves up. The A+ student, for instance, may go into a depression if he or she gets a B+ on an exam. Such students think of themselves as no good and a failure because they magnified the negative and discounted the positive. Another trap is to personalize everything. Some people, for example, take responsibility for actions they have no control over. Let us say that a well-loved baseball player strikes out at a key moment. If a fan somehow blames himself for this event, this would be an instance of irrational thinking. Getting overly upset if a local team loses is another example.

Beck has identified what he calls the cognitive triad of depression—I am no good, the world is no good, the future is horrible—as the cause of most people's depression.

Both Beck and Ellis suggest reevaluating maladaptive thinking patterns so that the person is made aware of the nonrational reasons for his or her unhappiness. These psychologists suggest identifying negative or dysfunctional automatic thoughts that tend to inhabit the psyches of the modern-day individual.

Another cognitive psychologist who has elaborated on these ideas is Tony Robbins, the infomercial guru. Robbins has created a series of "PowerTalk" tapes that are filled with excellent advice on the topics of positive thinking and optimum states of consciousness.

Robbins states that *each of us is responsible for our own present state of consciousness*. The way we feel, as Beck and Ellis would also say, is not due to outside circumstances but to how we respond to these circumstances. Take, for instance, two Vietnam veterans who have lost an arm and a leg. One ends up selling pencils on the street corner; another becomes a U.S. Senator, Max Cleland. Some people "who could not manage their state," Robbins suggests, were Marilyn Monroe, Elvis Presley, and John Belushi. All three achieved tremendous success in their respective fields of acting, music, and comedy, but all three died at young ages because of their inability to achieve an inner sense of happiness to correspond with the material wealth and outer success they had attained.

It is one thing to intellectualize and agree that "we create our own reality." It is quite another thing to viscerally recognize how profound this idea really is.

Robbins uses as an example a very unhappy lady who had approached him at one of his seminars. She was depressed, he suggested, for the following reasons:

1. Her carriage: she had her shoulders down and walked at a lethargic pace.
2. Her facial expression: she was frowning.
3. She was creating negative images in her mind.

Now, certainly there are many people who are depressed for legitimate reasons, and neither he nor I would suggest that these people deny the natural emotion when it arises at times when it should. But too many people are depressed because of programming and ultimately because they make themselves depressed. By doing the three things above, Robbins would argue, anybody would become depressed.

His cure for depression is simply to reverse the process:

1. Put a *smile* on your face every day, whether you are happy or not. It is Robbins's contention that the very act of smiling will send messages to the brain to inform the brain that it is happy. This is a neurophysiological process that supercedes psycho/emotional action.
2. Put your shoulders back and walk with a sense of purpose. Robbins suggests pretending you have a cape attached to your shoulders and to walk like you are king of the world.
3. Most importantly, put *happy* pictures in your mind.

People who are depressed had to work hard at it, says Robbins. These three simple steps will cure the everyday variety of depression that plagues so many people in today's culture.

Robbins goes even further into the topic of unhappiness vs. happiness. He wants us to become aware of the rules we set up for ourselves in order to be happy. What has to happen to be happy? He suggests "softening" the rules. As one example, he mentions the fellow whose rule is: "Any day above ground is a happy day." Robbins wants people not to dwell on the negative, and he also wants people to take some time to look at the *vocabulary* they use to describe themselves.

> "Hey, how are you feeling?"
> "I'm okay."

Robbins suggests changing the response.

> "I'm feeling fantastic!"
> "I'm feeling outrageous!"
> "I'm feeling dynamite!"

If we make a consistent effort to change our vocabulary to more positive words, and if we stay with positive people as opposed to negative people, our state of consciousness will change in corresponding fashion.

Another way to change one's state is to use contrasts. He mentions the story of the man who complained about having no shoes until he saw a man with no feet. I have found, in general, that many people are jealous of people that are similar to them. For instance, if a person's next-door neighbor wins the lottery, that event is more apt to make a person jealous than if Tom Cruise were to earn $65 million for his next movie.

If instead of looking at others, a person truly counts his or her own blessings, that person is more apt to be and stay happy. The only kind of success that matters, ultimately, is internal happiness, not external achievement.

The only reason a person does not have the joy in his life is because
he has not claimed it.

TONY ROBBINS, 1993

"We have already won the race" by being born, says Robbins. Out of
the millions and billions of sperm and eggs that fall by the wayside, we,
the living, represent the few that have already succeeded. So in order
to be happy, we simply should be happy. It is our choice. Happiness is
not determined by outside events, or even by achievement; it is simply
determined by perspective and attitude on life.

Robbins suggests a number of powerful techniques to alter the way
we view the world. Take, for instance, a particular unpleasant memory.
Maybe it is a boss from years back that still bugs you. Robbins suggests
reframing your perception of that person so that when you think of
him or her, instead of being angry, you are happy. For instance, he suggests that you could shrink the person down to the size of a mouse in
your mind, place big rabbit ears on his head, and a put corkscrew tail on
his backside. If that vision is impressed into your mind, then whenever
you see or think of that person, instead of tuning in to the negatives
that are associated with him, this new vision can replace it. This may
sound dumb, but really this is quite an effective way to handle past dis-
appointments. You have changed the way you view/interpret the past.
It is merely a shift in perspective. My guess is that many top politicians
use this kind of technique all of the time, because they have to be mentally armed to battle against the brutal treatment they often receive in
the press and world at large.

> You don't have to give up being an achiever and a doer to make
> things happen to make you happy. You can bliss out while you work.
> What a concept! You can feel so good while you build that empire.
> You don't have to wait to feel good. If you feel good along the way
> you are liable to build the empire bigger.
>
> TONY ROBBINS, 1993

Another technique he suggests is to stack happy events in a mental vault that you can access whenever you perform some simple ritual, like snapping your fingers in a special way.

Take out a sheet of paper. Think back on your life and write down five truly great times. Memorize this list. Place it in your mental vault. Then when you need to feel upbeat and be on top of your game, refer to this list, and this will change your state to a more optimum one.

One such event that always makes me happy, that puts a smile on my face, is a particular wave I rode on a surfboard out by Point Judith, Rhode Island, way back in 1970. Sure, it was a long time ago, but so what? It makes me happy to think about that perfect moment when I was right with the world. So write this list out and stack these great events in your mental vault!

Robbins ends one of his tapes with a deep idea. Joy resides, by birthright, inside each of us. Our goal is not only to enjoy our own lives, but also to create enjoyment in the lives of others.

> I think there is a reason why our brains want to move towards pleasure. It's because it leads us to a place where we are really connected with our creator. That may sound weird to you; but I think there is a reason why human beings are wired the way they are wired. And I think that the easiest way to get to your creator, the easiest way to have that joy, is to know those feelings are available now, and to hold yourself to a standard where you cause yourself to have those feelings on a regular basis, not because you have to, but because you deserve to.
>
> TONY ROBBINS, 1993

Implied here is the idea that if we live a life of joy, we are making our creator happy. As Tony Robbins says when he ends each of his tapes, "Live with passion!"

31
Quantum Jumps:
Uri Geller

I was in Scientific Laboratories at Stanford Research Institute investigating a rather amazing individual, Uri Geller. Uri's ability to perform amazing feats of mental wizardry is known the world over. We in science are just now catching up and understanding what you can do with exercise and proper practice. Uri is not a magician. He is using capabilities that we all have and can develop with exercise and practice. After the Geller work, I was asked to brief the director of the CIA, Ambassador George Bush (later to become President of the United States), on our activities and the results.

EDGAR MITCHELL, ASTRONAUT AND
THE SIXTH MAN TO WALK ON THE MOON

AN INTERVIEW WITH URI GELLER

In the early 1970s, Uri Geller entered the world scene. Having performed telepathy and bent small metal objects like spoons and keys psychokinetically in Israel for a number of years in theaters and before VIPs like Prime Minister Golda Meir, he was brought to the attention of Andrija Puharich, a medical doctor and parapsychologist. Since Puharich had studied other individuals who had exhibited paranormal abilities, he realized that if Geller were ever to be taken seriously, he would have to be tested. And so Puharich set Geller up at laboratories around the world, including several military labs in America. In every case, Geller was able to exhibit telepathic and psychokinetic abilities, and because of this, he gained the credibility to be accepted on the world scene.[1] In short order, Geller appeared on a variety of TV talk shows like Merv Griffin and Mike Douglas and also met such luminaries as Salvador Dali, Mohammad Ali, Elvis Presley, Roselyn Carter, Al Gore, and Henry Kissinger. The following interview and demonstration occurred in 1975 on a segment of *The Today Show,* which starred Barbara Walters. This segment begins with Barbara Walters holding a key while Uri gently strokes it.

URI GELLER: Okay, I'll touch it very gently. I'm rubbing it. You can feel that there's no force.

BARBARA WALTERS: Very lightly. Very lightly [*she says looking at the key and concurs*].

URI: [*long pause . . . deep impatient breath*] Wait—hold it like that. [*long pause*] I always say, why do you let me down when I'm on television? [*impatient breathing*] Hold it here. Gently here.

BW: It seems to me it's already bending.

URI: No, it was . . .

BW: It's bending [*her voice is soft and reflects awe*].

URI: It is?

BW: Yes. I'll show you. I'll put the both of them together and show you.

URI: Wait, I know what I'll do. . . . I'd like you to go like that.

BW: What do you mean, like what?

Uri: Move also this piece, rub it.

BW: Rub it?

Uri: Yeah, but open so everyone will see. Hold it [*unintelligible*].

BW: I think that's enough to show people.

Uri: Yes, it's going! . . . [*Walters places the key down*] . . . Look, it's bending more.

BW: It's continuing to bend! This is the one Uri did, which is continuing to bend. . . . I'm not even touching it and it's . . .

Uri: Look, it's . . . you see, it's plastic [*applause from audience*]. I wish people would see it's not a break, even. It's . . . it looks like puddley wax. . . . It's like the energy eats the metal from inside. Can you see it?

BW: Yes, I see it.

Barbara Walters TV show
For Women Only, ca. 1975

The terms "paradigm" and "paradigm shifts" were placed into general usage by Thomas Kuhn in his book *The Structure of Scientific Revolutions.*[2] Kuhn shows clearly that accepted premises, observations, laws, and theories are influenced by the prevailing worldview.

Utilizing the word "myth" to describe obsolete scientific theories, Kuhn states, "Normal science . . . often suppresses fundamental novelties because they are necessarily subversive of its basic commitments."[3] However, as contemporary "laws" of science are to some extent "arbitrary" by their nature, eventually they yield to new and more comprehensive tenets.

> To no one type of mind is it a given to discern the totality of truth. Something escapes the best of us—not accidentally, but systematically, and because we have a twist. The scientific-

academic mind and the feminine-mystical mind shy from each other's facts.[4]

WILLIAM JAMES

When the American psychologist William James would discuss the problem of proving the existence of ESP, he talked about the "white crow." One only needs one white crow to establish that crows can be white. If telepathy or psychic metal bending occurs only once, that is enough to establish that these phenomena indeed exist. In the case of Israeli paranormalist Uri Geller, although his ESP abilities have been tested positively with no detection of fraud at some of the greatest think tanks in the West, such as Stanford Research Institute in Menlo Park, California; Naval Surface Weapons Center; White Oak Laboratories in Silver Springs, Maryland; Lawrence Livermore Laboratories in California; and at other labs and physics departments in England, Canada, France, South Africa, and Denmark,[5] the backlash by the skeptical community against Geller had been too great. The end result is that although scientists were seriously studying the full range and potential of human consciousness throughout the 1970s, in part in reaction to the wake-up book *Psychic Discoveries Behind the Iron Curtain*,[6] today almost no university will even consider the topic, even though the ramifications of such studies would be profound.

I have watched Uri Geller spin the keys and things like that. . . . I have seen that so I am a believer. It was my house key and the only way I would be able to use it is get a hammer and beat it out back flat again. So there are certain energy things that are outside of the norm.

ACTOR AND ACADEMY AWARD–WINNING
DIRECTOR CLINT EASTWOOD

Scientific revolutions, for Kuhn, occur when a bright scientist is finally able to fit the "anomaly" into a new workable model. A qualitative shift takes place in accepted views and "a new set of commitments [becomes the] new basis for the practice of science."[7]

Kuhn's premise is that most scientific revolutions are caused by individuals who threaten the endemic construct reality (e.g., Copernicus, Newton, Lavoisier, Einstein). Therefore, they are first met with vehement resistance. The end result, however, in each case is a reversal, whereby of necessity, the "community . . . rejects [the] time-honored scientific theory and adopt[s] . . . the new one."[8] Society, in turn, becomes "qualitatively transformed [and] . . . quantitatively enriched."[9]

The group fantasy is a powerful vehicle for structuring consciousness and either guiding or restricting the behavior or life goal of the individual and society in question. The direction in which history proceeds is also influenced.

> I was introduced to Dr. Werner von Braun by a NASA astronaut, Captain Edgar Mitchell. Ed was the man who stood on the moon and tried to send back telepathic messages. He taught me to hold a seed in the palm of my hand and will it to sprout. I was escorted to Dr. von Braun's office, where he had masterminded the U.S. space program, and while he held his gold ring in his fist, I bent it psychically. "I have no scientific explanation for this phenomenon," he remarked.
>
> I was not aware until later that von Braun had also designed the V1 and V2 flying bombs that killed thousands during World War II. When Germany was defeated, his team was very close to creating atomic weapons. He had worked enthusiastically for the führer, and I believe he deserved to stand trial—if not for his scientific work, which had murderous intent, then for his use of Jewish slave labor. Instead, he was brought to the U.S., with dozens of other Nazis, to have his slate wiped clean before setting to work on America's nuclear missile research. If the Axis powers had defeated the Allies, von Braun would have been their guiding genius.[10]
>
> URI GELLER

32
Waking

Returning to Gurdjieff, one can see that the entire field of advertising, including the selling of almost every product (or politician), and also the entire thrust of the capitalist system of rewarding workers at the end of the week after they have completed their tasks are the engines that run our society. So indeed most men can be considered machines, and most behavior can also be seen as pretty much automatic. This, for Gurdjieff, is called the "waking sleep" state, the state of autopilot that most humans routinely operate on. Gurdjieff says that there are two states above this and one state below it:

> Objective Consciousness
> Waking
> Waking Sleep
> Sleep

The first stage, sleep, refers to actual sleep. The second stage, the waking sleep state, is the state in which the world operates. We think we are awake, but in actuality our lives are ruled by mechanical actions and also by the wishes and desires of other more powerful entities than us (i.e., society at large). In order to wake up, that is to stop being a machine, we must *remember* our *selves,* and learn through intentional suffering to control our fate. This can only be achieved through self-knowledge and exercise of one's own willpower. Gurdjieff does not deny psychic abilities. He just doesn't emphasize them because the most important thing to do is to optimize your self in the real world.

> Can you govern your emotions? No. You may try to suppress them or cast out one emotion by another emotion. But you cannot control it. It controls you. Or you may decide to do something—your "intellectual I" may make such a decision. But when the time comes to do it, you may find yourself doing just the opposite.[1]
>
> GURDJIEFF, *VIEWS FROM THE REAL WORLD*

How do we know we are asleep? When we are shocked into a sudden sense of awareness, or during the few other occasions when we awaken. We knock our hand to our head and proclaim, "Gosh, I've been asleep!" It's at *that* moment when we realize that we really have been asleep, that our lives really do operate for the most part on autopilot.

Gurdjieff wants us, first of all, to face the hard truth that we do not know ourselves. Through self-observation in all situations, we can begin to recognize how mechanical our actions really are. Part of this process is also to come to grips with the idea that we think that we are one person, but really we are many. This concept is what Gurdjieff calls "the imaginary I." Objectively observing ourselves as we go through life will lead us to see that we really have many I's, a number of which are in constant conflict. "Man," Gurdjieff says, "is a plural being."[2]

I will give you an example from my own life. Friday night I tell myself that I would like to get up early Saturday morning to get a jump-start on the day, so I set my alarm to 6 a.m. When the alarm goes off the next morning, I clearly see the two I's and woefully announce that I do not care what that guy said Friday night. This guy, the one lying in bed, is not ready to get up at 6 a.m.

Gurdjieff's view on the imaginary I is unique to psychology. We want to believe that we are one person, but according to this view, we really just blow with the wind, with the whim of the moment, and most people are slaves to their emotions. "We are not our emotions." Gurdjieff would say.

I had a powerful instance of this realization a number of years back. It was shortly after I completed my doctoral dissertation, a psychohistory on the inventor Nikola Tesla, which ran 725 pages. I had caught a wicked flu that left me incapacitated for over a week. This was highly unusual, because most flus, when I get them, last two or three days at most. As one of the symptoms of this flu, I became depressed, and I remember distinctly looking at the dissertation and saying to myself that I could not imagine that this entity, me, wrote even *one* page of that treatise, let alone 700+ pages. At that instant I realized that my mind was being swayed by the illness and that there was another part of me that was clearly separate from that self that was in a terrible state. Emotions operate the same way. Many people "become" their emotions. Look at the harshness of political debate for instance, or the fervor in the stands at some sporting events, or the ancient ethnic hatreds that prevail in so many regions of the world. People get caught up in the craziness of a moment. But Gurdjieff wants us to realize that this is just another imaginary I, mistaken as the one central I, which, in reality, for the common man, does not exist.

Gurdjieff also discusses at length the destructive aspect of negative emotions. Essentially, all negatives take away from the system and all positives add to the system. Many people are dominated by such emotions as hate, envy, and fear. When a negative emotion arises, through the dual process of self-remembering and nonidentification, one can begin to separate oneself from the emotion. As Harry Benjamin suggests in his superb primer *Basic Self-Knowledge,* during these instances, the negative emotion needs to be recognized. If we then separate from this emotion, and "make personality passive,"[3] this will allow essence to be activated.

The idea, of course, is to coordinate all the many I's and create one central controlling I, but this can only be done after first of all realizing that we have been living under the illusion that we are one self. We are not. We are many.

Benjamin's book explains in clear fashion Gurdjieff's idea of essence, personality proper, and false personality. Our *essence* is really our soul, our core, which we are most in touch with when we are children. People who live close to the land are often more in touch with their essence. Personality comes in after birth and involves the programming we receive from society. Some programming is good, such as the skills we learn and the education we obtain. All of this adds to what is called *personality proper,* and this is beneficial, because these skills will enable us to operate successfully in society. However, we are also painted with *false personality,* which feeds on essence. Pride, vanity, jealousy, self-conceit, and daydreams about ourselves are all linked to false personality. Worrying too much about superficial aspects of life, such as one's hair color, the type of car we drive, social status—all of this adds to false personality. In humanistic psychology, false personality would be linked to the idea of alienation from the real self, which Gurdjieff calls essence. In order for essence to grow, false personality must be abandoned. One movie that aptly portrays this division is *Roman Holiday* with Audrey Hepburn and Gregory Peck. Hepburn, stuck in an isolated and overprotected existence as a princess, longs to taste real life and is able to do so when she escapes and meets the straight-thinking and charming Peck.

Another film that carries this theme to a more powerful conclusion is the 1937 classic *Captains Courageous.* Child actor Freddy Bartholomew, a cultured, spoiled brat, ends up on a fishing boat where he meets down-to-earth sailor Spencer Tracy. As the film progresses, living as a deck hand, Freddy must give up more and more of his false personality. At first he resists, but then he begins to see what is really important in life, and he sees that Spencer Tracy's simple existence and link to the sea is much more important than all the fake trappings of his well-to-do yet artificial existence. The gut-wrenching accident that occurs at the climax of the film drives home the point Gurdjieff is making: don't short-change your life. See through the veil to find out what is really important.

The idea of essence is linked to a higher realization and Aristotelian view that the universe has purpose, that there is a reason for life. Where ordinary man is ruled by mechanical action and false personality, the man of substance is ruled by essence, purpose, self-direction, and self-transformation.

"A man who sleeps cannot do," says Gurdjieff. "In order to do, a man must die voluntarily and be born again,"[4] so that he can change and evolve while he is alive. Ordinary man has no conception of the huge reservoir of energy available to the man of substance. I have likened this to the *second wind effect*. A person who, for instance, is jogging may hit a wall. The ordinary man stops jogging, but the man of substance works through it and finds a reserve of energy many times more powerful than the surface energy that he had been tapping. The hardest thing of all to do, Gurdjieff teaches, is to change the self, but that is the task. Transformation is possible through work on oneself.

He evolved. He embraced change. He always wanted to be better than he was.

CAPTAIN PICARD REFERRING TO THE HUMANOID
DATA IN *STAR TREK 10: NEMESIS*, 2003

All of life is ruled by the *Law of Will*, which Gurdjieff states has three divisions:

> God's Will
> Big Brother's Will (updated term!)
> One's Own Will

God's will rules life and death, disease, acts of nature, the seasons, and so on. Big Brother's will refers to entities more powerful than you.* Your boss, the phone and oil companies, the mass media, the political power system, society at large. Since we are asleep, we therefore tend to be ruled by other people's will, and thus also the law of accident.

For example, there is a cut in defense contracts. A thousand workers

---

*The term "Big Brother" came from Orwell's book *1984,* which was written about the same time Gurdjieff passed away.

are laid off and local businesses close. These catastrophic events occur regardless of the acts of the individuals who have been so adversely affected. In essence, they had no say in their own destiny because they live under the dictates of entities more powerful then they.

Higher states of consciousness for Gurdjieff are directly related to activation of one's own willpower, an area of the psyche completely neglected by Western religion and psychology. Look at the index of any major psychology textbook and try to find a section on the will. You will be hard-pressed to find one.

Whereas Freud placed the unconscious in the center of the personality, Gurdjieff placed the will. Consider the difference. The idea of will is, of course, anathema to the behaviorists, but as stated above, it is also completely ignored by essentially the whole of mainstream academic psychology. The will lies on that magical boarder between the mental and physical realms. Yet if we were to use a psychoanalytic paradigm for unifying Gurdjieff with Freud, the ability to self-remember and the will, as such, could be considered as ego functions.

According to Gurdjieff's view, man is the only animal able to evolve during the course of his life. Each of us can attain higher states of consciousness by, first of all, seeking out and attaining worthwhile goals and by remembering ourselves. But this involves (1) the harsh realization that we really do operate mechanically, even though we are under the constant illusion that we are in control; and (2) the ability to see through the false aspects of society and of ourselves, and thus tap back into our essence. Sacrifice and super efforts are involved for the "crystallization of the soul" to take place.

During the Russian Revolution, Gurdjieff was able to put his teachings into practice. Following the "way of the sly one," as reported by Thomas de Hartmann in *Our Life with Mr. Gurdjieff,* Gurdjieff was able to obtain passports for his many students by placing one of them, a lawyer, into a Soviet governmental position. He also wrote to the "council of Deputies, making a formal request for aid in organizing a scientific expedition to the region of Mount Induc in the Caucasus."[5]

Funded by the crumbling government, this supposed "scientific expedition" enabled them to leave Essentuki only three weeks before a reign of terror began. Gurdjieff had not only saved the life of the aristocrat Thomas de Hartmann, but he also persuaded a crumbling government to fund their departure and supply train tickets as well! This is only one of many examples of the extraordinary achievements attained by Gurdjieff.

In the early 1920s, Gurdjieff settled with his students in Paris where he remained until his death in 1949, able to survive Nazi occupation during part of this period. Having founded the Institute for the Harmonious Development of Man at the Chateau du Prieure at Fountainbleu, students from Europe and America came to learn his teachings. Visitors included D. H. Lawrence, Gertrude Stein, A. R. Orage (editor of *The New Age*), Mrs. Enrico Caruso, and Margaret Anderson (editor of *The Little Review,* a showcase periodical for such writers as T. S. Eliot, Ezra Pound, Orage, and Ernest Hemingway). A few years after the founding of the Institute, there was a disagreement with Ouspensky. Nevertheless, the writer most responsible for the mystic's success continued to support and refer students to Gurdjieff for the following two decades, although they never actually met again.

Fritz Peters, a nephew of Miss Anderson, spent his youth at the school and has written of his unique experiences in two colorful books, *Boyhood with Gurdjieff* and *Gurdjieff Remembered*. Peters often discusses the lack of real substance in many of Gurdjieff's students, but also describes the guru's extraordinary knowledge concerning man's possible evolution.

> He talked to me for a very long time that morning, and emphasized the fact that everyone had usually a particular recurring problem in life. He said that these problems were usually a form of laziness, and that I was to think about my laziness, which took a fairly obvious physical form, as in the case of the garden. I had simply put off doing anything until someone had taken notice of that fact. He said that he wanted me to think seriously about my laziness—not the outward form, which was unimportant, but to find what it was. . . . "Must ask

yourself, whenever you see your own laziness; 'What is this laziness in me?' If you ask this question seriously, and with concentration, [it] is possible someday you will find answer. This important and very difficult work I give you now."

I thanked him for what he had said and added that I was sorry that I had not done my work in the garden and that I would do it properly in the future.

He brushed aside my thanks and said it was useless to be sorry. "Is too late for that now, and is also too late to do good work in garden. In life never have second chance, only have one chance."[6]

Gurdjieff made repeated trips to the United States throughout the 1920s. Appearing at Carnegie Hall, he presented sacred dances from the Sarmoung Brotherhood and helped raise money for his school. In 1935, he traveled to Washington, DC, to meet with Senator Bronson Cutting from New Mexico with the idea of obtaining funding for the Prieure and spreading his schools to America. Unfortunately, the senator died in a plane crash on his way to the meeting.

33

Education of the Will

The gravest form of evil . . . is "langor of the mind" which manifests itself in the young man. He sleeps several hours too long, he does not feel very fit, he has no inclination for work. His laziness is apparent on his very face. . . . There is neither vigor nor precision in his movements. After this lost time, he lingers over breakfast reading the newspaper through even the advertisements, because that occupies him without requiring any effort . . . In the afternoon some of his energy is soon wasted in useless discussion and in gossip. . . . Lazy people inflict upon their lives the emptiest lives imaginable. . . . All happiness presupposes [initiative] of some effort.

JULES PAYOT, *EDUCATION OF THE WILL,* 1909

One theoretician who attempts to combine the teachings of Freud and Jung with that of Gurdjieff is Roberto Assagioli (1888–1974), an Italian psychologist who corresponded with Freud and met with Jung on a number of occasions. Assagioli's work is taken directly from Assagioli's *Psychosynthesis* and from Sam Keen's remarkable interview, which was conducted for *Psychology Today* during the last year of Assagioli's life (December 1974).

One key difference from Freud is that Assagioli wants to resurrect the will as a key component of the ego, which he equates with the self. His criticism of Freud is that he "neglected the higher reaches of human nature." This self, which he sees as constantly growing, is often faced with choices. One's values play a crucial role in determining which choices are taken and which are discarded. Where Freud sees choices as stemming from or in reaction to the primitive id, Assagioli sees the will as "the source or origin of all our choices, decisions, and engagements."[1]

The WILL differs from drives, impulses, and desires. It is composed of the following phases:

> Deliberation
> Motivation
> Decision
> Affirmation
> Persistence
> Execution

The existential experience of the SELF is directly related to the expression of will. The next step would be to learn how to develop and strengthen it. Similar to Freud, who says that the ego can split off and observe the self, Assagioli also realizes that the self can be aware of internal as well as external reality. But he is going a step further to link the willing self to one's identity. How does one experience oneself? It is through self-observation, introspection, and active doing that one truly confronts the self.

The self, for Assagioli, cannot live in isolation. He makes a distinction between being lonely and spending time alone. The self grows by spending time with itself and by actively making conscious decisions, but it must also learn to live in harmony with others and deal with the will of others. And yet the self must learn to deal with the self as well! Assagioli wants us to have a dialogue with and interact with the self. His "psychosynthesis" is a technique for integrating social interactions with one's goals and one's will. How, he asks, does one achieve a goal? By "analyzing the value and motivation of the goal," by "deliberating, deciding, affirming, planning, and executing" one's goal. Each of these areas can also be developed.

In pursuit of goals, conflicts often arise. Energies are wasted in wrongheaded emotions, misguided sexual pursuits, and through power struggles or combat with others. For Assagioli, the way out of this malaise is through sublimation and creative achievement. Part of the way is to get in touch with our "superconscious" or spiritual side, a part of the self that has recuperative and transformative aspects.

Similar to Gurdjieff, Assagioli has come upon various techniques to "disidentify" with negative and destructive emotions. For instance, instead of saying, "I am discouraged" or "I am depressed," say, "A wave of discouragement has swept over me." In this way, the person is separate from the emotion. As Gurdjieff has said, "we are not our emotions." And just as Gurdjieff wants us to be aware of self, Assagioli wants us to develop a "vigilant self" that does not submit to these detrimental feelings.

A vigilant self "critically surveys those impulses (e.g., discouragement or anger), looks to their origin, foresees their deleterious effects and realizes their unfoundedness." The goal is to "disintegrate harmful energies" and become self-aware so that these negative emotions do not take hold.

These ideas are very similar to those of Gurdjieff, who also discusses at great length how to disidentify with negative emotions and remember the self. All negatives take away from the system, and all positives add to the system. As Uri Geller often says, "Stay positive!" Where Assagioli differs from Gurdjieff or combines these ideas with a Freudian paradigm is in his recognition that many negative impulses can have an unconscious origin. Just as in psychoanalysis, Assagioli wants us to "unmask, understand, and resolve" these dark emotions. In many cases, we need to "recognize their stupidity." True, this is easier said than done, but certainly worth the effort. We could say that this is all part of what Gurdjieff calls "the work," meaning the work on oneself.

Where Gurdjieff sees multiple I's, Assagioli "sees the will as standing above the multiplicity. It directs, regulates and balances all the other functions." Once one "cultivates the certainty that one has a will, with that comes a realization of an intimate connection between the will and the self." Assagioli tells us we need "cold, impersonal observation as if these impulses are a natural phenomena acting outside ourself." In this way we can create a "psychological distance" between ourself and these negative complexes. The goal is to create a "critical faculty" of self-awareness, "but not too critical!"

Having taught psychology for over thirty-five years, I continue to be amazed that the will is completely ignored by mainstream textbooks in the field. For all intents and purposes, the will is never discussed by Freud or Jung, and certainly not by the behaviorists! Thus, it is of historical interest to realize that one of Freud's closest associates, Otto Rank, wrote a considerable amount about the will. Rank goes so far as to say that "the human being experiences his individuality in terms of his will."[2] For Assagioli, and I would imagine for Rank as well, one should "take a vow" to affirm and express the will.

However, when it comes to defining precisely what the will is, both Assagioli and Rank state that ultimately it is undefinable. It is easier to experience the will than to define it. Nevertheless, Rank does make an attempt. "We cannot prevent our birth or death," Rank says, but we can choose how to live our life during the interim. The will is "the integrated personality as an original creative force." It is "the impetus that strives for affirmation and control." Quoting Jessie Taft, an associate active in the women's movement, Rank stated, "Will is not merely the drive of a predominant instinct or combination of instincts. It is that central integration of the forces of the individual that exceeds the sum of the parts, a unity which can inhibit as well as carry through to realization the instinctual urges." Will is a "positive, guiding force" responsible for the integration of the self. It "represents the life center of the human being, something primal and ultimate."[3]

I can't make you love me if you don't.
LINE FROM A BONNIE RAITT SONG,
WRITTEN BY MIKE REID AND
ALLEN SHAMBLIN

Jules Payot, in his classic book *The Education of the Will,* takes a different approach. Payot realizes that expression of the will along a single path will lead one to success. However, "even good ideas are no match against the brute strength of natural inclinations and tendencies."[4] Payot has uncovered a powerful hard truth, namely that *the will is no match against the emotions.* Spencer notes, "the world is led by emotion."[5] "The power that emotional states have over our wills cannot be exaggerated. They can even make us face suffering and death without hesitation. . . . [Even intelligence] submits docilely to emotional states."[6]

Since "the will is not fond of receiving cold orders from intelligence," Payot realizes for the will to become successful, it must tie itself to an emotional state. History is replete with "the feeble effect of abstract ideas contrasted with the power of emotion." Thus is the "Comedy of Life."[7]

Payot also realizes that "all communication with the outside world must necessarily be through the action of the muscles." This involves "an expenditure of energy."[8] Much like Gurdjieff's teachings, Payot suggests, "men who are masters of themselves are extremely rare." Similar to Gurdjieff's idea of mechanical man, Payot notes that most men are "marionettes." "When powerful emotions and violent thoughts take over, we stand by helplessly."[9] He then hits the reader with the harshest of truths. True self-mastery, he says, "is a delusion." The will "has only a mock power over the brute forces with which we must struggle."[10]

The reason Payot comes to this conclusion has to do with our biology. Emotions are primary, but so are physical states. And when physical states affect the mind, the exertion of will over such states becomes extremely difficult—and in most cases essentially impossible.

However, one advantage the will has is the ability to perceive the future and consider its consequences. Here is Payot's "Kingdom of Intelligence": *The secret for approaching self-mastery is to fuse our plans with positive emotions.* The only way for an intellectual idea to have power is to find an emotional state to attach to it. That is how to increase willpower. Essentially, what Payot is saying is for the will to succeed, the head must work with the heart. This is what Tony Robbins means when he drumbeats us to "live with passion."

"All volition involves resolution" and commitment. But for true success to be achieved, we must "cultivate enthusiasm" and choose a path that will lead to enjoyment. The secret to triumph and exultation lies in knowing how to direct one's own thoughts and feelings in the direction that leads to a happy existence.[11]

But happiness also involves "effort." In other words, a person must work for happiness. If you like homemade coconut custard pie, then don't go to the store and purchase one. Make it yourself. The effort involved has a payoff.

E. H. Anderson, metaphysician and hypnotist from Toledo, Ohio, and contemporary of Jules Payot, looks at will in a different way. For Anderson, the will is a resultant force. What one really wants to cultivate is the force behind the will, which Anderson says is INTENTION. "The will is an expression of a force." Intention involves resolve, contemplation, planning, aim, purpose, goal direction, fixed determination, or in Anderson's words, "conscious deliberation. . . . *Intention directs the will.*"[12]

In order to develop intention, one must learn CONCENTRATION. This is a technique closely linked to meditation, learning to withdraw into one's silence. Anderson tells the initiate to "relax your mental tension, banish random associative thoughts" and learn to concentrate. *"Silence is one of the great factors in all psychic work."*[13]

Anderson is telling us to learn how to get in touch with our real selves by meditating and by concentrating. He also recognizes that for intention to be maximized, the subject must approach his goal with CONFIDENCE. "Confidence begets confidence." Confidence involves faith and belief in oneself. Doubts and fears need to be set aside. "I can't" should never be part of one's vocabulary. "When you rely on yourself, you are relying upon the universal power that is expressing itself through you. . . . Know thyself and you will be self-confident."

In Chögyam Trungpa's book *The Sacred Path of the Warrior,* Trungpa suggests, "people don't appreciate themselves. Having never developed sympathy or gentleness towards themselves, they cannot experience harmony or peace within themselves."[14] Trungpa says that we often see the world as "burdensome or depressive." "Instead of appreciating one's life, we take our life and our existence for granted." We need to relax more and learn to "appreciate our mind and body." Trungpa wants us to seek tranquility and learn that our lives are "wonderful and precious."[15] Express gratitude for the gift of life. Give yourself a break. When necessary, forgive yourself. Realize that humor has a healing effect. Appreciate the irony and even nuttiness of existence. Become a friend and be gentle with yourself.

A first step toward increasing self-awareness and the ability to concentrate involves learning how to MEDITATE. Part of this process is to learn how to *stop thoughts*. Three easy ways are as follows:

1. Sit in a quite place and concentrate on your breath. That's it. Think only about your breath. This allows you to slow yourself down and get into a meditative mode.

2. This should be done outdoors: Find a special spot, perhaps in your backyard, in a forest, or on a hilltop. Sit quietly and listen to the sounds around you. The quieter you are and the more you listen, the more unwanted thoughts will disappear and the more open your mind will become.

If you perform this second exercise correctly, you will begin to extend your hearing senses, and by this process, an entirely different level of awareness will be attained. You will note, for instance, that dogs and birds communicate with each other over distances exceeding several miles.

Both of these techniques are simple but powerful ways to learn how to draw into one's silence so that concentration can take place. And with concentration comes contemplation, deliberation, intention, and acts of will. Where Freud sees humans as being motivated by two key drives, sex and aggression, Assagioli wants to add the spiritual quest as a third primary drive. Associated with this third drive is a desire for self-transformation, and the vehicle for obtaining this is the will. Successful expression of the will involves tying the head with the heart, pairing your goals with positive emotions.

3. The third way was derived from the teachings of Silva Mind Control, Uri Geller, and E. H. Anderson, who devotes a chapter in his book *Psychical Developments* to what he calls autohypnosis and healing. The idea is to create a spiral stairway down into your mind, say ten floors. At the bottom floor create a room with a set of tools and a stage, and on that stage place a screen. On this screen you can project a part of your body or someone else's body you need to heal. Surround that image with a vision of healing light. This space is your workplace. Use the sacred room and the projection screen for a moment of prayer and a variety of visualized goals.

Quoting Maslow, Assagioli recognizes that through self-actualization, peak experiences can be achieved. These spiritual encounters are associated with the feeling of transcending time, being in synch with the self and one's destiny, and feeling at one with the world.

For Anderson the only way for the soul to "manifest itself on the physical plane is through the physical organism."[16] The old cliché "the body is the temple of the soul" comes to mind. "Remember," Anderson says, "man is at one with the universal, his natural condition is that of harmony with all of nature. Now he is estranged, it is his duty to again become in rapport with the soul of the race,"[17] to allow the "universal intelligence to manifest itself through him, and it is this condition of eternal peace that brings him into a condition of peace with all around him."[18] For Anderson, "the expression of this peace is grace."[19] Through will and the realization of one's oneness with the universal intelligence, thought can be directed and "greatness" can be achieved.

As Assagioli told Sam Keen, "By denying the centrality of the will, modern psychology has denied direct experience of the self."[20] We must become aware of the notion of being a "willing self" as this first step toward self-transformation.

34

Last Days

Gurdjieff's last few years were spent in Paris with his students. Dorothy Caruso, wife of Enrico, writes of this time in her book *A Personal History:*

> No matter how late each night in the salon, after dinner, Gurdjieff took his little accordion-piano on his knee and while his left hand worked the bellows, his right hand made music in minor chords and haunting single notes. But one night in the aromatic store-room he played for five of us, alone, a different kind of music, although whether the difference lay in its sorrowful harmonies or in the way he played, I do not know. I only know that no music had ever been so sad. Before it ended, I put my head on the table and wept. "What has happened to me?" I said. "When I came into this room I was happy. And then that music—and now I am happy again."
>
> "I play objective music to make you cry." Gurdjieff said. "There are many kinds of music—some to make [you] laugh, or to love or to hate. This is the beginning of music—sacred music—two, three thousand years old."[1]

During these same last days, J. G. Bennett returned after an absence of over twenty years.

On the Saturday before he died, I had two hours alone with Gurdjieff. . . . At one point I said I could never repay him for all he had done for me and my wife. He was silent and then, looking very hard into my eyes, he said: "Only you. Only you can repay for all my labors."[2]

After reading through most every book on Gurdjieff, this writer would have to agree, for Bennett's book *Gurdjieff: Making a New World* is a masterpiece of insight as well as a historical compilation of the roots of high-level Muslim and Sufi thinking and of a life so enigmatic and crucial to the twentieth century. In the chapter titled "Gurdjieff's Question," Bennett gives the answer to "What is the sense and significance of life on Earth?" Explaining Gurdjieff's most difficult and cumbersome work *Beelzebub's Tales to His Grandson,* Bennett discusses the concept of *reciprocal maintenance,* whereby man feeds God and God in turn feeds man, but also, "every class of existing things produces energies or substances that are required for maintaining existence of other classes."[3]

Gurdjieff uses the terms *involution* and *evolution* to describe the process. Involution is the transformation process in which a high level energy acts on lower energies through an apparatus [such as a human body], and

Evolution is the reverse process. It is the production of high-level energy from a lower-level source. This also requires an apparatus, but of a different kind, for the "upgrading" of energy is improbable and cannot occur at all unless some high-level energy is present. Life is an evolutionary process that goes against the direction of probability. The work by which man is transformed is evolutionary.[4]

But the evolutionary process, according to the Gurdjieffian view, can only occur with "help from above," involution. This is for him a guiding component. Yet at the same time, every level is mutually dependent on every other level, so that the higher strata needs the lower strata, just as the lower needs the higher. Gurdjieff understands that for evolution to take place, involution must be in operation. The higher energy is already present as a potentiality, and also as a guiding principle.

Here is the component missing from the generally accepted modern view of evolution. In this model, an animal does not blindly evolve based on simply chance mutation and survival of the fittest. There is another component, analogous to what Henri Bergson calls the "élan vitale," that is also a motivating force underlying and in that sense guiding the process.

> If this were all that the doctrine of reciprocal maintenance was about, it would not be a revolutionary idea. The sting . . . comes with the inclusion of man as a class of beings whose lives also serve for the maintaining of something great or small in the world. . . . Like every living or nonliving thing, man is an "apparatus for the transformation of energy" and he is specifically required to produce sensitive and conscious energy needed for maintaining the harmony of the solar system. He can produce energy voluntarily or involuntarily. The first way is by "work on oneself" that is striving for self-perfection. The second way is by dying.[5]

Gurdjieff is suggesting here that organic life and (especially) man are both essential for the evolution of the earth and for maintaining cosmic harmony. Each part depends on the other. But man plays a special role because of his high state of consciousness. We have *consciousness* for a reason. If we evolve while alive, we help transform the planet because the planet is a dynamic entity growing as well. According to this idea, humans are mechanisms for transforming energies for the evolving cosmos. This is a very powerful idea, which is an extension of the kabbalistic concept of being in partnership with God. Since the universe has purpose, and since man's talent involves mental activity, the way we help the planet is by transforming ourselves and raising our level of energy to a higher realm.

Gurdjieff's idea of evil can be discussed here in relationship to, for instance, the Nazi wish to create a master race. For Gurdjieff, the *conscience* is inborn. It is objective. Murder is wrong in all societies, and so if a people kills by repressing their conscience, then they are not fully conscious, because to be fully conscious is to be in touch with the conscience. Thus, the Nazi wish to create a master race by wiping out other races can only occur through lack of realization of the total self. In this case, evil can be seen as really unconscious behavior (i.e., not operating with a full deck). It is ultimately the product of ignorant action.

Above the waking state of self-remembrance and willful activity is objective consciousness. This state involves the understanding of essential truths, comprehending eternity, and of living with conscience, purpose, and partnership with our creator.

> A long and difficult journey is before you. You are preparing for a strange and unknown land.
>
> GURDJIEFF

In line with this idea of reciprocal maintenance, MIT professor of computer sciences and self-made millionaire Ed Fredkin has linked the concept of consciousness to the very fabric of matter. He sees DNA, which is made up of atoms of hydrogen, oxygen, nitrogen, carbon, and phosphorous, as "a good example of digitally encoded information." It is Fredkin's hypothesis that the conscious component is even more primary than matter and energy. Subatomic particles, according to this view, can be seen as "bits of information . . . [just like those found inside] a personal computer or pocket calculator. . . . The behavior of those bits, and thus, the entire universe," Fredkin says, is "governed by a single programming rule." Through eternal recapitulation and incremental transformations, the "pervasive complexity" that we see as life emerges.

> The Hermetic Teachings are that not only is everything in constant movement and vibration, but that the "differences" between the various manifestations of the universal power are due entirely to the

varying rate and mode of vibrations. Not only this, but that even THE ALL, in itself, manifests a constant vibration of such an infinite degree of intensity and rapid motion that it may be practically considered at rest, the teachers directing the attention of the student to the fact that even on the physical plane a rapidly moving object (such as a revolving wheel) seems to be at rest.[6]

David Chalmers, in a watershed article on consciousness in *Scientific American,* echoes this idea by stating, "The laws of physics might ultimately be cast in informational terms. . . . It may even be that a theory of physics and a theory of consciousness could eventually be consolidated into a single grander theory of information."

If we add to this view the idea of teleological action/purposeful action, this would come close to Gurdjieff's concept of involution, that is, where the higher energy is already present in the lower, and the lower, in this case man, aspires to attain the higher.

The difference for Chalmers between information encoded in atoms as compared to brains is the "experiential" aspect. What Chalmers calls the "hard question" is linked to "how physical processes in the brain give rise to *subjective* experience [emphasis added]." In the movie *2001: A Space Odyssey,* the "hard problem" of how consciousness gives rise to subjectivity is driven home. A monolith, no doubt produced by an advanced species, has been discovered on one of the moons of Jupiter. To maintain a sense of calmness on Earth, the public is kept uninformed. Even the astronauts on board the ship traveling to the site do not know about it. Only HAL, the computer, knows. Because the mission is so important, HAL takes it upon himself to commandeer the ship, and there is a standoff between the one remaining astronaut, Dave, and this electronic entity. HAL has self-knowledge. It is that aspect that makes the film so amazing. Dave needs to shut off HAL's higher centers in order to take back the ship. In essence, he needs to murder HAL, and while he is in the process of unplugging the higher centers HAL manages to say, "Stop, Dave, stop. I'm afraid, Dave." These are some of the most haunting lines ever put on film. Note the use of the concept "I."

That is the key to I-dentity and the hard problem that Chalmers is concerned about. How do we get that sense of I?

Gurdjieff discusses the kabbalistic notion of a partnership with God. He links this to Leibniz's monad theory whereby the microcosm (the self) reflects the macrocosm (cosmos).

This idea was wonderfully expounded upon by kabbalistic Rabbi Joseph Gelberman at an amazing new age conference held the very weekend of the Jonestown massacre in November of 1978. Other speakers included Nobel Prize winning physicist Eugene Wigner, mathematician Charles Musés, Sufi Pir Vilayat Khan, and hospice pioneer Elisabeth Kübler-Ross. The rabbi told a story about God meeting with a group of angels with the task of figuring out where to hide himself on the earth. One small angel suggested hiding God inside every person. "They'll never look there," she exclaimed.

35

I Am

Moses said to God, "Suppose I go to the Israelites and say to them, 'The God of your fathers has sent me to you,' and they ask me, 'What is his name?' Then what shall I tell them?" And God said unto Moses: "I AM THAT I AM"; and He said: "Thus shalt thou say unto the children of Israel: I AM hath sent me unto you."

Exodus III

Rudolf Steiner expands upon this idea in his book *An Outline of Occult Science* when he discusses the *language of the soul* and the relationship of one's sense of self-identity to the motive power that runs the universe. With the realization of the *self* comes direct knowledge of our connection to the source. We are made in God's image; as above, so below.

> In the whole range of language there is only one name that, through its very nature, distinguishes itself from every other name. That name is "I." . . . The "I" as designation for a being has meaning only when this being applies it to itself.[1]

Steiner outlines the ancient's teachings regarding the realization of man's connection to the Godhead by exploring the biblical name for

God given to Moses during his meeting with the burning bush: the "I AM THAT I AM." Unable to say "I" for another:

> I am an "I" to myself only. The true nature of the "I" is independent of all that is external. . . . Those religious denominations that have consciously maintained their relationship with supersensible perception designate the "I" as the "Ineffable name of God." . . . Nothing of an external nature has access to that part of the soul with which we are concerned here.[2]

The understanding of the meaning of "I" involves one's own connection to the internal world of the psyche. Not only is it an identification with the totality, it is realization of this identification. We are linked to cosmic consciousness through knowledge of our selfhood. This is the highest state of consciousness not present in lower realms. Using the symbol of the mandala, God lies in the center, and each of us are spokes on the wheel. All are connected through identification with the source. Access to the source can be achieved through meditation, dream interpretation, and teleological action.

The act of becoming conscious is a complex process, and consciousness as a concept is not one "thing." Man may be the most "conscious" being on the planet; however, principles of his consciousness are also imbued into the atoms that comprise his being and into the very fabric of the ordered universe that he inhabits.

Embedded in Gurdjieff's teachings is also an ancient concept that can be found in the Christian idea of heaven. If a person is able to transform his or her self through work on the self and intentional suffering, a new "Kesdjan body" or astral shell, which existed as a potentiality, is created, which will enable that person to leave the earth plane at death. In this view, heaven, in a sense, must be earned. If a person, however, leads a low existence, his energy state is such that he returns to the earth and becomes fertilizer for the next crop. Gurdjieff uses the analogy of the acorn and oak tree. He tells Fritz Peters that out of the thousands of acorns that drop, only a few will become oak trees. The other acorns will go back into the earth and will be used as food for the growing oak. "My teaching is not fertilizer," Gurdjieff says.

Fritz Peters describes the man's final days in *Gurdjieff Remembered:*

> The day I was to leave, Mr. Gurdjieff said that I would probably never see him again. "As you can see with own eyes," he said, "I now very tired and I know that when I finish my last book my work will be done. So now I can die, because my task in life is coming to an end." He looked at me gravely and continued, "This also mean that I can do nothing more for you. . . . So when you get out of the army do not come back here but go home to America."[3]

However, Peters saw Gurdjieff once again. After returning to Paris a number of weeks later:

> I found him alone at his apartment. He opened the door for me himself and was wearing a night shirt, looking very sleepy. He gave me what I can only describe as a "cold" look and asked me what I was doing here. . . . "Can not say good-bye again—this already done," he said.[4]

Peters turned and left.

This chapter is an expanded version of my article, "Gurdjieff," published in *MetaScience Quarterly,* 1, no. 3 (Autumn 1980): 348–52.

36

His Holiness
the Dalai Lama

DEFENDER OF THE FAITH

Cultivating an attitude of compassion and developing wisdom are slow processes. As you gradually internalize techniques for developing morality, concentration of mind, and wisdom, untamed states of mind become less and less frequent. You will need to practice these techniques day by day, year by year. As you transform your mind, you will transform your surroundings. Others will see the benefits of your practice of tolerance and love, and will work at bringing these practices into their own lives.

THE DALAI LAMA, *HOW TO PRACTICE THE
WAY TO A MEANINGFUL LIFE*, 2002

In the early part of the 1900s, Dr. W. Y. Evans-Wentz journeyed from Oxford University in England to Ceylon and India and up through the Himalayas in his quest for holy men. During his five years of wandering, he visited perhaps the most mystical place on the planet, Tibet. Nestled between Nepal, Bhutan, and Sikkim, this land has always maintained the aura of mystery associated with the very highest states of existence.

Having sat with high lamas for a number of years, and working with Tibetan translator Lama Kazi Dawa-Sandup, Evans-Wentz "in the spirit of true devotion and humility" undertook the "sacred trust" and published in 1927 the *Bardo Thodol* or *Tibetan Book of the Dead*.

In presenting the work to the West, Evans-Wentz asked Carl Jung to write a psychological commentary. Jung's insight into Freudian psychoanalysis and its impact on our thinking coupled with his knowledge of transcendent states of consciousness helps shed much light on the development of Western thought even today, half a century later. With Freud's fear of metaphysics, the "black tide of occultism,"[1] Western man on the one hand discovered the reality of the subconscious mind. This became labeled the personal unconscious, the storehouse of one's experiential memories. On the other hand, inquiry into one's own individualized past helped also to obscure the realization that other layers of the unconscious transcended the individual's psyche. This realm, which Jung called the collective unconscious, contains preexistent and metaphysical states of consciousness. "At-one-ment" (with the Universal Mind) can only be achieved by integrating Eastern or Buddhist thinking, Jung suggests.

Unable to comprehend the "voidness of nothingness," Western man stays rooted in the "neuroticism of the Sidpa (or rebirth) state." Insight, Jung tells us, lies in the realization that each soul is actually "the radiant Godhead itself. . . . The soul is the light of the Godhead, and the Godhead is the soul."[2] It is the "primacy of the soul" that leads one, through direct experiences, to self-realization.

Although the *Tibetan Book of the Dead* is believed to have been first committed to writing in the time of Padmasambhava in the eighth century CE, nevertheless its message is probably many centuries older. Below is a summary of some of its fundamental teachings:

- Enlightenment results from realizing the unreality of existence.
- His doctrine (Buddha) is not unique. It is the same doctrine that has been proclaimed in the human world for the giving of salvation, for the deliverance from the circle of rebirth and death, for

the realization of Nirvana since immemorial time, by a long and illustrious dynasty of buddhas who were Guatama's predecessors.

- The goal is and can only be emancipation from Samsara (worldly existence).
- Such emancipation comes from the realization of Nirvana (transcendence through the extinguishing of desire and individual consciousness).
- Nirvana is non-Samsaric, being beyond all heavens, hells, and worlds.
- This is the ending of sorrow, the realization of reality.[3]

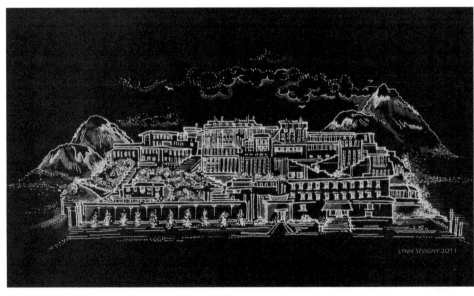

Fig. 36.1. The Potala. Drawing by Lynn Sevigny.

A SHORT HISTORY OF TIBET

Tibet is the highest country in the world, twice the size of Texas. It lies on a plateau thirteen to twenty thousand feet above sea level and is surrounded by mountains. It is also the source of several important rivers that flow through India and China. Up until 1959 it was a theocracy. Today Tibet is ruled by the Communist Chinese.

Tibetan Buddhism is led by lamas, priests, or monks who practice their religion in places of worship called lamaseries. The most important religious and thus governmental figure is the Dalai Lama who, until 1959 resided in Lhasa in the Potala. Next in line is the Tashu Lama, head of the great Tashu Lamasery.

About twelve hundred years ago Tibet's people converted to Buddhism. Four hundred years later the Mongols took control, but their stay was short-lived. In the fifteenth century the first Dalai Lama was born. His name was "Gedun Truppa, a nephew and leading disciple of Lama Tsongkhapa who founded the Getupa, or 'yellow hat' sect of Mahayana Buddhism. Translated literally Gelugpa means 'those of the way of virtue.'"[4]

In 1720 the Manchus of China conquered Tibet, and one way or another, the Chinese have maintained control ever since. When the Manchus were overthrown in China in 1911, the Tibetans revolted, but they were only partially successful in forcing the Chinese out. After opening up trade links with the British in India in 1914, Britain attempted to have a treaty signed that would place Tibet under external control of China but allow Tibetan internal autonomy. Refusing to sign the document, the Chinese maintained, in theory, their right of ownership, whereas Tibetans declared themselves free and independent. However, this declaration was more a wish than an actuality, as the Chinese have continued to oversee Tibet throughout the twentieth and now the early part of the twenty-first centuries, although internal autonomy was in existence until the 1950s.

In 1933, the thirteenth reincarnation of the Dalai Lama died and so the search for the new incarnation began. From Tibetan Lama Rato Khyongla Nawang Losang, we learn how the government knew where to find the next Dalai Lama. Only seven years old, Losang, himself the reincarnation of the ninth Khyongla of Tibet, visited the Potala in Lhasa, the capital:

The chapel containing the tomb [of the thirteenth Dalai Lama . . .] was three stories high facing south. . . . [It had] an enormous glass window that provided much better light than could be found in any other chapel of the palace. The Dalai Lama's body reposed on a throne within its second story surrounded by relics, books and images that had been placed there before the ceremony of sealing took place. A life-sized gilded copper image of the seated Dalai Lama, holding in his right hand a lotus and in his left the Wheel of Law, was set against one wall of the chapel. . . . In the corners of the room square pillars supported the chapel ceiling, and on the northeastern pillar, as the chapel keeper pointed out to us, there had grown a star-shaped meadow fungus, now protected by a glass box. We all studied the growth with curiosity. Although somebody remarked that it probably had grown because the wood of the pillar had not been dry enough when set in place, its appearance was nevertheless uncanny . . . later we came to realize that it was an indication that the new Dalai Lama would be found in Amdo, in the north east.[5]

After a vision from the regent, the next Dalai Lama, Lhamo Thondup, then only two years old, was brought to Lhasa in 1939. However, the Tibetan government had to pay the Chinese governor 400,000 Chinese dollars (about $92,000 American) for the privilege. "Renamed Ngawang Lobsang Tensin Gaytso—literally the eloquent, the wise, the defender of the faith, as deep as the ocean, he was enthroned on February 22, 1940, the fourteenth day of the first month of what Tibetans called the 'iron as dragon year.'"[6]

In 1955, Losang was forced to teach in an oppressed school run by the Chinese Communists. The young people were not allowed to learn about their religious and historical background. Because the country was basically a theocracy this situation became intolerable.

To my surprise, when I reported for work the next day instead of being introduced to a class, I was told I had been appointed to the Propaganda Office. At that time the Chinese were using Tibetans, whenever possible, to explain to villagers all the fine things our new rulers were going to do for us. . . . The first thing I saw on entering the room was blown up photographs of Stalin, Mao Tse-Tung, and Lenin staring out from the walls above the desks like supervising spirits.[7]

In March of 1959 Losang stated that "the Chinese general, commandant of the military post in Lhasa, had invited the Dalai Lama to attend a theatrical performance," to be presented in the forbidden zone inside the Chinese camp. At this same time hundreds of Tibetans were marching to proclaim their wish for freedom, their hatred of the Chinese approaching dangerous levels.

Fearing a kidnapping or assassination of the Dalai Lama, Losang realized the need for an escape plan and made his way to Norbulingka where his Holiness was staying. "As I hurried anxiously along, I heard the loudspeakers, which had been mounted on buildings occupied by the Chinese, warning our people not to revolt against their true friends, these same Chinese."

After notifying the Dalai Lama's tutors, Losang and a friend "casually sauntered past the camp, as though out for a stroll in the suburbs." They passed armed soldiers with big guns and pill boxes as they finally made their way beyond the Chinese lines.[8]

Joining many refugees, Losang fought through the difficult mountain trails and was happy to learn that the "Dalai Lama, disguised as a soldier [had] left the palace, walked to the river Kyi Chu, crossed it on a public ferry boat, and joined supporters to head for India."[9]

"The day after we arrived," Losang added, "we heard a helicopter flying overhead and were told that the Indian government was delivering rice to us."[10] Prime Minister Nehru granted the Dalai Lama political asylum. During the skirmishes that followed over ten thousand Tibetans were killed by the Chinese. Today, there are about thirty thousand Tibetans living as refugees in a town called Dharamsala in northern India with their beloved Dalai Lama.

IN PERSON, THE DALAI LAMA

Conference Report

On Friday, October 12, 1979, His Holiness the fourteenth reincarnation of the Dalai Lama appeared at Brown University, Providence, Rhode Island. He began his talk in Tibetan, stopping periodically to allow the translation to take place. The talk was divided into two parts. An aura combining almost childlike curiosity and radiant happiness surrounded the humble speaker, as his melodic voice began with part one.

"When we look on the surface (of peoples) there are many differences; but if we go deep down I feel we are the same. We are all members of the Human Family. We all same, no differences. All humans want happiness, no one want suffering.

"The essence of all religion," he continued, "is respect for each other, love, compassion, harmony, and Godliness. On one side there is hate and anger and too much attachment, and thus unhappiness. On the other side there is love, kindness, and the invitation for inner peace. For example, if two people experience identical tragedies there will still be great differences in [the] amount of suffering. This is due to spiritual development and inner attitudes. All racial, ideological, and international problems are man made. They are created by ourselves."

As the translator continued, the Dalai Lama would get impatient. Suddenly and quite unexpectedly, he burst into English. "If we can adopt a correct mental attitude, we can overcome these problems. So we need human understanding and genuine mutual cooperation on the basis of love and respect for one another. The politician must become religious-minded, not strongly attached to his own religion, as that is also dangerous, but sincere, compassionate, and open minded.

"In science and technology we achieve a lot; but in terms of real human feeling, we are severely lacking. We need for real warm feeling here." (He pointed to his heart.) "Whether or not you believe in religion is your own matter. But all must have respect to kindness. If I show kindness then others show kindness in return. If from my side there is wrong attitude, then from other side the same attitude—and outcome is war. Without a moral principle society could not survive. Without inner development (i.e., compassion and love), we cannot achieve inner peace; and without inner peace we cannot receive worldwide peace."

The Tibetan paused and explained that this was the end of part one of his speech. The audience smiled.

I often tell people that this century should be the century of dialogue. Peace will not come from thought or from Buddha. Peace must be built by humans, through action. So that means, whenever we face problem—dialogue. That's the only way. For that, we need inner disarmament. So our work should make a little contribution to materialize a peaceful, compassionate world later this century. That's my wish. It will not come immediately. But we have to make the effort.[11]

"I would like now to explain something about action, karma, and its effects. Pleasure and pain come from one source: our own inner actions. So thus it is easy to explain karma. If you act well you will be happy. If you don't, you undergo pain.

"Karma is separated into three types: physical, mental, and verbal. In terms of time there are two divisions:

1. Building up motivation (i.e., thinking)
2. Actual performance

"Therefore, karma is being done all the time. Buddha teaches that you are your own action. This is to say, through virtuous or nonvirtuous actions, all is due to your own actions. All responsibility lies upon yourself. Whether you know this or not makes no difference.

"The perfect society would contain self-control and self-examination. The type of karma one accumulates is in your own hands right now, so practice wisdom and compassion."

During a question-and-answer period one person asked, "If Tibetans are following the laws of karma, action and reaction, how could there be suffering there now?"

The Dalai Lama answered that these people could be working out karma from former lives from "other nations, other worlds, or even other galaxies."

His Holiness then stated that the main problem lies with the six million people that remain in Tibet rather than with the refugees. Although invited by the Communists to return, he feels that he can serve his country better from the outside.

Answering a question about anger he suggested that correct thinking and control of anger will allow it to dissolve. If it is let out, it gradually gets worse.

"How can we learn from our enemies?" someone else queried.

"We can learn tolerance," he said, "and learn to test our inner strength, courage, and determination. Paradoxically, it is through suffering that you become closer to reality. If life were very easy, you could never touch reality. Your enemy is your own best teacher."

With a broad smile and a bow to the audience, His Holiness, the fourteenth reincarnation of the Dalai Lama, departed with his small entourage.

This text was originally published in *MetaScience Quarterly* 1, no.3 (Autumn 1980): pp. 313–17.

Epilogue

This volume and its companion book, *Transcending the Speed of Light,* contain articles and ideas spanning forty years of my life. I am grateful for the technology, which preserved much of my thinking, and a bit amazed at the amount of work that I had done on this material as far back as the 1970s. Large sections were part of my master's thesis and, eight years later, my doctoral essays. What has changed since then? I think, in many ways, metaphysical thinking has retrogressed particularly through mainstream channels. For instance, one would be hard-pressed to come upon any advanced texts in parapsychology or consciousness research like *Psychic Explorations* edited by Edgar Mitchell and John White, *The Tao of Physics* by Fritjof Capra, or *Dream Telepathy* written by Ullmann, Krippner, and Vaughan. I haven't seen the Seth books by Jane Roberts in years, nor are the works of Lobsang Rampa, Wilhelm Reich, J. B. Rhine, D. Scott Rogo, Gurdjieff, or Ouspensky readily available. Yes, all of these works can be obtained online, but there is a big difference between hands-on browsing in a modern bookstore as compared to browsing through out-of-print works on the web.

I did not start out as a psychology major. I simply had a talent for the topic. Through the years I have been fortunate to work with some of the most advanced thinkers in the field, such as Dan Anthony, an expert in the field of graphology at New School University; at the University of Chicago, Dr. Herbert Meltzer, Dr. Daniel G. Freedman, and Dr. Bruno Bettelheim, a student of Sigmund Freud, who at the time, was the world's leading psychoanalyst; at Saybrook Institute, Dr. Stanley Krippner, leader in the fields of dreams and consciousness research; and at Providence College, Dr. Edwin Gora, a physicist whose teachers included Arnold Sommerfeld and Werner Heisenberg. Books that influenced me greatly included *Wit and It's Relation to the Unconscious* by Sigmund Freud; *New Model of the Universe* by P. D. Ouspensky; *Human Personality and Its Survival of Bodily Death* by F. W. H. Myers; *Unfinished Symphonies* by Rosemary Brown; *The Geller Papers* edited by Charles Panati; *Beyond Telepathy* by Andrija Puharich; *Knowledge of Higher Worlds and Their Attainment* by Rudolf Steiner; the writings of Carl Jung, J. B. Rhine, Lobsang Rampa, E. H. Anderson, Aristotle, Leibniz, Descartes, Kepler, Newton, Tesla, Einstein, Mach, Charles Musès, Arthur Koestler, Heinz Hartmann, Otto Fenichel, David Rapaport, Ivan Pavlov, Alexander Luria, Thomas Kuhn, and Gurdjieff; and the book *Thirty Years That Shook Physics* by George Gamow.

Taken as a gestalt, these writers helped me shape a model of mind essentially built on the works of, in order, Freud, Jung, Leibniz, Myers, Rhine, Ouspensky, and Gurdjieff. We start with the conscious, and beneath that are the preconscious and personal unconscious, and then Jung's collective unconscious. At the top end, in what Freud calls the ego, one can place much of the thinking of the cognitive psychologists like Beck, Ellis, Robbins, Assagioli, and Gurdjieff. Activation of the will and the process of self-observation can be neatly fit into the Freudian model.

A big question, not completely resolved, is where the individual mind ends. If divine energy is embedded inside the center of each of us, then the very highest states of consciousness can be accessed only through self-knowledge, which would include meditation, contemplation, lucid dreaming, and the idea of self-transcendence.

Rudolf Steiner sets up an interesting premise, namely that the archetypes of the collective psyche are essentially angels, higher beings living in the astral plane. My premise is that there is a hierarchy of consciousness, and man is somewhere in that hierarchy, but not at the top. We restrict our thinking by oftentimes punishing the extraordinary individual, or the one who threatens the prevailing worldview; Roger Bacon, Copernicus, Galileo, Nikola Tesla, and J. B. Rhine are cases in point.

I do not understand why there is such a vehement attack against the field of parapsychology. Telepathy is an easily provable phenomenon, and yet no mainstream college psychology or neurology text takes this phenomenon seriously. Frankly, this herd mentality is untenable for the simple reason that there are many scientific benefits to be had in understanding this process, benefits in such fields as psychology, neurophysiology, physics, and philosophy. The first step would be to set up telepathy experiments using EEG equipment and the MRI, and then try to figure out the neurophysical mechanisms involved. There is much to be learned.

The mistake many people make is equating unusual abilities with "miracles." On this account, I agree with Spinoza. I do not believe in miracles. My premise is that everything must follow natural law. Something is called a miracle only because we do not understand the underlying processes involved. For example, consider the Shroud of Turin. If we assume that it is a fake, the game is up, but if we take the premise that such an artifact was caused by a heretofore-unknown process, this kind of event, much like the Geller metal-bending phenomena, can then be seen as an *opportunity* for learning more about the underlying structure of the universe. See *Transcending the Speed of Light* for further discussion.

With regard to humans and the process of THINKING, it seems self-evident that this ability was already present as a potentiality before we arrived on the planet. My guess is that a conscious component, some teleological aspect, existed at the start of this universe. This component, the seed of our intelligence, is evident in DNA, a highly organized system that not only designs all aspects of the physical structure of life but also directs the growth of an organ—our brain—which not only produces all the levels of thought processes discussed in this treatise but also produces a process for studying its own existence.

I agree with Aristotle and Gurdjieff. We are headed somewhere.

There is a reason for life. Order presupposes conscious design. Freud's view, often forgotten, was that there is a universe of infinite dimensions present in the psyche of everyone. We glimpse this vast realm when we dream. All are linked to the One at the source, all have access to the source, but there may also be mediators, who, for the most part, leave the earth alone. If man screws up, God will not step in. Nazi Germany is a case in point. We have free will, but man also has a conscience, and thus, in the end, he must answer to the entity that placed this in his psyche. I like the kabbalistic/Gurdjieffian notion that we are in a partnership arrangement with the One. Call it Mother Nature, and that we breathe together.

Notes

CHAPTER 1. THE PHILOSOPHERS

1. Bennett, *Gurdjieff: Making a New World,* 57.
2. Ibid., 42.
3. O'Connor and Robertson, "Roger Bacon," www-gap.dcs.st-and.ac.uk/~ history/ Mathematicians.
4. Koestler, *The Sleepwalkers.*
5. Gora, "Pythagorean Trends in Modern Physics, Part II," 3.
6. Ibid.
7. Koestler, *The Sleepwalkers,* 27.
8. Ibid., 30.
9. Hothersall, *History of Psychology,* 25.
10. Mishlove, *Roots of Consiousness,* 25.
11. Gora, "Pythagorean Trends in Modern Physics, Part II," 14.
12. Sufismjournal.org, 2002.

CHAPTER 2. THE INDUSTRIAL REVOLUTION

1. O'Connor and Robertson, "Roger Bacon," www-gap.dcs.st-and.ac.uk/~ history/Mathematicians.
2. Wikipedia.
3. Brennan, *History and Systems of Psychology,* 109.
4. Ibid.
5. Hothersall, *History of Psychology,* 46–49; Brennan, *History and Systems of Psychology,* 86–87.
6. Leahey, *A History of Psychology,* 144.
7. Ibid., 145.
8. Hothersall, *History of Psychology,* 56.
9. Brennan, *History and Systems of Psychology,* 82.

10. Ibid., 125.

11. Loemker, *Struggle for Synthesis,* 55.

12. Bohm, "On the Intuitive Understanding of Nonlocality as Implied by Quantum Theory."

13. Mates, *The Philosophy of Leibniz,* 45.

14. Ibid., 41–42.

CHAPTER 3. THE LAWS OF HISTORY

1. Heisenberg, "The Copenhagen Interpretation of Quantum Theory."

2. Wikipedia, List of Journalists Killed in Russia.

3. Vico, "The New Science," 10–21.

4. Kant, "Ideas of a Universal History from a Cosmopolitan Point of View," 21–32.

5. Condorcet, "The Progress of the Human Mind."

6. Hegel, "Philosophical History," 62–64.

7. Ibid., 63.

8. Gardiner, *Theories of History,* 83.

9. Mill, "Elucidations of the Science of History," 92.

10. Ibid., 96.

11. Ibid., 101–4.

12. Buckle, "History and the Operation of Universal Laws," 114.

13. Ibid., 112–22.

14. Marx, "The Materialist Conception of History," 126.

15. Gardiner, *Theories of History.*

16. Ibid.

17. Ibid., 128.

18. Ibid., 131.

19. Ibid., 129.

20. Ibid., 131.

21. Ibid., 134.

22. Ibid., 135.

23. Tolstoy, "The Problem of Free Will and Necessity," 174.

CHAPTER 4. THE ROLE OF TECHNOLOGY

1. Hegel, "Philosophical History," 126.

2. Tesla, "The Problem of Increasing Human Energy," 175.

3. Ibid., 178.

4. Tesla, "The Transmission of Electrical Energy Without Wires," 429–31.

5. Tesla, "The Problem of Increasing Human Energy," 178.

6. Ibid.

7. Ibid., 179.

8. Spengler, "The World as History," 194.

CHAPTER 5. MODERN PSYCHOHISTORY

1. Manuel, "The Use and Abuse of Psychology in History," 43.
2. Dilthey, "The Understanding of Other Persons and Their Life Expressions," 213.
3. Ibid., 218.
4. Ibid., 219.
5. Febvre, *Combats pour l'histoire.*
6. Manuel, "The Use and Abuse of Psychology in History," 46.
7. Ibid.
8. Ibid.
9. Freud, *Totem and Taboo.*
10. Freud, *Civilization and Its Discontents.*
11. Freud, *The Future of an Illusion.*
12. Freud, *Leonardo da Vinci, A Study in Psychosexuality.*
13. Freud and Bullitt, *Thomas Woodrow Wilson, A Psychological Study.*
14. Freud, *Totem and Taboo,* 808–9.
15. Freud, *The Future of an Illusion,* 10.
16. Mick Jagger and Keith Richards, "You Can't Always Get What You Want," 1968.

CHAPTER 6. SOCIOLOGY, PSYCHOLOGY, AND HISTORY

1. Kren and Rappoport, eds., *Varieties of Psychohistory,* 1.
2. Mazlish, "What Is Psychohistory?" 18–19.
3. Ibid.
4. Erickson, *Young Man Luther.*
5. Erickson, *Gandhi's Truth.*
6. Erickson, *Life History and the Historical Moment,* 20.
7. Ibid.
8. Manuel, "The Use and Abuse of Psychology in History," 51.
9. Erickson, *Life History and the Historical Moment,* 22; Manuel, "The Use and Abuse of Psychology in History," 5.
10. Erickson, *Life History and the Historical Moment,* 24.
11. Ibid., 27–29.
12. Ibid., 24.
13. Erickson, *Young Man Luther,* 17–24, 165.
14. Erickson, *Life History and the Historical Moment,* 45.
15. DeMause, "What Is Psychohistory?" 179–84.
16. DeMause, *The New Psychohistory,* 13.
17. Ibid., 12.
18. DeMause, "What Is Psychohistory?" 180.
19. DeMause, "The Fetal Origins of History," 1–89.

20. Ibid, 15.

21. Ibid., 2.

22. Ibid., 68.

CHAPTER 7. CRITICAL THEORISTS

1. Held, *Introduction to Critical Theory*, 29.

2. Adorno, "Culture Industry Reconsidered," 3–7.

3. Fromm, *Escape From Freedom*.

4. Horkheimer, *Critical Theory: Selected Essays*.

5. Marcuse, *Eros and Civilization*.

6. Held, *Introduction to Critical Theory*, 15.

7. Ibid., 31.

8. Ibid., 33.

9. Ibid.

10. Ibid., 68; Marcuse, *Eros and Civilization*, 430.

11. Held, *Introduction to Critical Theory*, 69.

12. Ibid., 68.

13. Ibid., 71.

CHAPTER 8. THE CRITICS

1. Capps, "Psychohistory and Historical Genres: The Plight and Promise of Eriksonian Biography."

2. DeMause, *The New Psychohistory*, 9.

3. Kren and Rappoport, *Varieties of Psychohistory*, 65.

4. Manuel, "The Use and Abuse of Psychology in History," 43.

5. Kren and Rappoport, *Varieties of Psychohistory*, 65.

6. Stannard, *Shrinking History*, xix.

7. Ibid., 150.

8. Freud, *Leonardo da Vinci, A Study in Psychosexuality*.

9. Stannard, *Shrinking History*, 147.

10. Ibid., 149–50.

11. Freud, *Leonardo da Vinci, A Study in Psychosexuality*, 120.

12. Mannheim, *The Sociology of Knowledge*, 143–44.

CHAPTER 9. NINETEENTH-CENTURY PSYCHOLOGY

1. Boring, *History, Psychology and Science*, 95.

CHAPTER 10. THE MYSTERY OF HYPNOTISM

1. Ellsworth, *The Key to Hypnotism*, 11.

2. therapeutictouch.org.

3. Ellsworth, *The Key to Hypnotism,* 11–12.

4. Ibid., 35–36.

5. Ibid., 39.

6. Ibid., 70–82.

7. Ibid., 118.

8. Ibid., 104.

9. Ibid., ii.

10. Sidis, *Psychology of Suggestion,* 129.

11. Ibid., 138–39.

12. Ibid., 245–46

13. Ibid.

14. Ibid., 252.

15. James, *William James on Psychical Research,* 34.

16. Ellenberger, *Discovery of the Unconscious,* 386–88.

17. Seifer, *Levels of Mind.*

CHAPTER 12. BRAINWAVES AND DREAMS

1. Lu Zhang, Liu, Soong, and Diasio, "Relationship of Circadian Rhythm to Toxicity."

2. Herbert Meltzer, lecture at the University of Chicago, 1972.

CHAPTER 13. MEMORY, ENGRAMS, AND MRNA

1. Hyden, "RNA: A Functional Characteristic of the Neuron and its Glia."

2. Seifer, *Levels of Mind.*

3. Abstracted from Hyden, "RNA: A Functional Characteristic of the Neuron and its Glia."

4. Gruzeiler, "Hypnosis from a Neurobiological Perspective," 111–32.

5. Jouvet, "The States of Sleep," 62–68; Jouvet, "Biogenic Amines and the States of Sleep," 32–34.

6. Gruzeiler, "Hypnosis from a Neurobiological Perspective," 123.

7. Ibid., 112.

8. Luria, *The Working Brain: An Introduction to Neuropsychology.*

9. Ibid.

CHAPTER 15. A PSYCHOANALYTIC MODEL OF MIND

1. Freud, *The Interpretation of Dreams.*

2. Jung, *Memories, Dreams, Reflections.*

3. Hall and Lindzey, *Theories of Personality,* 35.

4. Ibid., 35.

CHAPTER 17. FREUD'S PSYCHOSEXUAL STAGES OF DEVELOPMENT

1. Cloninger, *Theories of Personality*, 49.
2. Ellis and Abrams, *Personality Theories: Critical Perspective*, 103.
3. Freud, *Collected Works*, 582.
4. Cloninger, *Theories of Personality*, 51.

CHAPTER 18. CONSCIOUS, PRECONSCIOUS, AND UNCONSCIOUS

1. Freud, *Collected Works*, 542.
2. Jolley, *Leibniz and Locke: A Study of the New Essays on Human Understanding*, 104.
3. Freud, *Collected Works*, 518.
4. O'Leary, *Door Number Three*, 17–18.

CHAPTER 19. JUNG AND FREUD

1. Jung, *Memories, Dreams, Reflections*, 12.
2. Parker, *Women and Carl Jung: Sabina Spielrein*, Jungcurrents.com.
3. Jung, *Memories, Dreams, Reflections*, 149.
4. Ibid., 158.
5. Ibid., 159.
6. Ibid., 157.
7. Ibid., 160.
8. Freud, *Collected Works*, 185.
9. Brome, *Jung: Man and Myth*, 120.
10. Ibid.
11. Freud, *The Interpretation of Dreams*, 184.
12. Freud, *Civilization and Its Discontents*.
13. Jung, *Memories, Dreams, Reflections*, 71.
14. Hall and Lindzey, *Theories of Personality*, 83–84.
15. Ibid., 84–85.
16. Ibid., 86.
17. Jung, *Memories, Dreams, Reflections*, 106.
18. Ellis and Abrams, *Personality Theories: Critical Perspective*, 150.
19. Freud, *The Interpretation of Dreams*, 497.
20. Ibid., 972.
21. Ibid., 950.
22. Ibid., 960.
23. Ibid., 938.
24. Ibid., 941.

25. Ibid.
26. Ibid., 974.
27. Ibid., 974–75.
28. Ibid., 968.
29. Ibid., 974.
30. Ibid., 970–71.

CHAPTER 20. THE DYNAMICS OF MIND

1. Freud, *Wit and Its Relation to the Unconscious.*
2. Freud, "The History of the Psychoanalytic Movement."
3. Freud, *Collected Works,* 965.
4. Hartmann, *Ego Psychology and the Problems of Adaptation.*
5. Freud, *Collected Works,* 542.
6. Fenichel, *The Psychoanalytic Theory of Neurosis.*
7. Janov, *The Primal Scream.*
8. Reich, *Character Analysis.*
9. Freud, *The Interpretation of Dreams,* 938.
10. Reich, *The Function of the Orgasm,* 45.
11. Reich, *The Mass Psychology of Fascism.*
12. Bennett, *Gurdjieff: Making a New World.*
13. Whyte, *The Organization Man.*

CHAPTER 21. COLLECTIVE CONSTRUCT REALITIES

1. Whyte, *The Organization Man.*
2. Adorno, "Culture Industry Reconsidered," 3–7.
3. Held, *Introduction to Critical Theory,* 68.
4. DeMause "What Is Psychohistory?" 172.
5. Ibid.
6. Ibid., 180.
7. Ibid., 172.
8. Feinstein and Krippner, "Personal Mythology as a Paradigm for Holistic Health," 198–217.
9. Ibid.
10. Ibid., 198.
11. Ibid., 3.
12. Ibid., 4.
13. Ibid., 7.
14. Ibid., 13.
15. Jung, *Portable Jung.*

CHAPTER 22. DREAMS AND THE COLLECTIVE PSYCHE

1. Brown, *Unfinished Symphonies*, 18.
2. Heywood, *Reach of Mind*.
3. *Playboy* interview conducted by Marcia Seligson, January 1976.

CHAPTER 25. THE CULTURAL MYTH

1. DeMause, "What Is Psychohistory?" 178–79.
2. Ibid.
3. Janis, "Groupthink Among Policy Makers," 316.
4. Ibid.
5. Ibid., 318.
6. Seifer, *Transcending the Speed of Light*.
7. Gamow, *Thirty Years That Shook Physics*, 119–20.
8. Seifer, *Transcending the Speed of Light*, 71–73.
9. Janis, "Groupthink Among Policy Makers," 318–19.
10. Ibid.
11. Ibid., 321.

CHAPTER 26. THOUGHT TRANSFERENCE

1. *Publishers Weekly* review of *Psychic Discoveries Behind the Iron Curtain* by Sheila Ostrander and Lynn Schroeder, 1970.
2. Ullman, Krippner, and Vaughn, *Dream Telepathy*, 108.

CHAPTER 27. OCCULT SCHOOLS, AVATARS, AND SEED MEN

1. P. D. Ouspensky, *New Model of the Universe*, 29–30.
2. Ibid.
3. Dane Rudhyar, *The Sun Is also a Star*.
4. Ibid., 245.
5. Evans, *Cults of Unreason*.
6. Ibid., 10.
7. Ibid., 14.
8. Ibid., 219.
9. Ibid., 175.
10. Ibid.
11. Ibid., 247.
12. Swann, *To Kiss the Earth Goodbye*.

CHAPTER 28. GURDJIEFF (1874?–1949)

1. Gurdjieff, *Beelzebub's Tales to His Grandson*, 27–30.
2. Ibid., 35.

3. Gurdjieff, *Meetings with Remarkable Men.*
4. Ibid., 263–64.
5. Bennett, *Gurdjieff: Making a New World,* 27.
6. Ouspensky, *In Search of the Miraculous,* 7.
7. Ibid., 18–19.

CHAPTER 30. TONY ROBBINS ON
THE CAUSE AND CURE OF DEPRESSION

1. Ellis and Abrams, *Personality Theories: Critical Perspective.*

CHAPTER 31. QUANTUM JUMPS: URI GELLER

1. Panati, *The Geller Papers.*
2. Kuhn, *The Structure of Scientific Revolutions.*
3. Ibid., 5.
4. James, *William James on Psychical Research,* 27.
5. Panati, *The Geller Papers.*
6. Sheila Ostrander and Lynn Schroeder, *Psychic Discoveries Behind the Iron Curtain.*
7. Kuhn, *The Structure of Scientific Revolutions,* 6.
8. Ibid.
9. Ibid., 7.
10. Geller and Boteach, *The Psychic and the Rabbi,* 111.

CHAPTER 32. WAKING

1. Gurdjieff, *Views from the Real World,* 75.
2. Ibid.
3. Benjamin, *Basic Self-Knowledge: Based on the Gurdjieff System of Development.*
4. Gurdjieff, *Views from the Real World,* 70.
5. De Hartmann, *Our Life with Gurdjieff,* 49.
6. Peters, *Boyhood with Gurdjieff,* 163–64.

CHAPTER 33. EDUCATION OF THE WILL

1. Assagioli, *Psychosynthesis.*
2. Rank in Lieberman, *Acts of Will: The Life and Work of Otto Rank,* 126.
3. Ibid., 357–58.
4. Payot, *The Education of the Will,* 61.
5. Ibid., 80.
6. Ibid., 70–77.
7. Ibid., 81.
8. Ibid., 83–84.

9. Ibid., 86.

10. Ibid.

11. Ibid., 379.

12. Anderson, *Psychical Developments*.

13. Ibid.

14. Trungpa, *The Sacred Path of the Warrior*.

15. Ibid.

16. Anderson, *Psychical Developments*.

17. Ibid.

18. Ibid.

19. Ibid.

20. Assagioli, *Psychosynthesis*.

CHAPTER 34. LAST DAYS

1. Caruso, *A Personal History*, 178.

2. Bennett, *Gurdjieff: Making a New World*, 7.

3. Ibid.

4. Gurdjieff, *Beelzebub's Tales to His Grandson*, 146.

5. Ibid., 146–47.

6. Anon., *The Kybalion: Hermetic Philosophies by Three Initiates*.

CHAPTER 35. I AM

1. Steiner, *An Outline of Occult Science*, 34.

2. Ibid., 34–35.

3. Peters, *Gurdjieff Remembered*, 110.

4. Ibid., 116.

CHAPTER 36. HIS HOLINESS THE DALAI LAMA

1. Jung, *Memories, Dreams, Reflections*, 150.

2. Evans-Wentz, *The Tibetan Book of the Dead*, xxxix.

3. Ibid., 66–67.

4. Grimes, "For Tibetans an End to the Long Exile?" 33–40.

5. Losang, *My Life and Lives, The Story of a Tibetan Incarnation*, 45–46.

6. Grimes, "For Tibetans an End to the Long Exile?" 33–40.

7. Losang, *My Life and Lives, The Story of a Tibetan Incarnation*, 182.

8. Ibid., 201.

9. Grimes, "For Tibetans an End to the Long Exile?" 33–40.

10. Losang, *My Life and Lives, The Story of a Tibetan Incarnation*, 215.

11. Mathison, "A Conversation with the Dalai Lama," 54–59.

Bibliography

Adorno, Theodor. "Culture Industry Reconsidered." *New German Critique* 6 (1975): 3–7.

Anderson, E. H. *Psychical Developments.* Toledo, Ohio, 1901.

Anonymous. *The Kybalion: Hermetic Philosophies by Three Initiates.* 1908.

Assagioli, Roberto. *Psychosynthesis.* New York: Penguin, 1981.

Barnett, Lincoln. *The Universe and Dr. Einstein.* New York: Time, 1962.

Barrow, John, and Frank Tipler. *The Anthropic Cosmological Principle.* Oxford, England: Clarendon Press, 1986.

Beck, Aaron. *Cognitive Therapy and the Emotional Disorders.* New York: International University Press, 1976.

Benjamin, Harry. *Basic Self-Knowledge: Based on the Gurdjieff System of Development.* York Beach, Maine: Weiser Books, 1995.

Bennett, J. G. *Gurdjieff: Making a New World.* Santa Fe, N.Mex.: Bennett Books, 1992.

Boheme, Kate. *Realization Made Easy.* Holyoke, Mass.: Elizabeth Towne Company, 1917.

Bohm, David. "On the Intuitive Understanding of Nonlocality as Implied by Quantum Theory." *Foundations of Physics* 5 (1975).

Boring, Edwin. *History, Psychology and Science.* New York: John Wiley, 1963.

Brennan, James. *History and Systems of Psychology.* Upper Saddle River, N.J.: Prentice Hall, 1998.

Brome, Vincent. *Jung: Man and Myth.* New York: MacMillan, 1981.

Brown, Rosemary. *Unfinished Symphonies.* New York: William Morrow & Sons, 1971.

Buckle, H. T. "History and the Operation of Universal Laws." In *Theories of History,* edited by P. Gardiner. Glencoe, Ill.: Free Press, 1959.

Capps, D. "Psychohistory and Historical Genres." In *Childhood and Selfhood,* edited by P. Homans. Bucknell: Buckness University Press, 1978.

Carter, Brandon. *Large Number Coincidences and the Anthropic Principle in Cosmology.* Princeton: Princeton University Press, 1973.

Caruso, Dorothy. *A Personal History.* New York: Hermitage House, 1952.

Chalmers, David. "The Puzzle of Conscious Experience." *Scientific American* (December 1995): 80–86.

Cloninger, Susan. *Theories of Personality.* Upper Saddle River, N.J.: Prentice Hall, 2007.

Comte, A. "The Positive Philosophy and the Study of Society." In *Theories of History,* edited by P. Gardiner. Glencoe, Ill.: Free Press, 1959.

Condorcet, A. de. "The Progress of the Human Mind." In *Theories of History,* edited by P. Gardiner. Glencoe, Ill.: Free Press, 1959.

Dalai Lama. *How to Practice Meditation.* New York: Pocketbooks, 2002.

De Hartmann, Thomas. *Our Life with Gurdjieff.* New York: Penguin, 1972.

DeMause, L. *The New Psychohistory.* New York: Psychohistory Press, 1975.

———. "The Evolution of Childhood." In *Varieties of Psychohistory,* edited by G. Kren, and L. Rappoport. New York: Springer, 1976.

———. "The Fetal Origins of History." *Journal of Psychohistory* (1981): 1–89.

———. "What Is Psychohistory?" *Journal of Psychohistory* (1981): 179–84.

Dilthey, W. "The Understanding of Other Persons and Their Life Expressions." In *Theories of History,* edited by P. Gardiner. Glencoe, Ill.: Free Press, 1959.

Ellenberger, Henry. *Discovery of the Unconscious.* New York: Basic Books, 1970.

Ellis, Albert. *Reason and Emotion in Psychotherapy.* New York: Lyle Stuart, 1962.

Ellis, Albert, and Michael Abrams. *Personality Theories: Critical Perspective.* New York: Sage Books, 1999.

Ellsworth, Robert G. *The Key to Hypnotism.* Philadelphia: David McKay, 1902.

Erikson, E. *Young Man Luther.* New York: W. W. Norton, 1958.

———. *Gandhi's Truth.* New York: W. W. Norton, 1969.

———. "On the Nature of Psychohistorical Evidence: In Search of Gandhi." In *Explorations in Psychohistory,* edited by R. Lifton. New York: Simon and Schuster, 1975.

———. *Life History and the Historical Moment.* New York: W. W. Norton, 1975.

Evans, Christopher. *Cults of Unreason.* New York: Delta, 1973.

Evans-Wentz, W. Y. *The Tibetan Book of the Dead.* London: Oxford University Press, 1960.

Faraday, Ann. *Dream Power.* New York: Berkley Publishers, 1972.

Febvre, L. *Combats pour l'histoire.* Paris: A. Colin, 1953.

Feinstein, D. "Personal Mythology as a Paradigm for Holistic Health." *American Journal of Ortho-Psychiatry* (April 1979): 198–217.

Feinstein, D., and Krippner, S. *Personal Mythology: The Psychology of Your Evolving Self.* New York: Tarcher, 1988.

Fenichel, Otto. *The Psychoanalytic Theory of Neurosis.* New York: W. W. Norton, 1944.

Frayn, Michael. *Copenhagen.* London: Metheun, 2000.

Freud, S. *Civilization and Its Discontents.* London: Hogarth Press, 1930.

———. *Collected Works.* New York: Modern Library, Random House, 1938.

———. *Totem and Taboo.* New York: Basic Books, 1938.

———. *The Future of an Illusion.* New York: Liveright, 1949.

———. *Leonardo da Vinci, A Study in Psychosexuality.* New York: W. W. Norton, 1964.

———. "The Occult Significance of Dreams; and Telepathy." In *Psychology and Extrasensory Perception,* edited by Raymond Van Over. New York: New American Library, 1972.

———. *Wit and Its Relationship to the Unconscious.* Mineola, N.Y.: Dover Publications, 1993.

Freud, S., and W. C. Bullitt. *Thomas Woodrow Wilson, A Psychological Study.* Boston: Houghton Mifflin, 1967.

Fromm, Erich. *Escape from Freedom.* New York: W. W. Norton, 1941.

Gamow, George. *Thirty Years That Shook Physics.* New York: Anchor Press, 1966.

Gardiner, P., ed. *Theories of History.* Glencoe, Ill.: Free Press, 1959.

Gates, Bill. Interview. *Playboy,* September 1994.

Gauquelin, Michel. *The Cosmic Clocks.* New York: Henry Regnery, 1967.

Gazzaniga, Michael. *The Bisected Brain.* New York: Meredith Corp, 1970.

Geller, Uri, and Rabbi Boteach. *The Psychic and the Rabbi.* Naperville, Ill.: Sourcebooks, 2001.

Goethe. *Faust.* Cambridge, Mass.: Houghton, 1856.

Gora, Edwin. "Pythagorean Trends in Modern Physics, Part II." *MetaScience Publications.* Kingston, R.I., 1985 (unpublished).

Grimes, Paul. "For Tibetans an End to the Long Exile?" *Asia Magazine* (March/April 1979): 33–40.

Grossman, M. *Textbook of Physiological Psychology.* New York: John Wiley and Sons, 1968.

Gruzeiler, John. "Hypnosis from a Neurobiological Perspective." *Anales de Psicologia* 15 (1999): 111–32.

Gurdjieff, George Ivanovich. *Beelzebub's Tales to His Grandson,* vols. 1–3. New York: Dutton: 1973.

———. *Meetings with Remarkable Men.* New York: Dutton, 1974.

———. *Views from the Real World.* New York: Dutton, 1975.

Hadrat Abd al-Qadir al-Jilani. "The Seat of Thought." Sufijournal.org, accessed 2002.

Hall, Calvin, and Gardner Lindzey. *Theories of Personality.* New York: John Wiley, 1970.

Hartmann, Heinz. *Ego Psychology and the Problems of Adaptation.* New York: International Universities Press, 1964.

Held, David. *Introduction to Critical Theory.* Berkeley.: University of California Press, 1980.

Hegel, G. W .F. "Philosophical History." In *Theories of History,* edited by P. Gardiner. Glencoe, Ill.: Free Press, 1959.

Heisenberg, Werner. "The Copenhagen Interpretation of Quantum Theory." In *Physics and Philosophy.* New York: George Allen and Unwin, 1958.

Herder, J. G. "Ideas Towards a Philosophy of the History of Man." In *Theories of History,* edited by P. Gardiner. Glencoe, Ill.: Free Press, 1959.

Heywood, Rosalind. *Reach of Mind.* New York: E. P. Dutton, 1974.

Homans, P., ed. *Childhood and Selfhood.* Bucknell, Penn.: Bucknell University Press, 1978.

Horkheimer, M. *Critical Theory: Selected Essays.* New York: Herder and Herder, 1972.

Hothersall, David. *History of Psychology.* New York: McGraw Hill, 1995.

Hyden, Holger. "RNA: A Functional Characteristic of the Neuron and its Glia." In *Brain Functions,* edited by Mary Brazier. Berkeley: University of California Press, 1964.

James, William. *William James on Psychical Research,* edited by G. Murphey and R. Ballou. New York: Viking Press, 1973.

Janis, I. "Groupthink Among Policy Makers." In *Varieties of Psychohistory,* edited by G. Kren and L. Rapapport. New York: Springer, 1976.

Janov, Arthur. *The Primal Scream.* New York: Dell, 1972.

Jolley, Nicholas. *Leibniz and Locke: A Study of the New Essays on Human Understanding.* Oxford: Clarendon Press, 1984.

Jones, R. S. *Physics as Metaphor.* Minneapolis: University of Minnesota, 1982.

Jouvet, Michael. "Biogenic Amines and the States of Sleep." *Science* 163 (January 1964): 32–34.

———. "The States of Sleep." *Scientific American* (February 1967): 62–68.

Jung, Carl. *Memories, Dreams, Reflections.* New York: Vintage, 1963.

———. *Portable Jung.* New York: Viking Press, 1971.

Kant, I. "Ideas of a Universal History From a Cosmopolitan Point of View." In *Theories of History,* edited by P. Gardiner. Glencoe, Ill.: Free Press, 1959.

Keen, Sam. "Interview with Roberto Assagioli." *Psychology Today,* December 1974.

Koestler, Arthur. *The Sleepwalkers.* New York: Macmillan, 1958.

Kren, George M., and Leon Rappoport, eds. *Varieties of Psychohistory.* New York: Springer, 1976.

Krippner, Stanley, and David Feinstein. *The Mythic Path.* Santa Rosa, Calif.: Energy Psychology Press, 2006.

Kuhn, Thomas. *The Structure of Scientific Revolutions.* Chicago: University of Chicago Press, 1990.

Leahey, T. H. *A History of Psychology.* Englewood Cliffs, N.J.: Prentice Hall, 2000.

Leibniz, Gottfried Wilhelm. *The Monadology.* www.knuten.lieu.se/monadology. Text translated by Robert Latta in 1898.

Lieberman, James. *Acts of Will: The Life and Work of Otto Rank.* New York: Free Press, 1985.

Lifton, R. J., ed. *Explorations in Psychohistory.* New York: Simon and Schuster, 1975.

Loemker, L. E. *Struggle for Synthesis.* Boston: Harvard University Press, 1972.

Losang, Rato Khangla Nawang. *My Life and Lives, The Story of a Tibetan Incarnation.* New York: E. P. Dutton, 1977.

Luce, Gay Gaer. *Biorhythms in Human and Animal Physiology.* New York: Dover, Publishing, 1971.

Luria, Alexander R. *Higher Cortical Functions in Man.* New York: Basic Books, 1966.

———. *The Working Brain: An Introduction to Neuropsychology.* New York: Basic Books, 1973.

Machiavelli, N. *The Art of War and the Prince.* New York: AMS Press, 1967.

Mannheim, Karl. *The Sociology of Knowledge.* London: Routledge, Kegan and Paul, 1952.

Manuel, F. "The Use and Abuse of Psychology in History." In *Varieties of Psychohistory,* edited by G. Kren and L. Rappoport. New York: Springer, 1976.

Marcuse, Herbert. *Eros and Civilization.* Boston: Beacon Press, 1966.

Marrow, H. *The Meaning of History.* Baltimore: Helicon Press, 1959.

Marx, K. "The Materialist Conception of History." In *Theories of History,* edited by P. Gardiner. Glencoe, Ill.: Free Press, 1959.

Mates, Benson. *The Philosophy of Leibniz.* New York: Oxford University Press, 1986.

Mathison, Melissa. "A Conversation with the Dalai Lama." *Rolling Stone,* August 4, 2011.

Mazlish, B. "What Is Psychohistory?" In *Varieties of Psychohistory,* edited by G. Kren and L. Rappoport. New York: Springer, 1976.

Mill, J. S. "Elucidations of the Science of History." In *Theories of History,* edited by P. Gardiner. Glencoe, Ill.: Free Press, 1959.

Mishlove, Jeffrey. *Roots of Consciousness.* New York: Random House, 1979.

Musès, Charles, and Arthur Young. *Consciousness and Reality.* New York: Avon Books, 1972.

Myers, F. W. H. *Human Personality and Its Survival of Bodily Death.* New York: Longmans, Green and Company, 1903.

Nicol, Maurice. *Gurdjieff and Ouspensky: Psychological Commentaries,* vols. 1–4. Boulder and London: Shambhala, 1984.

Nott, C. S. *Teachings of Gurdjieff: A Pupil's Journal.* New York: Arkana/Penguin, 1990.

O'Connor, J. J., and E. F. Robertson. "Roger Bacon." www-gap.dcs.st-and.ac.uk/~history/Mathematicians.

O'Leary, Patrick. *Door Number Three.* New York: Tor, 1995.

Ornstein, Robert. *The Psychology of Consciousness.* New York: Viking Press, 1972.

Ostrander, Sheila, and Lynn Schroeder. *Psychic Discoveries Behind the Iron Curtain.* New York: Prentice Hall, 1970.

Ouspensky, P. D. *The 4ᵗʰ Way.* New York: Vantage Press, 1957.

———. *In Search of the Miraculous.* New York: Harcourt and Brace, 1960.

———. *New Model of the Universe.* New York: Harcourt and Brace, 1960.

Panati, Charles. *The Geller Papers.* New York: Houghton Mifflin, 1976.

Parker, Stephen. *Women and Carl Jung: Sabina Spielrein.* www.Jungcurrents.com, accessed November 2010.

Patterson, William P. *Struggle of the Magicians: Why Uspenskii Left Gurdjieff.* Fairfax, Calif.: Arete Communications, 1996.

Payot, Jules. *The Education of the Will.* London: Funk and Wagnalls, 1909.

Peters, Fritz. *Boyhood with Gurdjieff.* Santa Barbara, Calif.: Capra Press, 1980.

———. *Gurdjieff Remembered.* Santa Barbara, Calif.: Capra Press, 1984.

Progoff, Ira. *Jung, Synchronicity and Human Destiny.* New York: Julian Press, 1973.

Puharich, Andrija. *Beyond Telepathy.* New York: Anchor Press, 1973.

Rapaport, David. "Activity and Passivity of the Ego with Regards to Reality." *Collected Writings,* edited by Morton Gill. New York: Basic Books, 1967.

Read, Herbert. *Origin of Form in Art.* New York: Horizon Press, 1965.

Reich, Wilhelm. *The Mass Psychology of Fascism.* Rangeley, Maine: Orgone Institute Press, 1946.

———. *Cosmic Superimposition.* Rangeley, Maine: Orgone Institute Press, 1953.

———. *The Function of the Orgasm.* New York: Noonday Press, 1972.

———. *Reich Speaks of Freud.* Rangeley, Maine: Orgone Institute Press, 1972.

———. *Character Analysis.* New York: Farrar, Strauss and Giroux, 1984.

Robbins, Tony. *Life Management Systems.* Audiocassette. Guthy-Renker, 1996.

Roberts, Jane. *Seth Speaks.* New York: Bantam Books, 1972.

Rothman, Milton. *The Laws of Physics.* Greenwich, Conn.: Facett Publushers, 1963.

Rudhyar, Dane. *The Sun Is Also a Star.* New York: Dutton, 1975.

Runyan, William. *Psychology and Historical Interpretation.* New York: Oxford University Press, 1988.

Seifer, Marc. *Levels of Mind.* Masters thesis, Chicago, Ill.: University of Chicago, 1974.

———. *A Psychophysiological Model of Mind.* Kingston, R.I., 1975 (unpublished).

———. "Lobsang Rampa." *Ancient Astronauts* (July 1976): 8–10.

———. "Uri Geller: Handwriting Analysis; Exposé." *ESP Magazine* 1, no. 3 (September 1976): 14–18, 48–49.

———. "Wilhelm Reich." *MetaScience* 1–2 (Winter 1980): 73–76.

———. "The Mind of the Skeptic and the Hierarchy of Doubt." *MetaScience* 1, no. 3 (Autumn 1980): 285–95.

———. "Gurdjieff." *MetaScience* 1, no. 3 (Autumn 1980): 348–52.

———. "An Interview with Uri Geller." *MetaScience* 1, no. 3 (Autumn 1980): 335–45.

———. "His Holiness: The Dalai Lama." *MetaScience* 1, no. 3 (Autumn 1980): 313–17.

———. "The Belief in Life on Mars: A Turn-of-the-Century Group Fantasy." *Proceedings: Sixth Annual International Psychohistory Convention.* New York: City College of New York and International Psychohistory Society, 1984.

———. "The Inventor and the Corporation: Case studies of Nikola Tesla, Steven Jobs and Edwin Armstrong." Edited by S. Elswick. *Proceedings of the 2nd International Tesla Society,* Conference. Colorado Springs, Colo.: ITS Press, 1986.

———. "A History of Psychohistory." Edited by J. Atlas. *Psychology and History.* New York: Long Island University and International Psychohistory Society, 1986.

———. *Nikola Tesla: Psychohistory of a Forgotten Inventor.* Doctoral dissertation, San Francisco: Saybrook Institute, 1986.

———. Book Review: *Uri Geller: Mystic or Magician?* by Jonathan Margolis. *Journal of Religion and Psychical Research* (Autumn 1999).

———. *Inward Journey.* Kingston, R.I.: Doorway Press, 2003.

———. *Transcending the Speed of Light.* Rochester, Vt.: Inner Traditions, 2008.

Seifer, Marc, and Howard Smukler. "The Puharich Interview." *Gnostica* (September 1978): 21–24, 78–81.

Sidis, B. *Psychology of Suggestion.* Kila, Mont.: Kessinger Publication, 2006.

Spengler, Otto. "The World as History." In *Theories of History,* edited by P. Gardiner. Glencoe, Ill.: Free Press, 1959.

Sperry, R. W. "Cerebral Organization and Behavior." *Science* 133 (June 2, 1961): 1749–57.

———. "The Great Cerebral Commissure." *Scientific American* 210, no. 18 (January 1964): 42–52.

Steiner, Rudolf. *An Outline of Occult Science.* New York: Anthroposophic Press, 1972.

Sui, Choa Kok. *The Ancient Practice of Pranic Healing.* Newburyport, Mass.: Red Wheel Weiser, 1990.

Swann, Ingo. *To Kiss the Earth Goodbye.* New York: Hawthorn, 1975.

Taylor, Alfred. "Meaning and Matter." In *Consciousness and Reality,* by Charles Musès and Arthur Young. New York: Avon Books, 1972.

Tesla, Nikola. "The Problem of Increasing Human Energy." *The Century* (June 1900): 175–211.

———. "The Transmission of Electrical Energy Without Wires." *Electrical World and Engineer* (March 4, 1904): 429–31.

"Three Initiates." *The Kybalion.* Chicago, Ill.: The Yogi Publication Society, 1940.

Tobin, Paul. "Is the Universe Tuned for Life?" www. geocites.com/paulntobin/fine-tuned.html#1.

Tolstoy, L. "The Problem of Free Will and Necessity." In *Theories of History,* edited by P. Gardiner. Glencoe, Ill.: Free Press, 1959.

Trungpa, Chögyam. *The Sacred Path of the Warrior*. San Francisco: Shambhala Press, 2007.

Vico, G. "The New Science." In *Theories of History*, edited by P. Gardiner. Glencoe, Ill.: Free Press, 1959.

Ullman, Krippner, and Vaughn. *Dream Telepathy*. New York: Penguin, 1974.

Vygotsky, Lev. *Lev Vygotsky Quotations*. www.pubpages.unh.edu, accessed 2011.

Watson, Robert I. *The Great Psychologists: Aristotle to Freud*. New York: J. B. Lippincot, 1968.

Whyte, L., et. al., eds. *Hierarchical Structures*. New York: Elsevier Publishing, 1969.

Whyte Jr., William H. *The Organization Man*. New York: Schuster, 1956.

Wright, Robert. *Three Scientists and Their Gods: Looking for Meaning in an Age of Information*. New York: Times Books, 1988.

Wolman, B., ed. *The Psychoanalytic Interpretations of History*. Englewood Cliffs, N.J.: Prentice Hall, 1973.

Zhang, Lu, Liu, Soong, and Diasio. "Relationship of Circadian Rhythm to Toxicity." *Icanar Research* (June 15, 1993).

Index

About the Author

Marc J. Seifer has a Bachelor of Science degree from the University of Rhode Island and did postgraduate work in graphology at New School University. He earned a master's degree in psychology from the University of Chicago and a doctorate in psychology from Saybrook University. He taught courses on consciousness at Providence College School of Continuing Education for fifteen years and presently teaches psychology at Roger Williams University.

An expert on the inventor Nikola Tesla and also in the field of graphology, Marc Seifer has lectured at West Point, Brandeis University, the United Nations, CCNY, Lucasfilms Industrial Light & Magic in California, Oxford University and Cambridge University in England, and the University of Vancouver in Canada, and at conferences in Israel, Serbia, Croatia, and throughout the United States. His articles have appeared in *Wired, Civilization, Parapsychology Review, Consciousness Research Abstracts, Psychiatric Clinics of North America,* and *Cerebrum.* Featured in *Brain/Mind Bulletin, New York Times, Washington Post, New Scientist, The Economist, Rhode Island Monthly,* and on the back cover of Uri Geller's book *Mind Medicine,* he has also appeared on National Public Radio's "To the Best of Our Knowledge" and on *The History Channel* and *Associated Press International TV News* and has been a consultant for *Biography,* the *BBC* and *The American Experience.*

Among his other published works, Seifer has three works of fiction (*Rasputin's Nephew, Doppelgänger, Crystal Night*) and four works of nonfiction (*Transcending the Speed of Light, The Definitive Book of Handwriting Analysis, Mr. Rhode Island,* and the biography *Wizard: The Life and Times of Nikola Tesla*). Called "a serious piece of scholarship" by *Scientific American,* "revelatory" by *Publisher's Weekly,* and a "masterpiece" by bestselling author Nelson DeMille, *Wizard* is "Highly Recommended" by the American Association for the Advancement of Science.